Governance, Grievance, and Violent Extremism in West Africa

Governance, Grievance, and Violent Extremism in West Africa

From the Caliphates to Great Power Competition

Zacharias P. Pieri and
Kevin S. Fridy

LYNNE
RIENNER
PUBLISHERS

BOULDER
BARNSLEY

Published in the United States of America in 2025 by
Lynne Rienner Publishers, Inc.
1800 30th Street, Suite 314, Boulder, Colorado 80301
www.rienner.com

and in the United Kingdom by
Lynne Rienner Publishers, Inc.
47 Church Street, Barnsley, South Yorkshire S70 2AS
www.scriptps.co.uk/rienner

The publisher's authorized representative in
the EU for product safety is Authorised Rep Compliance Ltd.,
Ground Floor, 71 Lower Baggot Street, Dublin D02 P593, Ireland.
www.arccompliance.com

© 2025 by Lynne Rienner Publishers, Inc. All rights reserved

Library of Congress Cataloging-in-Publication Data
Names: Pieri, Zacharias author | Fridy, Kevin S. author
Title: Governance, grievance, and violent extremism in West Africa : from
   the caliphates to great power competition / Zacharias P. Pieri and Kevin
   S. Fridy.
Description: Boulder, Colorado : Lynne Rienner Publishers, Inc, 2025. |
   Includes bibliographical references and index. | Summary: "Demonstrates
   the surprising linkages between global strategic competition and local
   counterinsurgency in West Africa and shows how resilient local
   governance structures have effectively managed the consequent
   challenges"— Provided by publisher.
Identifiers: LCCN 2025012286 (print) | LCCN 2025012287 (ebook) | ISBN
   9798896160267 hardcover | ISBN 9798896160274 ebook
Subjects: LCSH: Political violence—Africa, West—History |
   Radicalism—Africa, West—History | Islamic fundamentalism—Africa,
   West—History | Counterinsurgency—Africa, West—History | Africa,
   West—Strategic aspects
Classification: LCC HN820.Z9 V565 2025 (print) | LCC HN820.Z9 (ebook)
LC record available at https://lccn.loc.gov/2025012286
LC ebook record available at https://lccn.loc.gov/2025012287

British Cataloguing in Publication Data
A Cataloguing in Publication record for this book
is available from the British Library.

Printed and bound in the United States of America

∞ The paper used in this publication meets the requirements
of the American National Standard for Permanence of
Paper for Printed Library Materials Z39.48-1992.

5 4 3 2 1

Contents

Acknowledgments vii

1 Grievances, Governance, and External Shocks in West Africa 1
2 Precolonial Caliphates and Empires: Leveraging History 15
3 The Colonial Roots of Violence and Strategic Competition 39
4 Mobilizing Violence: Jihadist Strategies 61
5 Local Resilience in the Face of Violence 87
6 Enter Great Power Competition 117
7 International Actors, Local Dynamics 143
8 The Convergence of Violent Extremism and Great Power Competition 171

Bibliography 181
Index 203
About the Book 213

Acknowledgments

MOST, MAYBE ALL, ACADEMIC BOOKS ARE HARD TO WRITE. THIS ONE IS NO exception. You start with a puzzle that you find interesting and/or useful, design some research to get you the data you need to solve the puzzle, then hammer away at analysis and narrative until you are told it is good enough to stop. There are points of real intellectual curiosity and flashes of understanding. There is also a heck of a lot of work.

This book is fully cowritten. We would sometimes divvy up primary and secondary responsibility for a section, but even then, the secondary reader would do additional lifting to get the pieces to properly fit together. It was both a useful and a pleasant experience. We flipped a coin to see whose name would appear first on the title page. Zacharias won.

Authors with names on the front of a book bear sole responsibility for the words contained between the two covers, but credit for ideas and insights, wherever it is due, should be sprinkled more widely. Without the support of the Joint Special Operations University (JSOU), this work would have been impossible. Faculty and participants at a number of the university's short training conferences from 2018 to 2020 on violent extremism, great power competition, and African security offered feedback on many of the ideas that would eventually find their way into the book. All of the original survey data from Mali, Burkina Faso, and Ghana was funded by JSOU.

Marie-Claire Antoine at Lynne Rienner Publishers has been a pleasure to work with; she helped to shepherd the book from embryonic manuscript to final product and provided insightful feedback.

The two anonymous peer reviewers who provided constructive and encouraging comments helped us to emerge with a stronger final manuscript, and for that we are very grateful. We hope they will find the book better for their efforts.

Doing survey-data collection in northern Ghana, Burkina Faso, and Mali is no small feat. Sidiki Guindo in Mali, Mariame Compaore and Boubacar Beydouma Dicko in Burkina Faso, and Isaac Yen in Ghana led the teams of dedicated surveyors. From translation of concepts to case selection to surveying, these data collectors made this book possible. They braved Covid-19 restrictions, Ramadan fasting, heat, and a complex security environment for the research. We not only sing their praises, but are happy to put fellow scholars interested in survey research in the region into contact with them. More work for them keeps the valuable skills necessary for behavioralist social science research alive in the region.

Kevin would like to thank his wife, Sarah, and his daughter, Ruthie, for their patience. He enjoys fieldwork except for the absence from his family. When he is at home, he is not an easy writer and sometimes gets grumpy as he hacks away at the keyboard. Zacharias would like to extend his gratitude to the Johnsons of Utah, who opened their home to him while he wrote some chapters, and who encouraged breaks to visit the beautiful national parks and surrounding nature of the Beehive State. Elaine Begleiter spent a summer as a research assistant and was invaluable in helping with quantitative data analysis. She has since successfully graduated.

We dedicate this book to the respondents in our survey. This swath of West Africa is a really wonderful place full of resilient people whose perseverance in challenging times is admirable. May their futures be full of peace, progress, and possibility.

1

Grievances, Governance, and External Shocks in West Africa

WEST AFRICA IS NO STRANGER TO TURMOIL AND UPHEAVALS, YET THE PAST decade has been fraught even by the region's own historical standards. The Sahel area that intersects Mali and Burkina Faso has become a global epicenter of violent extremist organization (VEO) in the form of jihadist terrorism. Instability in West Africa has led to numerous coups, while external powers are becoming more comfortable commingling their longstanding economic competition in the region with renewed politico-military interests harkening back to the Cold War era as part of a regional trend of great power competition (GPC).

The rapid metastasizing of jihadist terrorism over the past decade has allowed groups affiliated with Islamic State and al-Qaeda to establish themselves as a permanent presence in the Sahel, with governments across the region proving unable to uproot the violence. Among the worst-affected places are Mali, Burkina Faso, and Niger where, in 2022 alone, over 9,000 people were killed in armed conflict (Wilkins 2022). Numbers for 2023 and 2024 suggest a significant rise in the death toll from these already historically high numbers (Nsaibia 2024).

Jihadist violence does not occur in a vacuum. Rather it capitalizes upon poor governance, rampant corruption, and a retreat of civilian rule where elected governments were usurped by military figures promising the end of jihadist terror. Since 2020 there have been coups in Mali, Burkina Faso, Chad, Guinea, Niger, and Gabon. In Mali and Burkina Faso especially, "the putsches have been followed by a spiral of deteriorating security" (*Economist* 2023a).

This security spiral opened the door for France to leave and Russia to enter as the preferred new global partner in the war on terror (McAlexander and Ricart-Huguet 2022).

The goal of this work is to understand how factors that are largely exogenous to communities contribute to local instability and violence in West Africa. Every society has problems and mechanisms to address these problems. Grievances vary from place to place in terms of substance, scope, and homogeneity. Governance mechanisms to address these grievances vary as well. They may be widely viewed as legitimate throughout the various segments of society, responsive to citizen demands, and have the capacity to fulfill their functions. They may not. Though no society has completely static grievance and governance constellations, and some flexibility is desirable to avoid stagnation and address novel concerns, stable and peaceful communities develop an equilibrium of respected and durable institutions to solve communal grievances (Lutz and Linder 2004). But what happens when powerful exogenous shocks are brought to bear on these grievances and governance institutions? In answering this question, we provide a lens that can be applied consistently across the VEOs and GPC security paradigms.

This monograph represents an effort to develop an analytical lens that examines the impact of exogenous shocks on governance using a bottom-up approach. In doing so, we seek to reveal the organic interlinkages between GPC and VEOs when viewed from the populations' perspectives to demonstrate how localized grievances can be amplified, redirected, and exploited into mobilizing narratives, and how VEOs and great power competitors can impact this process. Our research identifies effective local institutions and governance structures that provide models for stemming violence and instability in ways that make the most sense for the environment. Data is collected across three countries: Mali, Burkina Faso, and Ghana. These cases give us variance in terms of VEO activity, GPC, and local governance mechanisms, allowing us to isolate covariance between our independent variables (VEO activity and GPC) and our dependent variables (grievances and governance structures). We break this exploration down into three sections. First, we explore grievances and the institutional environment addressing these grievances in West Africa. Then we look at how VEOs and GPCs impact these processes individually. Finally, we explore how these two largely external actors interact in communities in which they both operate.

Two Global Challenges Cohabitating: VEO and GPC

Despite international efforts to stem the tide of jihadist terrorism, a number of jihadist movements not only continue to operate in Sahelian West Africa but are increasing their capacity. These include Jama'at Nusrat al Islam (JNIM) and Islamic State in the Greater Sahara (ISGS). JNIM is an umbrella organization that formed in 2017, unifying four al-Qaeda affiliated groups in the region: Ansar Dine, al Mourabitoun, Macina Liberation Front (also known at Kitaba Macina), and al-Qaeda in the Islamic Maghreb (AQIM). While consolidated in name, these groups retain a high degree of operational autonomy, and some are more potent than others. The Macina Liberation Front, for example, emerged as the most forceful group in central Mali and was, at the time of this writing, responsible for the majority of attacks in both the central region and increasingly into northern Côte d'Ivoire. The Macina Liberation Front's leader, Ahmadu Koufa, stands out as being an early user of technological platforms such as WhatsApp, Facebook, and Telegram to call for members of the Fulani community to rise up against the Malian Armed Forces, G5 Sahel countries, and France's Barkhane force (Lavallee 2019). Koufa, who in part operated through an irredentist lens, promised to mobilize people into action to erase nation-states whose borders the French and British drew during the colonial period, and to replace them with an Islamic caliphate modeled on the nineteenth century precolonial Fulani jihadist kingdom of Macina. ISGS has also found operational space with increasing lethality in parts of Niger, Mali, and Burkina Faso (Zenn and Clarke 2020).

Burkina Faso has emerged as one of the worst-affected countries in the region, with jihadist activity claiming more than 4,200 lives in 2022, and over 3,000 in the first four months of 2023. In 2023, Burkina Faso accounted for around a quarter of all terrorism-related casualties worldwide (Institute for Economics & Peace 2024). Jihadist groups are moving farther south, putting Burkina Faso's capital Ouagadougou, at risk (*Economist* 2023c). The enormity of the violence has meant that a significant proportion of the population, approximately two million people (or 10 percent of the population), have been displaced (Mednick 2023). In addition to this, immense pressure is impacting numerous community services, including schools, which have been disproportionately affected. According to some reports, approximately "200 schools are closing every month," and in the northern region of the country "almost 90% are already closed" (*Economist* 2023c). Burkina Faso's military government, which took power after two coups in 2022, has responded to the problem with heavy air strikes using Turkish drones and Russian attack helicopters.

Mali for a time was seen as one of the most promising countries on the continent having transitioned to democracy, yet this was revealed to be premature in 2012 when Azawad (a Tuareg name for Mali's northern region) was captured and occupied by Tuareg separatists and then by jihadist groups. French troops deployed to Mali in Operation Serval to eject jihadist groups from the north (BBC 2013). Peace accords were subsequently signed in Algiers in 2015, but conflicts continue in central Mali where the Fulani population regularly expresses feelings of disenfranchisement, and northern Mali where jihadist groups continue to operate. Despite concerted efforts to push back jihadists, as in Burkina Faso, they are threatening the capital, Bamako. The UN peacekeeping mission—Multidimensional Integrated Stabilization Mission in Mali (MINUSMA)—has left. MINUSMA's role, which included investigating allegations of severe human rights abuses in the country as well as protecting civilians from jihadist attacks, began withdrawing its 15,000-strong armed and civilian personnel in July 2023. This came on the back of increasing tension between MINUSMA's leadership and Mali's military government, partly over allegations of human rights abuses, but also over decisions by Mali's rulers to place more trust in the Russian-sponsored Wagner Group's mercenary forces.[1] While Mali and Wagner Group deny the allegations, in 2022 in Moura, a town in Central Mali, "white gunmen suspected to be Wagner mercenaries . . . killed hundreds of civilians, aided by the Malian military" (Mohamed 2023).

Though headlines of terrorist events and interethnic violence tend to dominate international press coverage of the region, the reality is far more complex. While an increasing number of communities are wracked by violence and disunity, many are largely peaceful and cooperative (Fearon and Laitin 1996). Causes of this disparity are undoubtedly complex and multivariate, but one likely piece of the puzzle is the process whereby solutions are found for communal grievances—that is, governance. Grievances refer to perceived or actual injustices that motivate individuals to demand change or to seek redress and are central to understanding the dynamics of social movements, conflicts, and revolutions. The types of grievances that fuel conflict extend beyond personal complaints and instead focus on collective sentiments that highlight a societal sense of injustice and which often lead to calls for some type of collective action to address the situation (Gurr 1970; Pieri and Grosholz 2023). Communal grievances can stem from a wide range of issues, including feelings of political disenfranchisement, economic inequality, social discrimination, and concerns around the lack of safety. Governance can either mitigate or aggravate grievances. There are many, sometimes contradictory, understandings of the concept of "governance" (Colebatch 2014), but an early and oft-used definition reads as follows:

> Governance is the sum of the many ways individuals and institutions, public and private, manage their common affairs. It is a continuing process through which conflicting or diverse interests may be accommodated and co-operative action may be taken. It includes formal institutions and regimes empowered to enforce compliance, as well as informal arrangements that people and institutions either have agreed to or perceive to be in their interest (Commission on Global Governance 1995, 2–3).

This definition covers governance processes across the national to local and formal to informal layers and follows problems to their ultimate solution providers. The relationships between jihadist activity, great power competition, and local governance is novel enough a focus that too much concentration at the national and formal layers is likely to leave important local and informal options out of view (Lijphart 1971, 692). This definition is also inclusive, identifying both formal and informal providers of governance. Broad interpretations of governance providers are a good match for an institutional environment where the formal state has been described as relatively weak and with a great deal of competition (Ekeh 1992; Schatzberg 2001; Herbst 2000; Boone 2005).

Communities in West Africa as in other parts of the world are not static, and neither is the nature of their governance. Most of the time there is considerable path dependency, meaning social patterns get locked in and repeated year after year (North 1990). More colloquially, problems around now often linger into later, influential people today are more likely to be influential people tomorrow, and solutions that have worked in the past will probably be tried again. Nevertheless, equilibriums of governance do change gradually and, under the right conditions, can change rapidly. These changes may be generated from within a community whose problems, members, and power change naturally over time; in the social sciences these are called endogenous factors (Mahoney and Thelen 2009; Beunen et al. 2015). Shocks from sources external to the community can also impact transformation processes; these are called exogenous factors. These exogenous shocks can vary from dramatic (e.g., foreign fighters associated with JNIM setting up an Islamic court or the UN establishing a base in the community) to subtle (e.g., youths finding a popular cleric from the Middle East on WhatsApp or new roofing sheets from China entering the construction market).

As a general rule, institutions of governance remain stable when those who have the power to change them lack the incentives to do so (Koning 2016, 650). But what happens when a new actor enters the system and alters the status quo grievances and balance of power? "Typically," Stiglitz (1999, 63) explains, "institutions (organizations) develop an internal coherency that is not too dissonant with the external environment they must face. When it becomes too dissonant, then institutions change." Intuitively students of African politics understand the trajectory of this answer. African history is often parsed into precolonial, colonial, and postcolonial categories because of just such shocks (Acemoglu, Johnson, and Robinson 2001). Postcolonial societies that creatively adapted informal governance institutions to retrofit ill-fitting formal, state-based institutions may be particularly vulnerable to rapid institutional change caused by exogenous shocks (Tsai 2006; Bratton 2007).

The history of the region remains crucial to understanding the ways in which contemporary dynamics around security and governance play out. The West African states of Mali, Burkina Faso, and Ghana were carved out and shaped through colonialism and are regarded by some as artificial. Prior to incursions out of Europe with aims at colonial reign, a plethora of states existed in the region, including a number of Islamic states such as the Macina Empire and the Sokoto Caliphate, which governed through sharia law, and which knitted together disparate communities in the region. The histories of these empires continue to reverberate in the region and have often been seized upon by jihadist groups such as JNIM, Boko Haram, or the Macina Liberation Front as examples of a golden age in the region—a time when communities were governed based on Islam, and in some cases where groups had their own ethno-religious states.

Though we do not claim that the West African jihads of the nineteenth century and those of today are analogous, we do argue that the two are linked through grievance construction. Contemporary jihadist groups invoke historical narratives and draw on religious ideologies that stem from the actions and works of such figures as Usman dan Fodio and Seku Ahmadu. The contemporary leaders of jihadist groups such as JNIM and Boko Haram frame their actions as a continuation of those previous jihads, arguing that it is their duty to complete the historical and religious reformations started by their predecessors, and especially in fighting against moral decay, corruption, and deviation from what they view as the correct practice of Islam (Pieri 2019; MacEachern 2018). While the historical, religious, and ideological aspects of jihad are stressed by movement leaders, it is also true that jihadist groups exploit and capitalize upon such narratives to legitimate their sociopolitical agendas. They use this strategy as a means of embedding their cause with local populations that are still culturally and historically connected to revered historical figures, and who might see a return to historic modes of governance as a way out from a series of socioeconomic calamities (Pieri and Zenn 2016; Walker 2016).

Though today's GPC in Africa is unlikely to reshape governance as quickly or dramatically as jihadist movements of the past, colonialism, or independence did, the magnitude of activities of the world's most powerful countries in the region is immense. GPC in West Africa can be viewed as part of larger global shifts in the global balance of power and attempts to reconfigure the post–World War II international liberal order. Great power rivalries have reemerged with actors seeking to redistribute regional dynamics to their advantage. In this way, West Africa is experiencing similar types of external attempts at influence at local levels that other regions across the world also face. Diplomacy, commerce, and security are areas of intense competition by external powers. Until recently, China, Russia, and Turkey have been investing, securing contracts, and lending to national governments in the region without much recognition from Western powers. China has emerged as the chief source of imports to the region, replacing France. Chinese investors own nearly one in every ten dollars of African mine production, and in 2017 the People's Republic of China opened its first overseas military base in Djibouti (Ericsson et al. 2020; Vertin 2020). Russia has stepped up covert activities on the continent and is widely speculated to be competing with the West for allies in the volatile Sahel (Ramani 2020b; Mackinnon 2020; Stronski 2019).

Where France was once the most dominant external power in the region, its influence has slipped and ire against what is perceived as French neocolonialism has been mounting, in part exploited by jihadist groups to pressurize French withdrawal from the region. France's contemporary activities in West Africa are often viewed through a historical microscope, and the former colonial metropole habitually finds itself as a convenient regional scapegoat. Of all the former colonial powers, it is the only one to maintain large-scale permanent military bases on the continent, and its intervention in the region's politics often on the side of elites perceived as corrupt by locals, undermines its position. This was seen for example in 2021 after France ignored the illegal seizure of power in Chad by Mahamat Idriss Déby on the death of his father, thus creating an inherited dictatorship. Such actions have served to create a direct association between France and the failures of governments in the region, which are often seen as propped up by France in the name of stability rather than for the prosperity of local populations. Authoritarian states such as Russia and China also capitalize upon such instances to highlight global inconsistencies with the West's position on democracy and democratization, and to further erode the international liberal order.

The ultimate shift to France's position came to a climax with France's departure from Mali in 2022. At the height of France's intervention in Mali in 2014 following an Islamist insurrection, and with an invitation from Mali's government, over 2,500 French soldiers were deployed to Mali as part of Operation Barkhane, successfully repelling a jihadist assault of Bamako. After initial successes, jihadist violence in Mali increased. Two coups in the country in 2020, followed by the "new junta's decision to hire mercenaries from Russia's Wagner Group, changed the calculation," and by August 2022 "all French soldiers had quit Mali" (*Economist* 2023b). Similarly, after Burkina Faso experienced its own coups in 2022, French troops were also asked to withdraw from that country, and again in 2023 from Niger. In November 2024, the government of Chad without warning ended its defense cooperation pact with France, while on New Year's Eve 2024, Côte d'Ivoire announced that all French troops in that country would leave in January 2025. Senegal soon followed suite with a 2025 withdraw mandate (RFI 2025). This marked the end of more than a decade of French military presence in the Sahel region and is also one of the most consequential shifts in regional security dynamics in recent memory.

In the past two decades, the United States has established an African Command, and the former commander of Theater Special Operations Command Africa (SOCAFRICA), Brigadier General (ret.) Donald Bolduc, reported in 2018 that special operations forces conducted approximately 100 activities a day on the continent (Gwatiwa and Van der Merwe 2020; N. D. F. Allen 2018). Additionally, Africa has been the largest recipient of US overseas development assistance, with the United States Agency for International Development (USAID) distributing figures approaching $10 billion annually to governments (Cook et al. 2017). These figures do not even account for the investments and engagements by other industrialized countries nor large corporations that also directly impact communities in multiple ways.

As the moniker implies, GPC has the capacity to create big ripples, altering grievances and changing power dynamics. The impact can be amplified in poverty-stricken and politically marginalized areas where even the most powerful local actor pales in comparison to great powers. These changes are likely to impact governance. This capacity is not, however, unique to GPC, as jihadist groups too can cause large ripples reshaping the problems a community identifies as first-order issues, the local actors with the power to address them, and the strategies a community chooses to resolve them. This monograph situates itself at the crossroads of VEOs and GPC where there is a contentious struggle for good governance, stability, and prosperity in the region.

Data Explored

The data used in this monograph stems from a range of sources, including violent events from ACLED; analysis of the speeches, communiques, internal documents, and media releases of jihadist groups; and figures on military, international assistance, and trade relationships. In addition to these publicly available sources, the monograph draws on a large-N survey designed by the authors and conducted in the first half of 2021. The survey, which informs much of the new empirical data presented in this book, drew its data from two border regions in West Africa (see Figure 1.1). One is located on

Figure 1.1 Map of Survey Sites

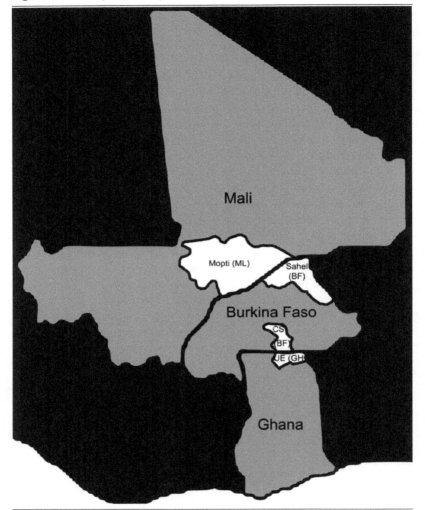

Note: Survey regions are shown in white. ML = Mali; BF = Burkina Faso; CS = Centre Sud Region; UE = Upper East; GH = Ghana.

the Ghana–Burkina Faso frontier in the land populated by descendants of Tohazie and the other at the nexus of Burkina Faso and Mali where the Macina Empire once reigned. Going east to west, these sites all fall on the longitude line −1. Going north to south, the area under consideration sits in the two climatic zones between the Sahara desert and the tropical forests along the Gulf of Guinea: the Sahel and Sudanian savanna. Religiously this transect cuts through populations that are generally more Islamic the farther north one travels and more Christian the farther south, with significant numbers of traditionalists and syncretists sprinkled along the way (Levtzion and Pouwels 2000). Major cultural groups inhabiting the region include Fulani, Dogon, Mossi, and various Mole-Dagbon communities (Ba 2010; Iliasu 1971). These majority populations are interspersed with a heterogeneous array of neighboring groups and immigrants. Socioeconomically, the median resident of these hinterland communities is quite poor by regional and global standards.

In Ghana the Upper East region is paired with the Burkinabé region Centre Sud. The Mopti region of Mali is paired with Burkina's Sahel region. These purposeful cross-border pairings allow for disaggregating national peculiarities from regional trends. If the data shows a correlation on both sides of the border, it is likely caused by something other than the political territory in which respondents reside. Within each of these four subnational units, between ten and a dozen research sites were purposefully selected. Some are located in areas known for their proximity to jihadist activity. Some are in areas with active and substantial great power presence (e.g., military bases or gold mines). Some are randomly selected.

Varying the sites by proximity to jihadist activity and GPC provides leverage to explore the relationships between these variables, sense of community, and governance. Our survey data achieves a large-N survey with thirty to forty respondents per site, yielding a total sample size of 1,368 respondents after quality control exclusions. These respondents were asked about communal problems and their perceptions of notable jihadist groups and global powers. They were also asked to compare their situation with those of their neighbors next door and in the wider regional context. Cognitive maps of local governance are constructed by asking people to solve hypothetical situations and inquiring who might be able to help them in their efforts. If residents of sites nestled near VEO or GPC activity consistently give answers unlike their neighbors farther away from direct VEO/GPC activity, there is good reason to believe this relationship is causal. Because actors associated with violent extremist organizations and great powers have so rarely based their activities in Africa on a careful reading of local conditions, it is likely that the causal direction goes from VEO/GPC to governance and not vice versa (Schmidt 2013; De Guttry et al. 2016).

Outline of the Book

Following this introduction, the focus of Chapter 2 is on the precolonial history of the region. We demonstrate that for jihadist movements, the historical and religious context of the region is still important and also resonates with local communities as a golden age of governance. The leaders of jihadist movements draw inspiration for their goals and actions today by drawing parallels with the actions of nineteenth century reformers who recast the sociopolitical and moral order of their time through violent collective action. Viewing history from the perspective of jihadist groups is important to understanding the drivers of violence in the region. Deciding which historical context is relevant, however, is complex. In West Africa the context predates the creation of contemporary nation-states, and in some cases stretches back to the ninth century with, for example, the formation of the Kanem-Borno Empire (in the Lake Chad basin and extending up into Sudanic Africa) and the arrival of Islam to the region (Pieri 2019, 12). The focus in this chapter, however, will be on the Islamic history of the areas of what are today the nation-states of Mali, Burkina Faso, and Ghana.

Chapter 3 looks at the roots of violence and great power competition in the region. Over the centuries, the regions we explore in this book have come under the dominion of a number of precolonial-, colonial-, and independence-era political entities. Populations have ebbed and flowed, and there have been several important migrations that have reshaped communities populating the region. Looking at GPC in this slice of West Africa across the precolonial, colonial, and independence eras, this chapter begins with the Sahelian kingdoms and concludes with the immediate post–Cold War period. Across these eras, we identify the most significant great powers operating in the region and describe the way they operated similarly or differently in the communities under investigation. Special focus is on how these great powers shaped local reactions and impacted power dynamics altering local governance.

The focus in Chapter 4 is on jihadist strategies in the region, both in terms of how they undermine existing forms of governance and the ways in which they offer alternative forms of governance. We provide an overview of most of the important jihadist factions—their core beliefs, goals, and actions—across Mali and Burkina Faso. Case studies of JNIM, the Macina Liberation Front, Ansarul Islam (founded in Burkina Faso), and ISGS are examined. We explain the ways in which these jihadist groups frame conflicts in the region and the extent to which they are successful in leveraging local grievances to advance their agendas.

In Chapter 5 we examine local resilience in the face of VEO violence using data gathered from our survey. We do this through exploring the relationships between community grievances in the tri-country region and the frequency of jihadist violence. As such, the chapter engages with the core questions of how grievances, governance, and violence might be interlinked.

In Chapter 6 we question the extent to which the presence of GPC shapes a community's grievances and the level to which international actors affect or rearrange local power dynamics to alter the ways these problems are solved. We describe the forms, magnitude, and locations of GPC in the three countries under investigation. We look at how the United States and China are managing their relationships with Mali, Burkina Faso, and Ghana across the issue areas of commerce, security, and foreign assistance. We also explore ways in which major (e.g., Russia, the European Union, and the United Kingdom), Middle Eastern (e.g., Turkey and Saudi Arabia), and regional (e.g., Nigeria) powers play into strategic competition in the region (Jones et al. 2020).

In Chapter 7 we build on the material outlined in Chapter 6 and explore the relationship between GPC and governance concerning international actors. GPC, for those who experience it in these hinterland communities, is about who brings the most utility to people and how they understand this utility. People are not synonymous with formal governments in the capital city. Certainly, bilateral relationships occurring on formal military-to-military and government-to-government channels can trickle down to impact individuals, but the character of this impact varies from place to place and issue to issue.

Chapter 8 concludes the book by knitting together more explicitly the ways in which VEO activity and GPC intersect to shape grievances and governance in the region. We find that VEO and GPC activities impact the sense of community in additive ways. Just because one makes a resident feel more or less comfortable and trusting, does not mean the other cannot amplify, mitigate, or reverse the impact.

Our analysis suggests ways in which viewing VEO and GPC through the same lens, as independent variables that can impact the nature of local governance, might be useful for scholar and practitioner alike.

Note

1. In 2024, Wagner Group's operations in Africa came under the newly formed banner of Africa Corps—though in this book we will continue to use Wagner Group.

2

Precolonial Caliphates and Empires: Leveraging History

ON MAY 3, 2015, A THEN LITTLE-KNOWN ISLAMIST GROUP, THE MACINA LIBeration Front (also known as Kitaba Macina), was propelled to international attention after some of its fighters blew up in Mali the tomb of the famous nineteenth century jihadist and founder of the Macina Empire, Seku Ahmadu (d. 1845). What is curious, however, is that the leaders of Macina Liberation Front claim to draw inspiration from Seku Ahmadu and even assert that their goal is to resurrect an Islamic state in the approximate region of the former Macina Empire. The Malian press reported that following a number of the movement's attacks, statements were released claiming a desire for "bringing back the old order" (Thurston 2015). Why then did the Macina Liberation Front blow up the tomb of their role model?

Unlike the West African jihadist movements of the past that were embedded in the theological institutions, Sufi brotherhoods, and Islamic learning of the time, the jihadist groups of today are somewhat disconnected from local longstanding traditions and instead orient themselves within an internationalist and austere form of Salafist Islam. The Macina Liberation Front demonstrated that the jihadist past of the region still resonates today. They draw inspiration from Seku Ahmadu's actions; however, they are also selective in their drawing on history and revisionist in their understanding of it, and their true allegiance is to ideology. Following the attack at the grave site, the fighters promised to "attack all those who did not follow the teachings of Islam's prophet" (Ahmed 2015). The attack, which was carried out using dynamite, mirrors attacks on graves of those considered as saints in northern Mali in 2012 when jihadists seized control of the major towns there.

Across parts of West Africa and the Sahel, jihadist groups have gained international prominence for seizing territory and attempting to establish Islamic forms of governance. Beyond the attempts of the Macina Liberation Front, two other noteworthy cases stand out. These were the takeover of territory by Islamist groups linked to al-Qaeda in northern Mali starting in 2012, followed by Boko Haram's annexing of large swaths of territory in northeastern Nigeria in 2015, where for a short period of time a strict form of Islamic law, which included amputation of limbs and public floggings, was applied (Pieri and Zenn 2018).

It was in 2010 that members of ethnic Tuareg groups in northern Mali founded the National Movement for the Liberation of Azawad (MNLA). This was a movement that sought to secure an autonomous state in the northern region. By January 2012 the MNLA launched a rebellion that reached into the northern regions of Timbuktu and Gao. This attempt at secession should be viewed as part of a much longer struggle between the Malian state and Tuareg dating back at least to 1963 (A. Morgan 2012). While successful in mobilizing Tuareg to the cause of an ethno-nationalist state, the MNLA was driven out of Gao, the largest city in the occupied area and the declared capital of Azawad, within just a few months by jihadist groups who saw an opportunity to carve out territory to be governed under Islamic law. Groups such as the Mouvement pour l'Unicité et le Jihad en Afrique de l'Ouest (MUJAO), managed to oust the MNLA and then set about establishing control over the region, making the imposition of Islamic law a priority (Lecocq and Klute 2013, 433). It was reported for, example that a couple who had a child outside of wedlock received 100 lashes of the whip, that a man imbibing alcohol was lashed 40 times, and a couple caught in extramarital sexual relations was stoned in the town center of Aguelhok (Agence France Presse 2012).

In Nigeria the seizing of territory by Boko Haram was part of what Abubkar Shekau, the group's then leader, declared as part of a Nigerian "caliphate." Boko Haram's leaders, both before and after their affiliation to the Islamic State (which formally occurred in 2015), saw jihad as a means to combat "corruption, poverty, nepotism, and bad governance and restore moral order, including ending the mixing of Islam with 'impure' concepts of democracy, secularism, and liberalism" (Pieri and Zenn 2016, 73).

Jihad in pursuit of territorial conquest is not, however, a novel or exceptional phenomenon in West Africa but rather has deeply rooted historical precedent and resonance in the region. Contemporary jihadist groups understand this and look to build their own cause on its foundations. Indeed, contemporary jihadist groups lay claim to a much longer tradition of violent action for sociopolitical change in the region stemming back to the eighteenth and nineteenth centuries.

During the late eighteenth and early nineteenth centuries reformist movements centered around Islamist visions of sociopolitical change arose almost simultaneously throughout not only West Africa, but also the broader Muslim world, with the aim of restoring society to what the religious scholars leading them believed to be a former greatness— or a golden age. These movements called for a pivoting of whole societies, orienting them to the highest ideals of Islam—a return to what was seen as the foundations of the religion as practiced by Muhammad, Islam's prophet, and his companions. It is without doubt that the most impactful of these were the Wahhabis of Arabia at the end of the eighteenth century, but perhaps more significant to West Africa were the three jihads of the nineteenth century.

During this period a number of Islamic scholars in West Africa proffered theological justification for violent action in pursuit of creating new sociopolitical spaces, breaching "established norms of political neutrality" (Syed 2021, 375). In the nineteenth century, West Africa witnessed the rise of the so-called Fulani jihads, waged by scholars from the Fulani ethnic group, against the Hausa and Bambara kingdoms. These movements resulted in the establishment of three pronounced confederations of emirates, each recognizing an *amir al-mu'minin,* or commander of the faithful (Smith 1962, 333). These three polities were as follows (H. Smith 1962, 333; Ibrahim 2017, 6):

1. The Sokoto Caliphate (1804–1903), in Hausaland and neighboring territories (what is now northwestern Nigeria). Founded by the Fulani scholar Usman dan Fodio (d. 1817) (hereafter known as dan Fodio), certain important elements persist in the governmental and social structures of the northern region of Nigeria down to the present day.
2. The Fulani Empire of Macina (1820–1863), centered around the Mopti region of Mali and occupying all the lands between the Inland Delta Niger and the Bandiagara cliff, and extended into Djelgodji to the east and Timbuktu to the north. It was

founded by the Fulani scholar Ahmad b. Muhammad (known as Seku Ahmadu).
3. The Tukolor Empire of al-Hajj Umar b. Said (d. 1893), which covered an area of some 150,000 square miles in the Upper Niger–Senegal region (including the land of the Caliphate of Macina which it destroyed). The empire was broken up by the French at the end of the nineteenth century.

In addition to these three polities, it is important to note that the long-established Kanem-Borno Empire, which extended from what is now northeastern Nigeria into parts of Cameroon, Niger, and Chad, was still a functioning Islamic state with some degree of influence in the region (Pieri 2019). H. Smith (1962, 333) further notes that the imamates of Futa Toro and Futa Jallon, which had been established through jihads in the eighteenth century, endured into the nineteenth century. Even right to the end of the nineteenth century and into the period of western colonization, the region was host to the scene of the campaigns of the Samori Ture (in Upper Guinea) and Rabih Zubayr in Borno (H. Smith 1962, 333).

The Importance of History

In this chapter we intend to show that contemporary jihadist movements in West Africa cannot be understood without first coming to grips with the history of the region, both distant and immediate, from which such movements draw inspiration for their goals and actions today. Viewing history from the perspective of these movements, and understanding the ways in which they interpret and reinterpret history, is important to understanding the drivers of violence in the region. Deciding which historical context is relevant, however, is complex. Here, the narratives gathered from the jihadists themselves tell us a lot about the ways in which they interpret history, and how these narratives come to form a part of their strategic discourses. In West Africa relevant historical context predates the creation of contemporary nation-states and in some cases stretches back to the ninth century with, for example, the formation of the Kanem-Borno Empire (in the area of the Lake Chad basin and extending up into Sudanic Africa) and the arrival of Islam to the region (Pieri 2019, 12). The focus in this chapter, however, will be on the Islamic history of the areas of what are today the nation-states of Mali, Burkina Faso, and northern Ghana.

While the contemporary emergence of jihadist movements in this region can, in part, be seen as a reaction to the state's inability to meet its statutory obligations to its citizens, this chapter places the movements within the historical trajectory of Islamic caliphates, empires, and jihads in the region. Modern movements such as the Macina Liberation Front and Ansarul Islam, among others, cannot be understood in a vacuum, nor as rogue movements bent on toppling the governments of the region simply because of socioeconomic concerns. Rather they must be seen as part of a longer tradition of revolutionary Islamist movements that came before them. Jihadist groups (at times opportunistically, and at others more meaningfully) look back to similar groups in the history of the region that were successful in reshaping the governance structures of the period, ushering in what they see as rightly guided governance based on Islamic law.

In this chapter we will provide an account of the Sokoto, Macina, and Tukolor jihads, arguing that many of the same grievance factors that spurred these movements in their own time have also been identified today by leaders of West African jihadist movements to legitimate their own violent action against the state. Jihadist leaders today, like their forebearers, amplify local grievances—corruption, nepotism, a failure to implement sharia (or Islamic law)—and fuse these within a framework of Islamic discourse that preaches sociopolitical change through violence. The jihads of the nineteenth century drastically altered the sociopolitical and geographic landscapes of West Africa—implementing theocratic systems under which people were governed through Islamic law. Figure 2.1 shows the extent of both the Sokoto Caliphate and the Macina Empire. Though abolished by colonial rulers, for many in the region these systems endure in conceptual resonance to this day. They are systems that are often seen as superior to the divisive politics of so-called democratic rule and as a solution to the ills of society.

Islamic History of the Sahel

While Islam has a long history in West Africa, having been introduced by trans-Saharan traders from northern Africa in the tenth century, early converts were limited to groups of merchants and certain members of the elite. The implementation and practice of Islam during these early years was far from orthodox, with Arabic-speaking travelers who had spent time in the region at the time describing a

Figure 2.1 Boundaries of the Macina Empire, Sokoto Caliphate, and Segu Empire

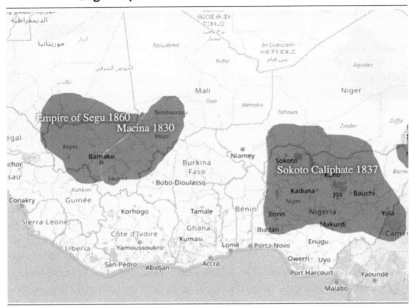

Source: Map generated with help from Michael Williams.

syncretic Islam shaped by local traditions and beliefs (Hill 2009). It was not until much later that Islam was to spread to the wider nonelite populations and was often imposed on them. A more orthodox form of Islam did not make it to the rural populations of the region until the seventeenth or eighteenth centuries during the era of the jihadis (MacEachern 2018, 103). Beginning in the 1690s and lasting until the 1890s, a series of jihads, wars predicated on the desire to install governance based on Islamic jurisprudence, fundamentally and irrevocably altered both Islam and governance in the region. These jihads, while rooted in the rhetoric of Islamic reform, were also informed by numerous other economic and social factors. The end of the trans-Atlantic slave trade, the growth of legitimate commerce, and the eruption of long-standing tensions resulted in Muslim reform movements led by charismatic religious leaders (Clark 1999, 152–153).

The period of history being examined in this chapter is one that was pregnant with messianic expectation and the idea that the end of times was near. Since the seventeenth century there had been a popular tradition that a religiously orthodox caliph, a man dedicated to renewing the faith, would appear in the region at the beginning of the nineteenth century, presumably to "recreate the idealized Gao Caliphate as a prelude to the advent of the Mahdi and the cataclysmic end of the world" (Brown 1969, 112). Similarly, Hiskett (1984, 157) advanced the argument that there was a belief that a Mahdi would arrive to "drive out injustice" and "bring true Islam," but before this could happen, "once every century, God would send a *mujadid*, a re-newer, to prepare the way for the Mahdi." It is sometimes easy to forget the religious fervor that existed during this time and the belief that people were living in an epoch of change. The year AD 1785 marked the start of a new Islamic century, AH 1200, and so there was "every reason to believe that a *mujadid* was near," and in West Africa "his arrival was awaited with anxious expectancy" (Hiskett 1984, 157).

Alongside such expectations were also understandings of Islam as a governing ideology and how Islamic jurisprudence should impact modes of governance, especially the implementation of justice in society. Muslim rulers, for the most part, had consistently failed to live up to the expectations of good governance, and thus became part of a recurring narrative around the notion of the apostate king—a ruler "nominally Muslim but judged by more Orthodox followers of Islam to be far too tolerant of traditional religious practices" (MacEachern 2018, 103). It was tolerance for pagan practices, especially, that emerged as a prominent accusation leveled against Hausa, Kanuri, Bambara, and other rulers by Islamic jihadists from the seventeenth century onward (MacEachern 2018, 103). It is in this context that the simmering up of jihads in the nineteenth century should be viewed.

Prior to the European colonization of West Africa and the carving out of states during the period of independence, there existed numerous empires, kingdoms, and sociopolitical groupings in the region. Of specific importance to this chapter are the precolonial Islamic states that existed in Mali and Burkina Faso, and particularly those affiliated with the Fulani jihads of the early nineteenth century. This is because much of the rhetoric of jihadist groups in the region today places an emphasis on this period of history as a golden age and as a period of Islamic governance that they wish to revive (Sangare 2019). Jihadist groups such as the Macina Liberation Front and Ansarul Islam look to the past and draw inspiration from states that existed to provide a blueprint for action today.

Usman dan Fodio and the Sokoto Caliphate

Of the jihads that took place in West Africa between the seventeenth and nineteenth centuries, the most consequential for the regions examined in this chapter were those of Usman dan Fodio in 1804, which toppled the Hausa kingdoms of northern Nigeria and in their place instituted the caliphate of Sokoto (which lasted until the advent of British colonialism in 1903), and the jihad of Seku Ahmadu in the Mopti region of Mali, which established the Macina Empire in 1820.

Dan Fodio (b. 1754) was an ethnic Fulani religious scholar who was concerned by moral decay and the departure from Islam as the guiding principle for state and society in the Hausa kingdoms during the late eighteenth century. He argued that only a return to governance based on Islam would rectify issues of corruption, judicial impunity, nepotism, and also what he regarded as lax moral standards, which he saw as rampant during that time (Pieri and Zenn 2016, 74–75). In his book *Kitab al-Farq*, dan Fodio made the case for how the rulers of the Hausa states were failing to rule as Muslims. He highlighted the lawlessness of the rulers; argued that laws rather than being on the side of the people were instead oppressive while at the same time contradicting the sharia; that excessive taxation was being implemented along with seizure of private property; that rulers were prone to corruption and bribes; and that they forced Muslims to fight in unjust wars (Eltantawi 2017, 54). The rulers were presented as presiding over a swamp, swindling the masses while themselves luxuriating in "voluptuous living, reveling in illegal music, wearing ornamented fineries, and accumulating women, often as many as a thousand in their harems" (Eltantawi 2017, 54).

Although the rulers of the Hausa kingdom of Gobir officially accepted Islam and claimed themselves as Muslim rulers, they were reluctant to implement Islamic law to its full extent, "such as applying shari'a or condemning polytheism and pagan practices" (Neggaz 2012, 125). Muslims, the reformers argued, were prevented by so-called Muslim rulers from living out an authentic Muslim lifestyle through, for example, laws forbidding veiling for women and turbans for men. Dan Fodio argued that Muslims had an obligation to look back at the examples of the prophet Muhammad and to strive to emulate him as a means of attaining worldly success and implementing necessary changes (Eltantawi 2017, 50). While originally calling for the rejuvenation of society in a nonconfrontational way, through preaching and attempts at providing advice to the rulers, dan Fodio changed his approach after an attempt on his life sanctioned by the ruler of Gobir.

It was at this point, after the attempt on his life, that dan Fodio came to believe that the most pressing issue facing Muslims in the region was the "hegemony of un-Islamic rule" and argued that change would necessitate Muslims having to "seize power" (Dallal 1993, 353). Firmly believing that change could now only occur through more assertive tactics and through collective action by Muslims, he led his followers on hijra, an emigration away from the capital of Gobir to a rural area near the borders of the state in 1804 (Pieri and Zenn 2016, 75). This emigration was a powerful statement—both symbolically and politically—through linking it to the actions of the prophet Muhammad, who himself led the early Muslim community in hijra from Mecca to Medina in AD 622, and from where the first jihad was launched. Through declaring an emigration and leaving the territory of Gobir, it in essence signified the ruler of Gobir as a wicked man and an apostate (MacEachern 2018, 173). In undertaking this emigration, dan Fodio and his followers who self-identified as "true" Muslims removed themselves from the temptations of the ruler's court to the borders of the country. They did so, however, "not to dwell in virtuous exile but rather to gather their forces to retake the capital and ruler's palace, thus transforming insurgents into a government and remaking society as a whole" (MacEachern 2018, 174).

The act of hijra is further important when considering dan Fodio's theological thought, spurring him to simultaneously develop an original theory of *takfir*. *Takfir* is the process of apostatizing Muslims and resembles a form of excommunication, or ejection, from the community of believers. Dan Fodio's innovation was that he argued that when it comes to *takfir*, both religious and political unbelief should be considered. Political *takfir* "could be pronounced against rulers who did not follow the shari'a and against whom waging jihad was legitimate" (Neggaz 2012, 125). Moreover, dan Fodio argued that once hijra was announced, it in effect became a binding form of collective action that every capable Muslim needed to engage in as a means of addressing the grievances that he had raised and with the end goal of restoring Islamic governance, which he viewed as more equitable. Any capable Muslim who failed to emigrate from a land of unbelief to one of belief with the community of believers in hijra, actively chose to belong to the land of unbelief and as such was required to bear the consequences of that choice (Dallal 1993, 354). This way of viewing *takfir* has been adopted by jihadist groups in the region today and is one of the ways used to challenge the legitimacy of political leaders, but it has also wreaked internal havoc in jihadist groups who also use the concept in internal battles over leadership, often apostatizing those within the movement whom they want to get rid of (Zenn and Pieri 2017). This type of religious fervor, then as now, was not easy to control once unleashed.

Dan Fodio's jihad of 1804 culminated in the formation of a new state built "on the ruins of an old social and political order" (Dallal 1993, 355). The Sokoto Caliphate was to be a centralized Islamic state based on the political thought of medieval Islamic scholars and had all the characteristics of the ideal model. It was a state in which "political power was delegated, but whose unity was guaranteed by the diffusion of a heterogeneous body of legal and administrative professionals" (Dallal 1993, 355). The jihad in Hausaland transformed Islam from a religion that rulers subscribed to when it suited them, into the official doctrine of the new state. The jihad also proved to religious reformers of the time that "a swift determined appeal to the sword could achieve much more than centuries of preaching" (Hiskett 1984, 166).

That dan Fodio was able to mobilize the Fulani of the region into armed insurrection against the existing authorities of his time, and to succeed in creating a state governed on Islamic principles, provided inspiration and a roadmap for other jihadist movements of the time, as well as to jihadist groups in the region today. This is true of movements such as the Macina Liberation Front, which seeks to mobilize Fulani in Mali and Burkina Faso to resurrect (or at least carve out) an Islamic state. It was also true of Boko Haram, a predominantly ethnic Kanuri movement, which argued that dan Fodio's methods for achieving structural change should be drawn upon in the contemporary period to transform the governance map of northern Nigeria (Pieri 2019).

Dan Fodio's successful defeat of the established Hausa states and the implementation of an Islamic state reverberated around West Africa in the early nineteenth century and was instrumental in being the locus of a number of other Fulani jihads in the region, the most successful being that of Seku Ahmadu, which established the Macina Empire in what is now the Mopti region of Mali. A smaller political entity known as Djelgoji was also established by Fulani inspired by dan Fodio, and linked to Macina, in what is now northern Burkina Faso. What is clear is that the jihads of the early 1800s in West Africa were directly tied to Fulani efforts to revive Islamic modes of governance. Today, many jihadist groups in West Africa seek to leverage this history and identity to exploit grievances among Fulani and broader Muslim populations to mobilize them for armed insurrection.

Macina

The history of the Macina region of what is now Mali is a complex one. Historical records show that there was a Fulani migration out of Mauritania to what is now the Mopti area of Mali in the fourteenth and fifteenth centuries. The Fulani settling in Macina at the time were cattle herders and followed their own animist religions, but over time they started to practice Islam after interacting with Muslims in the region. The Fulani of Macina, as with Fulani in other parts of Africa, increasingly adopted more orthodox forms of Islam, and it was from among this group that one of the most prominent Islamist reformers was to emerge in the early part of the nineteenth century, Ahmad b. Muhammad, known in this chapter as Seku Ahmadu (Hiskett 1984, 152).

Some scholars argue that the teachings of dan Fodio were the formative influence on Ahmadu's life, with the inspiration to reform his own society in Macina having stemmed from his participation in the early stages of dan Fodio's jihad in Gobir (Webster et al. 1967, 19). After Ahmadu left Sokoto he traveled south to what is today central Mali and settled in a village near Jenne (which at the time was a center of religious learning), but was expelled by its ruler for gathering around himself a group of followers who were inspired by ideas of Islamic reform (Trimingham 1962, 177). From Jenne, Ahmadu moved to Sebera, which was under the dominion of the ruler of Macina.

Ahmadu raised a number of concerns about the state of society, which included the issue that though Muslim in name, the rulers of the region did not practice Islam, that they freely patronized other forms of religious activity, and that people in positions of power often failed to defend trade from brigands, while also being prone to extortion and uncanonical taxation (Brown 1969, 110). In fact, Brown goes as far as to say that the rulers of the region "were hardly distinguishable from unbelievers" (1969, 110). Such accusations mirrored those that dan

Fodio had raised against the rulers of the Hausa states and which also laid the foundations for the subsequent call to arms.

Seku Ahmadu started to teach his own followers in the same way that dan Fodio taught his, placing an emphasis on Islam as an ordering principle and as a solution to the injustices of the existing system. It was because of this, that "his fame as a scholar, reformer, and devout Muslim spread until the king, fearful of losing his own position . . . appealed to his overlord, the Bambara king of Segu for assistance in crushing him [Ahmadu]" (Webster et al. 1967, 19). Muslim rulers in the region at the time would have been cognizant of the toppling of the Hausa states to the north of them and the creation of a new polity based on Islamic jurisprudence. Given the capacity for revolutionary ideas and action to spread, it is not unreasonable to believe that the Bambara rulers would have wanted to stop Ahmadu in his tracks.

While the situation was multifaceted, the immediate catalyst for conflict between Ahmadu and the ruling authorities came with an incident in which one of Ahmadu's followers was killed after an altercation with the son of a Fulani chief in the town of Simay, just north of Jenne (Nobili and Syed 2021, 4). It was at this point in 1817 that Ahmadu sought dan Fodio's banner before engaging in his own jihad. This is of particular significance because to request and receive a banner indicates that Ahmadu regarded dan Fodio as having at least some form of spiritual and temporal legitimacy in granting permission for his own jihad to extend into Macina. This would also explain why authorities in Sokoto later claimed that Ahmadu owed them his allegiance after establishing his Islamic state at Macina, and why Sokoto viewed Macina to be under their own jurisdiction and as part of the suzerainty of the Sokoto Caliphate (Hiskett 1984, 167). Brown, while arguing that Ahmadu was not able to resolve whether proper conditions for jihad existed and as such sent to Sokoto for approval as well as for the symbolic ensigns of the jihad, also notes that this last part of the story may be apocryphal (Brown 1969, 122).

After having attained dan Fodio's blessing (and possibly his flag), Ahmadu emigrated to the town of Hamdullahi. The importance of emigration as the forerunner to launching jihad was again of central importance in this case. Sensing that the deck was stacked against him, that the rulers would not implement the reforms he wanted, and that his own life was in danger, Ahmadu made the strategic calculation to emigrate with his followers. It was at Hamdullahi that Ahmadu was ultimately elected as "Amir al-Muminin" or Commander of the Faithful, by his followers (Webster et al. 1967, 19). Hamdullahi became the launch pad for jihad against the Bambara rulers and would eventually become the capital of the Macina Empire once Ahmadu was successful in defeating the armies sent against him. It was in March 1818, in Noukouma, south of Mopti, that an army composed of Fulani warriors and their Bambara allies from Segou, an overwhelming majority in numbers, attacked. "Against the odds, however, [Ahmadu and his partisans] were unexpectedly victorious," and then initiated a series of their "own battles that made, by mid-May 1818, Ahmadu the leader of a new, emerging polity centered in the Inner Niger Delta" (Nobili and Syed 2021, 4).

The Macina Empire was not, however, established in one fell swoop, instead being initiated over a number of different instances. Ahmadu needed to capitalize on his initial success through ensuring that his authority extended over the important city of Jenne, which was an important center of religious learning. The years following 1818 saw Ahmadu's armies engaging in extensive battles in the region, which resulted in his control of a large "state along the Niger and Bani rivers, occupying all the lands between the Inland Delta Niger and the Bandiagara cliff" by 1825 (Nobili and Syed 2021, 4).

Seku Ahmadu was first successful in defeating the armies of the Bambara king of Segu, and it was as a result of this that the religious scholars of Jenne invited him to take over the city, but the ruler of the city was unwilling to step down, and so the city was eventually captured through besiegement and conquest (Webster et al. 1967, 19). It was at this point that Fulani started to revolt in Macina, overthrew the ruler of the city, and like the scholars of Jenne, invited Ahmadu to take the reins of power. The role that the Fulani played was critical to Ahmadu's successes, with Fulani leaders in other areas coming out in support of Ahmadu, though this was at times as much of a political as a religious move (Webster et al. 1967, 19). It was not until 1819–1820 that Hamdullahi was established as the capital, and not until 1826–1827 that Timbuktu came under subjugation after a Fulani garrison was established in the city to protect it from Tuareg raids (Webster et al. 1967, 19).

There is some tension between the religious zeal of the jihad and the religious outlook of the established scholars in the region at the time. It was not just against the political elites that Seku Ahmadu's ire was directed, but also in part against the established scholarly class, which he saw as too scholarly (that is apolitical and somewhat invested in the existing order), advancing "an overly literate form of Islam, that neglected active reform in favor of excessive bookishness" (Hiskett 1984, 168). On the other side of the coin, the scholarly class, especially those in Timbuktu, which was regarded as a focal point of Islamic learning, considered Ahmadu to be ill-educated and lacking an understanding of the nuances of Islamic law. Whereas dan Fodio and his son Muhammad Bello published numerous books and Islamic treatises, Ahmadu is known to have authored only a single book, and his successors wrote none (Brown 1969, 104). The scholars of Timbuktu saw Ahmadu as a populist literalist who focused only on a small number of texts, and that the items he had branded as haram, or forbidden, such as women attending religious meetings, were actually allowed under Islamic law, and through condemning this, Ahmadu was in their view, showcasing his own ignorance (Hiskett 1984, 193). It is not surprising that such tensions also exist today between the leaders of jihadist movements and Muslim scholars and intellectuals. It is difficult to know what the religious scholars at the time must have thought once Ahmadu had become convinced that he was the promised twelfth orthodox caliph of the Sudan and recognized no higher earthly authority other than his own judgment and that of his own appointed council at Hamdullahi (Brown 1969, 138).

The jihad in Macina, as in the Hausa states, was at least partly a revolt of the people against the chiefly classes. Had the pagan masses loyally supported their rulers, the small Muslim communities could not have achieved success. It is probable that many people felt oppressed under multiple taxes, arbitrary justice, and corrupt officials. When the jihad commenced, they remained indifferent to the fate of their rulers, and even though they may not have been attracted to Islam as a religion, they could agree with the reformers' criticisms of the present system. Some animists even fought for the reformers, believing that they stood for a better life, honest government, and fair and just courts administering laws that could not be altered at a whim by the chiefly classes (Webster et al. 1967, 21).

The immediate consequences of the jihad were, first, to join together the broken fragments of a much older Islamic empire that had existed in the region—Macina, Segou, Kaarta, Timbuktu—into one single Islamic imperial unit. The second was to impose a strict codification of Islam on those who had previously been no more than faintly Muslim at best. Thus, like the jihadists in Hausaland, Ahmadu extended the domain of Islam in West Africa, but his reforms were slower to take effect among the ordinary people (Hiskett 1984, 168). Ahmadu called his empire a *dina* (that is, an Islamic state) and set up a council of forty ulema (or religious scholars) that supervised the work of governors appointed to rule the provinces, which consisted of five emirates. He prohibited all music and dancing, forbade the smoking of tobacco, and banned the wearing of dyed cloth. He inaugurated a program of mosque building, but decreed that mosques should have no towers, for he felt this to be showing off (Hiskett 1984, 178).

There was a concerted effort to implement Islamic law to its fullest extent, and it was this that resulted in pushback from different areas in the new empire. The Islamic code, regarding the number of wives and the prohibition of drinking and dancing, was rigidly enforced through the office of the Censor of Public Morals. In Timbuktu, it was in part the rigorous cleanup of the vices in that city that led to rebellions. Because of its location and prestige, Timbuktu attracted a large population of victors, especially young men seeking to satisfy carnal desires. Ahmadu's strict enforcement of moral codes "reduced the attraction of the city and its merchants' profits suffered" (Webster et al. 1967, 20).

Macina was a theocratic state—theocratic because it was ruled by the laws of God as laid down in the Quran; a state because it possessed a high degree of centralization, a supreme governing body that legislated for the entire nation, the emirates here resembling provinces rather than the largely autonomous emirates of Sokoto (Webster et al. 1967, 21). Upon Ahmadu's death in 1844, the succession passed smoothly from father to son: Ahmad II (1844–1852), and then to his grandson Ahmad III (1852–1862). Ahmad III was killed by the Tukolor conqueror, al-Hajj Umar (Webster et al. 1967, 22).

Extending Macina

After establishing his capital in Hamdullahi, Seku Ahmadu sought to extend his control over the two important cities of Jenne and Timbuktu—both centers of religious learning and commerce. Jenne was incorporated into the Macina Empire swiftly, but Timbuktu was able to resist for some time. A compromise was reached between Hamdullahi and Timbuktu whereby through submitting to Hamdullahi's rule Timbuktu could retain a degree of internal self-governance and, importantly, the right to keep a portion of taxes collected in the city and surrounding town (Clarke 1982, 129). Timbuktu was vital to Ahmadu's strategic intentions, not only because it was an ancient city of Islamic learning, but also because of its important trade routes and hub as a center of commerce. Initially the leaders of Timbuktu accepted Hamdullahi's rule over the city in the hopes that a Fulani garrison stationed in the city would protect its trade from marauding Tuareg, "but the rigidly enforced parochialism of the Fulani soon exacerbated the city's aristocracy" (Brown 1969, 141). Ahmadu's cleanup reduced the attraction of the city and its merchants' profits suffered. More than this, Ahmadu strictly prohibited the growth, importation, or the smoking of tobacco in his state. The Kunta tribe, to which the prominent Bakka'iyya scholars of Timbuktu belonged, held one of the most successful businesses in the procurement of tobacco in the Sudan, and as such Ahmadu's ruling directly impacted their wealth (Brown 1969, 139). On Ahmadu's death (1844) the people of Timbuktu repudiated his authority, trying to establish independence. His son, Ahmad II was, however, able to gain recognition in 1846 through reaching a deal that decentralized the city, allowing for all officials to be Songhai, with the exception of the supervisory tax collector, who was to be Fulani (Trimingham 1962, 180).

To the south, in what is now the very northern part of Burkina Faso, the Fulani jihads of the nineteenth century also had a profound impact. Ariotti and Fridy (2020) note that Ahmadu's Macina Empire penetrated into the area that is now Burkina Faso's Sahel Region. It was during the period of the Macina Empire that Fulani settlements like Djibo grew in power and solidified the displacement of Kurumba-speaking populations who predated Fulani speakers in this area of Burkina Faso (D'Aquino 1996).

While there is little scholarship on Djelgoji, what we do know is that in the eighteenth century, Fulani of Jelgoobe lineage started to arrive in the Djibo region of Burkina Faso and started to subjugate other Fulani clans that were already there. It was here that the Djelgoji emirate was created, and at the end of the eighteenth century it expanded into the emirate of Liptako around Dori (Bazemo 1990). While it is unlikely that there was any centralized form of control from Macina itself, it is more likely that Macina would have been viewed as a legitimate caliphate whose suzerainty extended to Djelgoji.

Since 2016, a jihadist group indigenous to Burkina Faso called Ansarul Islam rose in prominence, with its leader Ibrahim Dicko, drawing inspiration from the importance placed by the Fulani of the region to the now lost "ancient Fulani Kingdom called Djelgodji" (Bybee 2017). Ansarul Islam operates in the northern Burkinabé province of Soum, which is directly adjacent to the Mopti region of central Mali, which was once home to the Macina Empire. As Bybee (2017) notes, the area is home to a number of Fulani-led violent organizations, including Katiba Macina and Katiba Khalid Ibn Walid. Dicko has often framed the goals of Ansarul Islam through the lens of the "Fulani Struggle" in the broader region, as well as specifically to reviving the Djelgoji state, which was figuratively lost as a result of French colonization in the late nineteenth century.

The End of the Macina Empire and the Jihad of al-Hajj Umar

The Macina Empire established by Seku Ahmadu was perhaps the most authentically Islamic of the kingdoms that emerged from the nineteenth century jihads. The empire lasted for the reign of three rulers: the founding leader Seku Ahmadu (Ahmad I), his son Ahmad b. Ahmad b. Muhammad Lobbo (d. 1853; Ahmad II), and his grandson Ahmad b. Ahmad b. Ahmad Muhammad Lobbo (d. 1862; Ahmad III). In 1862, al-Hajj Umar Futi Tall (d. 1864), a prominent Muslim scholar and jihadist, conquered the empire, whereupon Ahmad III was captured and executed, thus ushering in a new era. (Nobili and Syed 2021, 4).

As with many states founded upon a revolutionary religious zeal, the leaders of the Macina Empire found it difficult to harness and sustain that initial impetus through the generations. Those born after the establishment of the empire and raised within the context of material power and military glory did "not share the austere religious outlook of many of the caliphate's founders" (Brown 1969, 152). At the same time, Ahmadu departed from the Muslim and Fulani traditions of designating one of his brothers as successor to the throne, instead opting for primogenital succession through his son (Clarke 1982, 131). It was partly as a result of the split between the older and younger generations that some of the more traditionalist minded saw the coming of al-Hajj Umar "as their sole hope for restoring the kind of religious attitudes and practices which they considered appropriate under Islam" (Brown 1969, 152). In addition to this, Ahmadu's brothers undermined the unity of the caliphate by regarding the invasion of Macina by al-Hajj Umar as a potential way to increase their own power after believing that their own brother had deprived them of their right to succession.

While the Macina Empire was invaded militarily by al-Hajj Umar and his forces, this move had to be justified within an Islamic framework. Why was al-Hajj Umar, an individual who identified as a correctly practicing Muslim, invading a Muslim territory that was itself established on the foundations of Islamic law through jihad? Under Islamic law it is forbidden to invade a territory that is already under Muslim rule. The question then becomes one of ascertaining what legitimate Muslim rule looks like. During the nineteenth century in West Africa, Islamic discourse suggested that a territory whose ruler was not a Muslim could also be considered as a non-Muslim territory even if the subjects of that land were Muslim. A territory defined as such could thus be regarded as legitimate for conquest as a means to bring it under the auspices of a Muslim ruler (Syed 2021, 366). This, for example, was also the pretext that the caliphate of Sokoto used to justify aggression against the Borno Empire, with dan Fodio's son Muhammad Bello arguing that the rulers of Borno tolerated pagan beliefs (Pieri and Zenn 2016).

It is in this context that al-Hajj Umar framed his own actions and legitimated his conquest of Macina. Al-Hajj Umar linked the situation in Macina to that of historical circumstances in Islam's formative years in Medina. He raised issues of both "idolatry" and "polytheism" as universal markers "of hostility," and a key reason for the actions followed by the prophet Muhammad (Syed 2021, 366). In a detailed examination of the topic, Syed (2021), recounts a series of exchanges between Ahmad III and al-Hajj Umar on this topic.

Ahmad III, seeking to solidify his own position, argued that "the Bambara have repented and turned to God. They have broken their idols and have constructed mosques, in accordance with what God demands of them" (Syed 2021, 368). This signified that the Macina Empire had instituted changes and made progress in implementing Islamic governance. In another exchange of letters Ahmad III asserted his legitimacy through arguing that it was "not possible to have two Muslim rulers in one single geographic area" and "that al-Hajj Umar was a stranger who had inserted himself into the social and political landscape" (Syed 2021, 369).

As with any change in the balance of power, it is often might that makes right, and al-Hajj Umar was fortunate both to have the necessary military power as well as to find the Macina Empire divided. He had the further advantage of holding a prominent position with the Tijani Sufi brotherhood, having been appointed by Muhammad al-Ghali as "one of the spiritual and temporal leaders of the order" and charged with sweeping away "all the remaining traces of paganism" in West Africa (Clarke 1982, 131). Because of his position, al-Hajj Umar had a significant base of support within the Macina Empire as well as within the wider region.

To further highlight the complex and interconnected ties between the territories that emerged from the nineteenth century jihads, it is interesting to note that al-Hajj Umar spent considerable time in the Sokoto Caliphate (1832–1838), where some accounts claim that he succeeded in convincing dan Fodio's son and successor, Muhammad Bello, in leaving the Qadiriyya for the Tajaniyya Sufi brotherhood (Clarke 1982, 132). To solidify relationships, al-Hajj Umar married one of Bello's daughters who bore his son and successor to the Tukolor Empire. In addition, he married into the ruling family of the Borno Empire (Clarke 1982, 132). The Tukolor Empire lasted until the imposition of French colonialism at the end of the nineteenth century, whereupon the empire was broken up.

Conceptualizing the Fulani

The Fulani have played a central role in this chapter as agents of change in West Africa during the jihads of the nineteenth century. Today, too, jihadist groups in the region have focused specifically on Fulani communities and have sought to repackage grievances in those communities into a vehicle for change, based on historical precedent and the historical role of the Fulani in religious renewal and political change. While the emphasis on the Fulani can be overstated, especially in the contemporary period, it is nevertheless important to examine the Fulani of West Africa in more detail.

The Fulani are widely dispersed throughout Western and Sudanic Africa, roughly along the latitude of contact from Senegal on the Atlantic coast to the border of the former Anglo-Egyptian Sudan (Gordon 2000). They are the largest people group—cultural, ethnic, or tribal—in Africa, with just under 40 million Fulani across fifteen countries in the Sahel and West Africa, extending into Sudan, Central African Republic, and Cameroon (Sangare 2019, 1). With regard to the countries examined in this book, the Fulani are much more varied in their concentration. The largest population exists in Mali at around 3 million or 16 percent of the population, followed by 1.2 million or 5 percent of the population in Burkina Faso, and just 4,600 or less than 1 percent of the population in Ghana (Sangare 2019, 1).

The Fulani are not homogeneous but rather a tribal entity comprising various cultural and social nuances through a dispersed population. After the advent of the colonial period in Africa, many of the tribes and ethnic groups that once had transregional ties (such as the Fulani) were often forced into new national identities, which continued with the establishment of nation-states in the postcolonial period. This has often caused feelings of irredentism, raising wider issues around the questions of citizenship and integration.

Much of the historical background as to the origins of the Fulani are vague—often including some fantastical theories, such as the Fulani being descendants of one of the lost tribes of Israel or of a Roman legion that had lost its way in the desert (Anter 2013). Those theories aside, what does seem consistent in the literature is the notion of the Fulani as not being indigenous to the areas they now inhabit. They are said to be a group that migrated from elsewhere and as such are usually seen as being distinct. Many of the early theories and attempts to categorize the Fulani were collected by Maurice Delafosse, a French ethnographer and colonial official. Delafosse noted that Fulani migration movement was from east to west, and it is only relatively recently (he was writing in 1904) that a few families "migrated from west to east under a conquering impulse, and imposed their rule upon countries where many of their race had long been present, and which they had originally entered from an easterly direction" (Delafosse 1904).

The Fulani have their own narratives as to their origins, which are important to consider, especially as they allow for the myths, memories, and symbols of the Fulani to emerge. In this regard, Johnston (1967) outlines the following origins legend that many Fulani cherish, noting that one version describes

> the marriage of a Moslem Arab, who is usually identified as Ukuba, to a woman of the Sudan called Bajjo Mangu. One day the mother goes to the well and leaves her youngest child in the care of its brothers. On her return she overhears the brother comforting the child in a strange language. She tells her husband, who predicts that this is a sign that the child will be the founder of a

new people who will not speak Arabic, but will nevertheless be the saviors of Islam.

The importance of this legend is that Islam emerges as the central component in Fulani identity. From the Fulani perspective, they were a people of whom great things were prophesied and who were expected to be the saviors of Islam. This can be seen as a resonant theme and even driver of the Fulani-led jihads of the late eighteenth and early nineteenth centuries. For Charles Davis, who investigated identity construction among Fulani, the noteworthy point is that it is not necessarily the factual origin of the Fulani (for the realities of this are lost to time), but rather the ways in which myths and memories around a sense of unique origin serve to reinforce "their sense of privileged status in relation to other tribal groups" (Davis 2012, 39). This unique nature of the myth of Fulani origin creates an aura around the Fulani as a distinct grouping. Davis goes on to argue that the "power of liturgy in forming identity and the shaping effect of narrative in one's understanding of oneself in relation to the world becomes evident in this embraced identity of mysterious origin" (Davis 2012, 39).

The most common arguments place the Fulani as having started to convert to Islam in the eighteenth century. Many of those who had not previously been converted started to abandon pagan beliefs at this time, and those who were already Muslim became emboldened in their religious identity (Johnston 1967). While Johnston does not explain this move toward deeper orthopraxy among Fulani in the eighteenth century, he did argue that the changes had important political results. Fulani held positions as important religious scholars in the courts of the Hausa chiefs. Fulani religious scholars "preached the Shari'a, taught in the palaces of the Hausa rulers, strove to rationalize the actions of the rulers and to moralize their conduct . . . their leadership qualities, sense of purpose, and religious fervor contrasted strongly with the nature of the Hausa" (Nur-Awaleh 2006, 95–114). Accounts from European explorers to Hausaland and the Borno Empire in the nineteenth century note that the "Fulani as Moslems, moreover, were generally much stricter than the more genial and worldly Hausas and Kanuri" (Johnston and Muffett 1973, 65).

By the nineteenth century, Islam had become so deeply embedded as a core component of identity for the Fulani that they began "manipulating their genealogies" to incorporate prestigious Arab Muslims into their ancestral lines, including the lineage of Muhammad, the clan

Quraysh, and the companions of Mecca and Medina who formed the early caliphate (Robinson 2000, 88–89). The argument has been made that the increase in religiosity and adherence to the tenets of Islam as encouraged by the Fulani throughout Hausaland and Macina helped to shift the balance of power toward Fulani ideals of governance. Spencer Trimingham continues this, noting that "Islam introduced an anarchic element [in society], that the law of God was absolute. Friction was therefore eminent between the ruling Hausa aristocracy and the ecclesiastic body composed mainly of the Fulani, who claimed to know the divine will of Allah. Fulani ulama and scholars had to stress religion as the new binding force and solicited the cooperation of the ruling Hausa elites to defend the faith" (Trimingham 1959, 56).

Because of the central importance of Islam, injustices against the Fulani were often therefore "seen as injustices not only against their ethnic group but also against the religion of Islam" (Adeleye 1971, 69). Prior to the nineteenth-century jihads that ushered in the Sokoto Caliphate and the Macina Empire, the Fulani were largely outside the pale of government, and with Islam playing so prominent a role in their identity, the "Fulani were more favorably placed to identify abuses against Islamic tenants than their counterpart indigenous Muslims, many of whom had vested interests in the existing system" (Adeleye 1971, 70). It is therefore not strange that religious reform should have found its staunchest votaries among the Fulani. Further to this, it is interesting to note that it is the identification of grievances against Islam that were motivating factors for social change and reform. Cline argues that the history of successful jihad at reforming society still resonates among some Fulani today (Cline 2021). The extent, however, to which this is a driver of Fulani recruitment to jihadist activity will be discussed in Chapter 4.

Conclusion

The sociopolitical and ethno-religious landscape of Mali, Burkina Faso, and Ghana are complex. Each of these states has had a unique history that has shaped the lived experiences of the population today. Though currently differentiated through nation-state boarders, these countries have longstanding shared experiences, including precolonial caliphates and Islamic empires that reshaped the identity of the region, colonization of the region by European powers and all of its impacts, and at times fraught postindependence periods with coups and the rise of jihadist terrorism.

Both Muslims in northern Nigeria and Muslims in the Mopti region of Mali have a shared understanding of the ways in which their histories were shaped by the jihads of the nineteenth century and how systems of governance were radically altered. There is recognition that just because the system is the way that it is today, it does not need to remain this way, and that there is inspiration to be drawn from the past, where Islam was mobilized as a factor that could radically change society from top to bottom. Brown, writing in 1969 on the Macina Empire, noted that at the end of the 1960s Fulani scholars and laymen took great pride in their history and culture and that the moral portrait of Seku Ahmadu that is preserved in the traditions of the region is not only that of a "classic Muslim saint, but also of a victorious Fulani noble" (Brown 1969, 98). There is no reason to assume that his analysis would be much different today.

We have argued here that the experience of a series of jihads in the early nineteenth century served to reshape the region and to create a space in which Islam as a religion was codified and implemented as the law of the land. For those leading the jihads, their vision was to combat the corruption and immorality of the ruling regimes and to create a new system, strictly based on Islamic law, and in which all people would have a stake. For some Fulani, both the Sokoto Caliphate and the Macina Empire represent a golden age in which Islamic governance was instituted to rectify a series of injustices identified at the time. The heritage these caliphates and empires included, in addition to the social structures they created, also changed the relationship between the Fulani and the religion of Islam. The Fulani went from being one of a range of actors in the socio-religious area to a group that were "perceived as supporters of a pure Islam . . . sensitive to a rigorous application of the precepts of the Qur'an" (Sangare 2019).

The jihads also renewed the focus over questions regarding the role of Islam in governance and shifted the religion from one of the elites, to one that encompassed almost every aspect of life across the Sokoto Caliphate and Macina Empire. Islam was instrumental in acting as an ideology of change through providing a blueprint for governance based on notions of justice. As MacEachern notes, the West African jihads of the nineteenth century were to a large degree revolts of the powerless, "those mocked as 'grass' and thought only to be fit to be grazed on by the horses of the nobles. . . . The millenarian aspects of dan Fodio's jihad, the image it provided of a future world more just and more good than the present one was evidently attractive to such marginalized groups" (MacEachern 2018, 105).

Historical memory, however, only takes us so far, and it is important to remember that history can be drawn upon selectively in order to emphasize certain narratives and themes, and as a means of mobilizing individuals to perceiving a "golden age" where one did not exist. The Macina Liberation Front, Ansarul Islam, and Boko Haram among others are VEOs operating in a globalized twenty-first century, and they need to be recognized as such. The West African jihadist movements of today, as MacEachern puts it, could not have emerged a century or two ago. These movements are products of their enmeshment "within a world of nation states" and developed "in a context of Westernization, urbanism, and other Islamist movements on other continents" (MacEachern 2018, 183). They are distinctly modern, yet at the same time they are also anchored within the contexts of local regions, with "the histories of these landscapes and the cultural understandings of human action that are generated by these histories" accounting for some of their unique and particular features (MacEachern 2018, 183).

The jihads of the nineteenth century were revolutionary because Muslim intellectuals, including dan Fodio, Seku Ahmadu, and al-Hajj Umar, breached long-established norms of maintaining pious distance from the political realm. Instead they articulated a new vision of power in the region that linked legitimate political rule with mastery over Islamic knowledge that they claimed only they had (Syed 2021, 359). While the violent action advocated by the jihadist groups of today in Mali and Burkina Faso should not be seen as directly mirroring the motives and methods followed by the leaders of the Sokoto Caliphate and Macina Empire, it does appear that selectively drawing on the Islamic history of the region, and the harking back to a so-called golden age of Islamic governance, has proved a popular form of mobilization in the region today (Sangare 2019). This theme will be picked up again in Chapter 4, in which we will explore the narratives and strategies of contemporary jihadist groups. In Chapter 3, we will continue with charting the history of the region, focusing on great power interactions across the precolonial, colonial, and independence eras, and the seeds for future violence that were planted during this time.

3

The Colonial Roots of Violence and Strategic Competition

IF THE WORLD IS ENTERING A NEW PERIOD OF GREAT POWER CONFLICT, Africans will likely have a front row seat. Unlike great power "backyards"—the Western Hemisphere for the United States, East Asia for China, and the former Soviet states of Eastern Europe and Central Asia for the Russians—Africa is often viewed as fair game for a diverse array of foreign powers (Meierding and Sigman 2021, 3). As China began to integrate Africa into its Belt and Road Initiative and Russia grew increasingly involved in African conflicts via its proxy, the Wagner Group, scholars seemed increasingly ready to adopt this reframing of African international relations. The post–Cold War period where the United States, its Western allies (especially France in its former colonies), and US-based multinational organizations influenced the terms and conditions of Africa's engagement in globalization with little competition is over (e.g., Blair et al. 2022; Denisov et al. 2019; French 2022; Hicks et al. 2022).

Leadership in global economic and military powers, who have likely been moving in this direction for some time, have gradually adopted this framing publicly. General Dagvin Anderson, Commander of US Special Operations Command Africa (2019–2021), stated: "Being able to partner with [African states] and address that security concern gives us access, gives us engagement opportunity and influence in order to then compete with these other global powers—China and Russia—to ensure we have access and the world has access to these resources as well that are vital to our economies" (J. Warner 2020). This stark framing of US strategic interests against Chinese and Russian interests in Africa acknowledges facts on the ground that have been building.

Between 2010 and 2020, Chinese financiers dedicated more than US$150 billion to African public sector borrowers. This made China the largest lender to African governments over the decade (Usman 2021). Though many of these loans have onerous terms for the borrowers, China has framed its engagement as one member of the Global South helping out another. "In the face of the various forms of hegemonic and bullying practices," Foreign Minister Wang Yi (2022) remarked at the Forum on China-Africa Cooperation, "China and Africa have stood with each other shoulder to shoulder." For its part, Russia has adopted a similar anticolonial rhetoric, with far less foreign assistance and loans and far more mercenaries (Marten 2019; Stronski 2019). In exchange for regime security, with a relatively small contingent of private troops operating under the auspices of the Wagner Group, Russia has managed to dramatically influence domestic and international politics in the Central African Republic and Mali (Cohen 2022).

Africans are no strangers to international influence. For a millennium, Sahelian kingdoms rose and fell based largely on their ability to manage trade between tropical Africa and civilizations to the north (Gomez 2018). Beginning in the sixteenth century international traders depopulated large swaths of the continent to send millions of Africans to the Americas as slave labor (Rodney 1981). The late eighteenth century brought colonialism. With few exceptions Africa was carved up and assigned to European metropoles (Mamdani 1996). Independence in the mid-twentieth century coincided with the Cold War. The United States and Soviet Union jockeyed for allies on the continent, often with little regard for the impact on Africans themselves (Schmidt 2013). In being connected to the international political economy, Africa is not unique (Wallerstein 1974). Its disadvantageous position within this political economy over the past several centuries does, however, put Africa regularly as an unfortunate outlier (Akyeampong et al. 2014).

Scholars largely view these international incursions into Africa from a geostrategic or national level. We know less about how these interactions impacted cities, towns, and villages differently depending on how the international event was experienced locally. How did these international actors impact local grievances and perceptions of international actors? How did they alter locally evolved grievance resolution mechanisms? Answering these questions is the work of this book. In later chapters, we use the contemporary tools of behaviorist social science to focus in on answers in the region stretching from northern Ghana to northern Mali. In this chapter, we turn our attention to periods before the present.

Because international competitors use weapons of both soft power (e.g., sports teams on tour, news networks broadcast via satellite, and multinational corporations selling their wares) and hard power (e.g., direct military engagement and quid pro quo loans), exploring the entire universe of great power competition activities is well beyond the scope of this monograph (Ibrahimov 2020; Nye 1991). Any narrowing of the range of competition is bound to be based on some arbitrary decisions. In this text, these decisions are made for both theoretical and practical reasons. Theoretically, activities that are widely viewed in the contemporary literature as consequential and impactful are preferred over those that are not. Though it is possible for any form of international intervention to have important ripple effects, with limited resources it makes sense to focus on those others have deemed most likely to have an effect. More practically, activities that vary in the region and can be reasonably measured are preferred. With these two overarching concerns, we focus on competition in the realms of military relations, development assistance, and extractive industries.

Looking at great power competition in this slice of West Africa across the precolonial, colonial, and independence eras, the remainder of this chapter begins with the Sahelian kingdoms and concludes with the immediate post–Cold War period. Across these eras, we identify the most significant great powers operating in the region and describe the way they operated similarly or differently in the communities under investigation. Special focus is on how these great powers shaped local reactions and impacted power dynamics altering local governance. This chapter lays the groundwork for subsequent chapters that explore the contemporary period. Today's external military interventions, development assistance, and extractive industries are not operating on a tabula rasa. Rather, communities are likely to understand and react to great power competition through the lenses of past experiences. In subsequent chapters, information here allows us to highlight aspects of the current era that are unique and those that may be better understood as sequels.

Sahelian Empires and the Precolonial Period

Beginning around the eighth century, trade across the Sahara was booming. In the north, salt was relatively abundant and gold relatively scarce. In the south, the situation was reversed. Transporting salt southward and gold northward could be lucrative business (Messier and Miller 2015). The Sahara is vast and treacherous, however. Given the technology of the day, it took the explorer Ibn Battutu two months to cross. Water was always a challenge. It is heavy to transport and there are few reliable sources along the route. Delays could result in death from dehydration. Caravans had to be large and well-armed for security. Failure to hire sufficient support left travelers susceptible to banditry. In a sea of sand and traveling at night to avoid the desert's daytime heat, one dune could look like the next. Those with experience traversing the Sahara stuck to known routes to avoid getting lost in the desert (Fauvelle and Tice 2018, 175–182; Hopkins and Levtzion 2000).

Given the lucrative nature and inherent challenges associated with trans-Saharan trade, powerful actors were incentivized to try and capture the trade. Being lucrative meant there was wealth to be gained. Being challenging ensured rogue traders would face onerous costs venturing from preferred routes. Though there were undoubtedly a number of communities trying to position themselves to get larger percentages of the wealth created via the trans-Saharan trade, eventually a group of Soninke speakers based perhaps in Koumbi Saleh, a town around 900 kilometers from the coast in present-day southern Mauritania, became the focal point. Wagadou, an empire often referred to as Ghana in the records of Arabic-speaking travelers of the time, dominated trans-Saharan trade for more than two centuries.[1] To fend off competitors, Wagadou developed a military reportedly of 200,000 men, many of whom were archers and on camels. To pay for this force, the Wagadou state taxed the trade it controlled (Gomez 2018, 32–38).

There are plenty of maps showing the purported outlines of Wagadou and the ensuing Sahelian empires. The empires appear as a color-coded irregularly shaped blob. This depiction suggests a uniformity that never existed. Wagadou's core would be the rulers and their immediate kinship network. Control along major trading routes and at extractive gold or salt sites needed to be strong to protect the empire's privileged position in the trade network. Outside the empire's core and zones of extraction would be communities connected to the empire by bonds of varying strength depending on proximity. The closer one was to the empire's core, the more demands for tribute and manpower could be exerted. There would also be pressure on leadership to mimic the core in things like religion, social norms, and governance to make compliance easier to enforce. As one moves further from the core, the ability to assert and ensure compliance becomes a bigger challenge. It takes resources to broadcast power across geographic and cultural differences. Wagadou would settle for less tribute and manpower and accept more heterogeneity by necessity. At the empire's margins, rulers could evaluate the strength of the core and modulate their compliance with demands accordingly (Gomez 2018, 32–42; Herbst 2000, 35–57; Isichei 1997, 218–227).

This pattern of building a state around potential chokepoints in the trans-Saharan trade was not unique to Wagadou. With only minor adjustments in sequencing, it fits comfortably within Tilly's (1985) war-making, state-making, protection, and extraction typology of state activities. Over the centuries Wagadou's privileged position in the trans-Saharan trade was challenged. Though the historical record is contested and evidence is sparse, there are several accounts of Almoravid invasions from the north and internal conflicts between the political center of Wagadou and hinterland areas (Gomez 2018, 32–38). By 1235, at the Battle of Kirina, Sundiata Keita and an army of Manding speakers from the current border regions of Mali and Guinea defeated the Sosso-speaking leaders who had recently moved into Koumbi Saleh from the Kaniaga commune of contemporary Mali (Stride and Ifeka 1971, 49).

Sundiata's Mali Empire, not to be confused with the contemporary state of Mali, positioned its center of political power nearly 500 kilometers south of the Wagadou capital, but its raison d'être remained more or less the same: control trade across the Sahara by taxing gold heading north and salt heading south (Wilks 1999). After defeating Wagadou, Mali Empire continued to expand, stretching from the Atlantic Ocean to Timbuktu with over a million square kilometers under dominion by 1350 (Conrad 2010, 116). By the middle of the fifteenth century, the Mali Empire had been weakened by challenges from the Portuguese along the Gambian coast and the persistent internal threats associated with its size and difficulty associated with broadcasting state power across such vast and challenging terrains (Herbst 2000, 49; Wilks 1982b).

Whereas Wagadou and the Mali Empire centered their empires in Mande-speaking areas, Songhai grew out of Gao nearly a thousand kilometers to the east in areas populated predominately by speakers of Nilo-Saharan languages. By the mid-fifteenth century Sonni Ali was leading the Songhai Empire in the capture of trade routes that once belonged to the Mali Empire. By this time Tuaregs had taken control of Timbuktu and Djenne, and Ali expelled them (Oliver 1977, 479). Successive leaders then turned their sights to the west, and by the turn of the sixteenth century nearly all territory the former Mali Empire had conquered was in the hands of the Songhai Empire. When Askia Muhammad's reign ended in 1529, Songhai had brought Agadez in Niger to the Senegal River under one political entity. The lucrative trans-Saharan trade belonged to them (Gomez 2018, 219–224).

This market dominance would soon be revealed as a pyrrhic victory as the perceived tax gains were eroded by competition along the coast. For at least a millennium, the demand for gold in the north and salt in the south incentivized political structures in the region. Beginning early in the seventeenth century, a new form of trade reshaped regional politics. Though the Portuguese had been dabbling along the coast of West Africa since the late fifteenth century, the Spanish, French, Dutch, and English had joined them by the seventeenth (Thornton 1998). They were interested in the same items sub-Saharan Africans had been contributing to the trans-Saharan trade for centuries. Gold, kola, ivory, and slaves were all items of interest to these new European buyers. There were, however, three significant differences in the Atlantic-focused trade routes in comparison to the trans-Saharan routes: markets were on the coast, buyers were relatively wealthy, and the percentage of trade dedicated to slavery increased substantially.

As trade was redirected to the coast, trans-Saharan trade declined and the Sahelian empires lost power. New centers of power arose in the forest belts and along the coasts in response to the altered regional power dynamics and to manage trade with the Europeans. Slaving kingdoms, the likes of Asante, Dahomey, and Oyo, were notable beneficiaries of this alteration of the status quo (Fage 1969, 63–80; Wilks 1982a, 1982b). Communities around these states had two new and significant concerns. First, as their wealth and power waxed, the kingdoms desired growth. This growth looked very similar to that engaged in by the earlier Sahelian empires, though transport challenges in the forest belt were more restrictive. At the center of the kingdoms would be the leadership and their extended kinship network who could be taxed directly and recruited for the military. In the far corners of the kingdoms would be communities that could be coaxed to pay tribute by force but not much more. If the kingdom showed weakness, these hinterland communities would be the first to extract themselves from its grip. Between these two poles was quite a bit of variance (Herbst 2000, 35–57; Wilks 1975). Second, as slaving kingdoms, neighbors were potential commodities. At the peak of the trans-Atlantic slave trade, between 50,000 and 100,000 people were sold to Europeans along the coast per year (Lovejoy 1982). Societies within reach of these kingdoms had not only to fear becoming tributary states giving money and labor to their metropole, but there was a real fear that they could be attacked so that slaving states could feed the voracious slave trade with captives (Diouf 2003; Klein 2001; Lovejoy 2011).

When we apply this precolonial history in the analysis of great power competition in the areas under close study (northern Mali, northern Burkina Faso, southern Burkina Faso, and northern Ghana), we see dramatically different experiences. During the great Sahelian empires, communities in northern Mali were participants in great power competition rather than recipients. By the time of the ancient Mali Empire, present-day northern Mali was part of the coalition of communities that maintained control over trans-Saharan trade. They were not, however, at the center of the empire. That privilege belonged to communities further west along the present-day Guinea/Mali border. Djenne was a major trans-Saharan trading center, but the historical record suggests the area was treated as a vassal state. Local authorities were given some leeway over local governance but were expected to pay tribute and tow the empire line on external matters (Levtzion 1973, 82). Things changed with Songhai's rise. Though Gao is considered the capital of the empire, Timbuktu and Djenne were conquered by Sonni Ali and brought into, if not the core of the empire, a very close ring around the core (Kaba 1984). Until trade was redirected to the coasts and Songhai weakened, communities in our sample of present-day northern Mali were great powers in terms of trade, military, and cultural matters (Niane 2016).

Areas of northern Burkina Faso were brought into the Songhai Empire, but as hinterlands. Gao is a mere 175 kilometers from what is today Burkina Faso's Sahel Region. Some Fulani, undoubtedly at least a few from this area, were taken into slavery by Sunni Ali and his forces (Gomez 2018, 211–212; Hunwick 1999, 95–96). Within Songhai, these Fulani female slaves became concubines and wives for many of Songhai's political, economic, and religious leaders. Men were funneled into the army, which was on constant campaign. Those Fulani left to live in current-day Burkina Faso would have understood their community as one in a tributary relationship with Gao and later Timbuktu and Djenne. Like those populated by Tuareg and northern Moors, Fulani communities were largely precluded from building large cities and urban areas during their time in the Songhai Empire. Cosmopolitanism in Songhai's larger cities did not tolerate inputs from nomadic neighbors considered déclassé by Songhai elites. The resentment this second-class status engendered manifested itself in swift opposition to the regime at the slightest sign of weakness (Abitol 1992).

For Mossi speakers in southern Burkina Faso and Dagomba speakers in northern Ghana, their origin stories are wrapped up in the breakup of one Sahelian empire and the rise of another. They were likely dabblers in slave raiding, mining, and petty trading of animal and agricultural products in the Niger bend area, and their services were authorized by Malian authorities whose trading network needed inputs. As the Mali Empire weakened and began to disintegrate, a group of Mossi speakers attempted to challenge Songhai for Timbuktu but were repelled. Songhai, led by Sonni Ali, looked to displace these networks loyal to Mali. Clerics went so far as to declare the largely non-Muslim Mossi and Dagomba as not only undesirable neighbors, but eligible for slavery (Gomez 2018, 305). These Gur speakers recognized the challenge Songhai posed to their existence and headed south to establish their own smaller tributary networks (Iliasu 1971). Once settled, they could trade with the Sahelian empire of the day but do so with a modicum of protection provided by distance.

Shortly after making this movement, however, these communities faced a new existential threat. Just as the trans-Saharan trade network waned, the trans-Atlantic trade in slaves was on the rise, and states like the Ashanti were in search of humans to feed this commercial activity. Dagomba and Mossi communities were both subject to raids and raiders themselves (Der 1998). Over time the Dagomba and Mossi developed stronger defenses to survive their new realities and warfare was replaced with trickery and neighbor selling neighbor as the primary source of slaves bound for the New World (Nunn and Wantchekon 2011, 3225–3226).

For the more than ten millennia that predates the arrival of European forts on West African coasts, these three great Sahelian empires were the regional great powers. Their activities fundamentally shaped international relations and local politics from the Mediterranean Sea to the Bight of Benin. For those who were in the center of these empires, this meant direct impacts. Taxes and military conscription were expected, but so too was fealty in who manned local government offices, how they interacted with local populations, and what the expectations were for compliance to cultural standards. As one moves from Wagadou to Mali to Songhai, the center of power moves closer to sites under close observation in this text. By the latter empire, areas of northern Mali were part of the center, and areas of northern Burkina Faso were quite close. In southern Burkina Faso and northern Ghana, residents lived outside the empire, but this fact did not shelter them from experiencing their might. They would have been acutely aware of the empires to their north and occasionally experienced their projections of power.

In terms of military operations, communities near the center of these empires were expected to donate treasure and men to the cause of building empire and maintaining it. For communities in the empire but outside of the center, these expectations would be interpreted less as a civic duty and more as an imposition. Sundiata Keita was born in the shadows of the Wagadou Empire, and Sonni Ali had a similar experience with regard to the Mali Empire. Growing up in hinterland communities or coming from a disfavored ethnic group came with fewer of the benefits of power. Outside the empires, communities were subject to raids for slaves and extraction of resources. The purpose of the Sahelian empires was to extricate as large a percentage of the trans-Saharan trade as possible. For areas in southern Burkina Faso and northern Ghana, where there were some gold deposits and less powerful kingdoms, this meant being squeezed as tightly as possible with threat of violence used as a deterrent from disrupting trade.

Direct and Indirect Rule During the Colonial Period

Early Europeans explored the coast without venturing far inland in numbers. In the first half of the fifteenth century, the Portuguese established trading posts along West Africa's Atlantic coastline. By the dawn of the sixteenth century, they had a fort in Elmina in present-day

Ghana and were rounding the Cape of Good Hope to explore ports in East Africa and onward to Asia. Caravelle sailing ships made the exploration possible (Unger 1995). A desire to cut Arab traders out of the loop in the valuable trade for slaves and gold from Africa and spice from Asia provided the motivation. As early as the middle of the fifteenth century, slaves from West Africa were being transported by Portuguese ships to the Canary Islands and Europe. Estimates for the volume of this trade were hundreds, but not thousands, of people per year. This volume increased dramatically by the middle of the sixteenth century when the Portuguese turned their attention to São Toméan and Brazilian sugar plantations, though most of these latter slaves originated in Central Africa and not West Africa. As slavery became a bigger admixture of Portuguese trade when the trans-Atlantic triangular trade was in full swing, other goods from the continent saw their role diminished (Manning 2006).

By the middle of the seventeenth century, Spanish, British, Dutch, American, and French sailors had joined the Portuguese in this lucrative transcontinental trade in slaves. Between the dawn of the sixteenth century and the close of the nineteenth century, an estimated 12.5 million Africans embarked on the journey to the New World as cargo on a ship flying one of these great merchant powers' flags (Eltis 2009).[2] Infrastructure to facilitate these operations in West Africa consisted of relatively small garrisons along the coast. These forts and their surroundings gave the European forces a place to organize their business transactions. This meant a place to safely store items they brought to Africa, which, by the heyday of the trans-Atlantic slave trade, consisted primarily of guns and gunpowder (Rodney 1981; Whatley 2018). It also meant a place to safely store human beings being shipped to the Americas until the next ship bound for the New World arrived. Europeans did very little capturing of slaves themselves. Rather they tapped into existing markets for slaves and provided the financial incentives to expand these markets and the weaponry needed to carry out slave raiding more efficiently. During the trans-Atlantic slave period, residents even hundreds of kilometers from the coast were potential victims of this trade. Communities were attacked by rivals and their residents sold into slavery. Slave raiders roamed the countryside looking for easy marks. Traditional leaders looking for personal gain would charge troublesome residents of their territory with a crime and send them away (Rodney 1967, 15).

In terms of great power competition, European forts along the coast were far enough from the geographic area under study here for there to be no direct effects. Europeans primarily relied on Africans to deliver slaves to the coast. The indirect effects, however, were immense. As discussed in the previous section, these coastal forts fundamentally redirected trade and the ripple effects both diminished the role of Sahelian empires and amplified the role of communities closer to the coast who would come to be known collectively as the "Slave Kingdoms" (PBS 1999). For communities under study who live in northern Mali, this meant being displaced as a regional power over relatively few generations. For communities who live in southern Burkina Faso and northern Ghana this meant the threat of predation from slave raiders was coming not from the north but the south, and the appetite of these raiders was intensified. Warfare, both from powerful neighboring states and raiders looking for slaves, was an increasing existential threat (Rodney 1967, 9).

Two technological advancements fundamentally changed this relationship between Europeans and Africans (Uzoigwe 1985). Though quinine's medicinal properties had been known to the Quechua people in South America before the arrival of Europeans and was available in Europe as a powder derived from the bark of the cinchona tree since at least the first half of the seventeenth century, it had not been packaged in standardized pharmaceutical doses until the middle of the nineteenth century (Rodríguez 2007; Roy 1998, 465). Quinine made it possible for Europeans to head inland in tropical Africa without the exceedingly high death toll malaria had heretofore extracted. The second advancement came in the form of Maxim guns, field artillery, and repeating rifles. One shot at a time, these weapons were no more deadly than weapons African armies would have had access to, but the rapidity with which European armies were able to deliver the next shot was a game changer. Just a few hundred troops and a few dozen of this new generation of rapidly shooting firearms could defeat armies numbering in the tens of thousands (Headrick 1979, 259).

These technological changes paved the way for colonial ambitions. What had been a relatively small footprint on the coast with serious reverberations caused by a change in the pattern and volume of the slave trade, turned quickly into full-scale colonialism. At the Berlin Conference of 1884–1885, the great powers of Europe met to reify their possessions along the coast and set the rules for claiming territory going forward in a manner that would not result in direct military conflict between European powers. Over the next decade, Africans and their land, with very few exceptions, were brought into a European colonial empire by treaty, private company, or war (Förster et al. 1988). In West Africa, this meant a long stretch of the Sahel came under the French flag with the British, Germans, Portuguese, and Liberians breaking up this block only along the coasts. Present-day Mali and Burkina Faso fell under the French flag. Northern Ghana represented the hinterlands of British-controlled territory.

On paper, this distinction between French and British West Africa amounted to much. A great deal of high-minded debate over their differing strategies of rule and the likely impact of each on Africans occurred. The French ruled directly. This meant many precolonial authorities maintained customary power over their subjects, but formal legal authority rested in Paris. All territory resting under the French flag was recognized as part of France, and compared to their British counterparts, French colonies had a disproportionately high number of French personnel from Europe on the ground. Despite governing a smaller population than the British in West Africa, the French sent nearly three times as many European administrators to West Africa as the British did (Crowder 1964, 197–199; Whittlesey 1937, 367).

For their part, the British ruled (for the most part) indirectly. Early in the scramble for Africa, British colonial officer Lord Lugard was tasked with maintaining effective control of the geographic area now known as Northern Nigeria. He had few men for the task, and the French were exploring areas upstream along the Niger River. To manage the situation, Lugard settled on an agreement with local authorities. If they acquiesced to flying the British flag and honoring the colonial tax system, local affairs would be left largely as the realm of traditional authorities. There were limits placed on local affairs for sure and plenty of anecdotes about British officers meddling behind the scenes, but by and large border communities agreed that British rule was less of an imposition (Crowder 1964, 199–202; Whittlesey 1937, 363–364). On the ground, these colonial proclivities had measurable effects on the aggregate, but they were far from uniform (Müller-Crepon 2020).

The Mopti region of Mali, once the epicenter of the Songhai Empire, had been relegated to relative obscurity by the time the French arrived in 1893 (Naval Intelligence Division 1944, 193).

Trans-Saharan trade saw its profitability diminished by European traders on the coast, and invaders from the north and west had picked apart the once powerful empire (Gomez 2018, 355–367). As the French approached, the Fulani Empire of Macina had been recently destroyed by Toucouleur forces led by al-Hajj Umar (Robinson 1985). Into this power vacuum came the French colonial authorities with their ideas of direct rule. The area, however, was viewed as a hinterland in this project. Areas along the coast received more attention than inland portions of the colony. When inland parts of French West Africa were separated administratively from the coast, partially in the form of French Sudan, the Mopti region remained far flung from the center of administration even then as the capital was set first in Kayes and later in Bamako.

Being a hinterland did not mean residents of the region were immune from the great power governing them. They were officially subjects of the French state and subject to taxation and forced labor. It does, however, mean a lighter touch in daily life. The way in which most residents of the region came into contact with the colonial state was via agriculture. There were experiments in imposed irrigated agricultural villages, but for the most part colonial authorities found it more convenient to rely on rain-fed agriculture operated by the patrilineal lineage-based networks that remained after the collapse of the Sahelian kingdoms and ensuing conflict (Becker 1994; Roberts 1996).

As a territorial unit, the existence of an entity now known as Burkina Faso was never a foregone conclusion during colonialism. In the late nineteenth century, the area had value to the French colonizers almost exclusively as a means to keep British and German ambitions at bay. Ruled as a backwater in their larger colonial project, it was not until 1919 that the French recognized Upper Volta (Burkina Faso's name until 1984) as a political unit to quell riots in the west over conscription, forced labor, and taxation. Unlike the Mossi kingdom to the east, the west had acephalous communities in the precolonial era and found it extremely difficult to acculturate themselves with the French centralized approach to authority (Sèni 1985). Then, barely a decade later, the French reversed course hoping to cut costs at the peak of the great depression. Upper Volta had relatively unproductive farmland and few natural resources the French coveted. It did have cheap labor, and this labor was needed in neighboring parts of the French colonial empire where colonial investments were higher

(Huillery 2009). Most of the colony was given to Côte d'Ivoire, with bits of the north going to what would become Mali and bits of the far east going to what would become Niger (Englebert 1999, 23–24). Reunification of France's Upper Volta colony came only in 1947, barely a decade before independence (Morgenthau 1964, 182–183).

Because of this marginality, the Burkinabé experiences in the north and the south had some commonalities. Nowhere in the country was bustling with Europeans like Saint-Louis, Dakar, or Abidjan. In 1910 Ouagadougou cercle had 5 Europeans per 100,000 residents and Dori cercle had 8. These cercles are where the present-day Centre-Sud and Sahel provinces would have resided. For comparison, Mopti had 26 Europeans per 100,000 residents in what were the hinterlands of French Sudan. Centers of French control like Dakar (6,918 per 100,000), Nouadhibou (2,125 per 100,000), Saint-Louis (1,670 per 100,000), and Bassam (907 per 100,000) were where high-minded conversations of assimilation happened, not in areas of present-day Burkina Faso.[3]

There were also, however, significant differences between north and south. The north of Burkina Faso was tied to French Sudan alongside neighboring, predominately Fulani-speaking, communities that would end up in independence-era Mali. Here the French rules against slavery were controversial among the elites and gave new rights to members of the Rimaibé caste. This led to population reductions as many formerly enslaved people left for their areas of origin or bigger urban areas (Klein 1998, 184). Migration in the south was even more intense. Colonial authorities in Côte d'Ivoire were desirous of cheap labor to work in agriculture. They viewed recently acquired portions of the disbanded Upper Volta colony as a potential source of this labor. In the competition between Britain and France for West African territory, southern Burkina Faso barely fell to the French, but by the first quarter of the twentieth century colonial policy had dramatically decreased migration just across the border into communities linked through precolonial ties and increased migration to Bobo and onward into Côte d'Ivoire (Gervais and Mandé 2000).

Britain formally declared northern Ghana a protectorate in 1901. The precolonial states of Dagomba, Mamprusi, and Gonja were in various states of decline. Just because Britain outlawed slavery nearly a century before, it did not mean the practices amplified during the Atlantic slave trade period ceased. With the powerful Asante state to the south and relatively weak states and decentralized societies to the immediate north, slave raiders like Babatu and Samori continued to roam what would become northern Ghana to cater to continental demand. The insecurity weakened the area's political institutions that variously benefited from the mercenary activities and were threatened by them (Benson 2007). For Britain the principal reason to colonize northern Ghana was to keep it out of the hands of the French and Germans. It was never viewed as a potentially revenue-generating part of their empire.

Despite finding weak states in disrepair, indirect rule was viewed as the financially prudent choice. Where leaders were feckless, they were propped up. Where there were no leaders, they were created. As long as there was no unrest, taxes were collected, and labor was given when called, local matters remained local matters and the colonial authorities were satisfied (Brukum 1999). "Native Tribunals," read the Northern Territories Administration Ordinance of 1902, "shall exercise the jurisdiction heretofore exercised by them in the same manner as such jurisdiction has been heretofore exercised" (Bening 1995, 228). So these fragile states faced little internal challenge, the British went so far as to ban Western education and Christian missionary activities in the north, only slightly relaxing these prohibitions over time (Bening 2015; R. G. Thomas 1974). Perhaps no figure better depicts the discrepancies between north and south in the British Gold Coast than school enrollment. In 1948, less than a decade before independence, Northern Territories could claim 3,970 primary school students enrolled and 80 at the secondary level. Southern portions of the colony, by contrast, claimed 282,718 and 6,410 students respectively (Austin 1964, 13–14). If northerners were going to contribute to the colonial cause, it would be in the form of forced labor, primarily in the south where roads were built, gold mined, and crops harvested (R. G. Thomas 1973).

Formal colonialism lasted approximately sixty years in the swatch of territory stretching from northern Ghana through northern Mali. There were two colonial powers and three different colonies. To paint such a large area geographically and temporally with a broad brush undoubtedly leaves out exceptions to the rule. For the most part, however, colonialism happened quickly and with relatively little armed local opposition. The communities in the region had been weakened by the fall of the trans-Saharan trade and/or the intense slaving that happened in the period immediately prior to formal colonization. Indirect or direct, colonial rule gave a great deal of autonomy to communities in the area as they inhabited colonial hinterlands with relatively little investment or European staffing. Traditional local governance was encouraged by the British and discouraged by the French, though these preferences had little force behind them.

Likely the biggest impact of the great power competition between the British and French was in the arbitrary boundaries drawn on a map and the location of colonial trading depots that would become independent Africa's mega-cities. It is here in part that seeds of future conflict were planted. Though power had migrated substantially, first to the east and then south, over the precolonial era described above, Lagos and Abidjan and Dakar as well as Accra and Ouagadougou and Bamako, once set as regional economic centers, have not budged. There is little evidence to suggest these locations were based on anything other than convenience for trade with the European metropole (Ricart-Huguet 2022). This would reify the hinterland status of the areas we investigate, routinely send residents elsewhere in search of work, and act as a significant anchor on development prospects (Huillery 2009).

Independence in the Age of the Cold War

Though much of the struggle for independence occurred in urban areas, there were undoubtedly members of the communities under investigation here who took part. They were, however, not the stars of the show. In the francophone countries, those roles went to elites like Léopold Senghor of Senegal, who did his university schooling in France, or Modibo Keïta of Mali and Maurice Yaméogo of Burkina Faso, who did their schooling at the elite French West African training college École William Ponty (Vaillant 2006; T. Warner 2016). Though some of these independence-era leaders came from hinterland communities, the French assimilation required to achieve these rarified academic credentials required time in urban centers spent early and often.

Though the anglophone agitators for independence in Ghana were slightly more heterogenous in their educational backgrounds, they were no less accomplished. Of Ghana's "Big Six" independence leaders, all went to well-regarded secondary schools in the south and did their tertiary education in the United Kingdom or United States. None hailed from a part of the Gold Coast colony's Northern Territories (Austin 1961). The seeds of colonialism's replacement were generally sewn in the most advantaged parts of the respective colonial empires. The Mopti Region of Mali, Sahel and Centre-Sud Regions of Burkina Faso, and Upper East Region of Ghana are not among these privileged corners.

For these hinterland communities, the biggest immediate impact independence had was on migration. There was a lot of movement of peoples during the precolonial era. If one part of West Africa became too inhospitable, entire extended families would pick up and travel until they found a spot more hospitable. Virtually every community has a story of a brave founder who settled nearby only after fleeing adversity some place else (Swindell 1995). Colonialism narrowed this migration, making it easier to move within the French or English or Portuguese sphere of influence than outside. Mopti is closer to Accra than Dakar. Po is closer to Accra than Abidjan. Colonial authorities in French West Africa knew British colonies were attracting entire communities with their more lenient rules early in the colonial era. They actively erected obstacles to working in anglophone countries and incentivized labor migration within the francophone colonies (Asiwaju 1976, 145; Gervais and Mandé 2000; Roberts 1996, 30).

Independence restricted migration routes even further. What had been a relatively choice-rich environment before, now had the path of least resistance indelibly marked toward the capital city. Overnight West Africa was transformed from an area where one could migrate easily within either anglophone or francophone colonies, to one with thirteen independent countries looking to control what went on within their borders (Herbst 1990, 188). Though there was early speculation on whether these borders would hold, they have been remarkably static and impactful over the ensuing decades (Herbst 2000). Despite being more than three times as far, residents in Ghana's Upper East region routinely travel to Accra to catch an international flight despite the fact that Accra is more than three times as far as Ouagadougou.

The effect of this status quo has been stagnation in the areas under study. At the time of colonization the communities in question were poor and agricultural. They left colonialism poor and agricultural. Though from time to time independence-era governments have mimicked colonial-era projects designed to commercialize cash crops in the regions, for much of this era farming has been predominately small-scale subsistence or destined for local markets (Bates 1981). These regions are some of the richest in the world in terms of gold, but the national governments preserve subterranean mineral rights for themselves, leaving localities with little leverage to parlay the wealth into local development. Instead, what little benefit is experienced happens in the capital (Andersson et al. 2015; D'avignon 2018; Stone 1920). It is in these large capital cities where population booms have been the subject of conversation from independence through the present (Gellar 1967; Heinrigs 2020). Much of this growth comes directly from more marginal areas of West Africa in terms of seasonal migration and longer-term resettlements in capital cities (McKay and Deshingkar 2014).

Great power competition in the form of the Cold War dominated the first three decades of the independence era. In Ghana and Burkina Faso this meant a steady stream of coups. Ghana experienced a successful coup in 1966, 1972, 1978, 1979, and 1981. Burkina Faso had theirs in 1966, 1974, 1980, 1982, 1983, and 1987 (McGowan 2003). Rumblings of Soviet and/or US involvement followed each event, though instability was more a marker of the period for each country than African socialism or pro-West sentiments. Not a decade went by with a regime intact. Mali only had a coup in 1968 where their leftist independence-era leader, Modibo Keïta, was replaced by a pro-West ally (Moussa Traoré). Though it was undoubtedly a blow to Soviet ambitions, compared to the overthrow of Kwame Nkrumah in Ghana it was received as a relatively minor loss (Telepneva 2018, 10).

As the Berlin Wall fell, Africa was washed over by democracy's fourth wave (Bratton and van de Walle 1997). Ghana's experiment with democracy brought it relative stability and prosperity. Mali too was largely considered a democratic success for a couple of decades. Though the country saw its first Tuareg rebellion shortly after independence, it would not be its last (J. S. Lecocq 2002). Tuareg rebellions threatened the country's stability in 1990–1995, 2007–2009, and in 2012 (Wing 2013). This last occurrence would become wedded to violent extremist groups and spiral into the contemporary era of conflict in Mali's north. Burkina Faso's former military head of state Blaise Compaoré was the only one capable of extending his rule past 2010, albeit in the role of a civilian. Shortly after his popular overthrow in 2014, Burkina Faso was engulfed in residuals of Mali's security troubles (Bonnecase 2015).

In terms of military relations, development assistance, and extractive industries, where Mali, Burkina Faso, and Ghana went, so too did the focus regions. So as not to steal the thunder of future chapters, we do not spend a great deal of time here delving into details on the contemporary status of great power competition in the four regions under study. The takeaway is when MINUSMA changes strategies in Mopti, the United States suspends aid to projects across Burkina Faso after a coup d'état, and Chinese entrepreneurs establish small holder rights to a mine in Ghana's Upper East, negotiations on the nature of these interactions is largely done in Bamako, Ouagadougou, and Accra respectively (Arieff et al. 2021; Crawford et al. 2017; Gauthier Vela 2021). The great power competition of today is at least substantially filtered through the results of the great power competition of yesterday.

Conclusion

Great power competition is not new to West Africa. Throughout the region's history, residents living in the areas stretching from just south of the Niger River's big bend to the convergence point of the Red and White Volta Rivers had to contend with powerful external actors influencing political, economic, and social outcomes at home. During precolonial history, this competition was driven by trade. For more than a millennium this trade primarily traversed the Sahara desert. When the Portuguese established footholds along the Atlantic and Gulf of Guinea coastlines, trade steadily redirected across the ocean. Communities responded to the incentives of this trade based on their power in relation to their neighbors. Near Mopti there was a period of time where residents were in close proximity to the center of regional power during the Songhai empire. For most of this period, however, the communities under consideration were more marginal. If they got too close to power, they could benefit tangentially from trade but were also subject to taxation and slave raiding.

As colonialism arrived in the late nineteenth century, trade was replaced by imperialism as the engine of great power competition. France got to present-day Mali and Burkina Faso first. Britain got to present-day Ghana. Once brought under a European flag, incentives to invest resources into the regions under focus here were few. Capital cities were established far away, and hinterland areas were most valuable as occasional labor reserves for infrastructure projects and large agricultural schemes. For the most part, lineage networks and customs were left alone as European education and religion were promoted more heavily in highly populated urban areas. Independence reified this hinterland status. Community members, who once had reasonably inexpensive exit options, lost the mobility they once had. Colonial borders shrunk their range, and national borders shrunk them again. These borders also tied communities like those in northern Ghana, Burkina Faso, and Mali to capital cities—a difficult day's journey away even with today's transport options. To formally engage with foreign policy, residents had to move away from their hinterland homes.

The relationship between residents of these areas and their local providers of governance were tousled over the years by these interactions with external actors. Though it is challenging to reconstruct the effects from intervention to intervention and from community to community, one can make some general observations based on how individuals can and do respond to negative changes to their environment by other actors. In the classic Exit, Voice, Loyalty game, citizens can passively accept the negative changes, protest said changes, or pick up and leave (Hirschman 1970). They will choose exit when it is relatively cheap, the proposed changes are bad enough, and/or the government is likely to ignore their protests. In the precolonial period, communities and individuals regularly chose this option. Over the eras, the incentives changed against this strategy. It is virtually nonexistent for communities today. For individuals it tends to come with a nonfungible refugee status, toward the national capital, or overseas (Joseph and Herbst 1997).

It is possible, though, that some communities found ways to respond to these external shocks that insulated them from the most negative of consequences. Their leadership, or institutions, or some bit of unanticipated luck made it so these interventions by powerful external actors resulted in positive effects or less negative ones. Damaging internal grievances were few and far between, and when they arose they were dealt with in a manner that satisfied all parties. What was different about these communities than those eviscerated by the trade wars of precolonial West Africa, the imposition of colonialism by European powers, or an independence that left them attached to a center but unmoored locally? Some external interventions were likely more detrimental to community governance than others as well. When there are big and reasonably well documented interventions in terms of geographical scope, it is possible to test this hypothesis with correlations between past events and contemporary opinions, behaviors, or characteristics (e.g., Acemoglu et al. 2001; Englebert 2000; Nunn and Wantchekon 2011).

Subtler and more poorly documented differences, however, cannot be incorporated into models. For years past we just do not know in a systematic way about a village's relative immunity to the pressures of regional trade during the Sahelian precolonial empires because of a particularly defensible geography, or a traditional leader's ability to avoid hut taxes because a quarrelsome neighbor regularly drew the attention of the colonial authorities, or a town's preference for homemade brooms over those imported from China because a popular religious leader advocated buying local. This makes the work done in later chapters so relatively unique. We take a snapshot of grievances and perceptions of local governance that can be compared with slighter forms of external interventions like the presence of an international mine in the vicinity, or a temporary base in the war on terror, or a Peace Corps volunteer everyone knows. This approach is challenging to do across time but is reflective of the heterogeneous ways in which great powers compete. Data on these subtle forms of competition that do not fit easily into known boundaries have been largely lost for previous historical periods.

Before we return to this topic, Chapter 4 explores the narratives and strategies of contemporary VEO groups in the region and identifies what jihadist groups see as the main grievances in local communities, their strategies for amplifying grievances as means for garnering violent collective action, as well as alternate modes of governance based on Islamic law that they put forward as solutions to grievances.

Notes

1. Wagadou is used here as a synonym for what many African histories refer to as the Ghana Empire. We go with the moniker Wagadou here for two reasons. First, a consensus has formed around the idea that Ghana was a mislabeling of the empire by outsiders. It was rather an appellation for the empire's

rulers. Wagadou was likely the name given the empire by its Soninke-speaking residents (Gomez 2018, 31–32). Second, though Ghana Empire is used more often in the literature than Wagadou, it is confusing. We spend a great deal of time on politics in the contemporary state of Ghana, which borrowed its name from the ancient empire. Though ancient Ghana and contemporary Ghana did not overlap geographically, the contemporary state derives its name from the ancient empire.

2. These large powers were joined by smaller powers operating companies like the Dutch. These included Danes, Swedes, and Brandenburgers (Fage 1969, 69).

3. Data on the number of Europeans in colonial era French West Africa taken from Huillery (2010).

4

Mobilizing Violence: Jihadist Strategies

IN 2019 THERE WAS A SHIFT IN THE GLOBAL DYNAMICS OF JIHADIST TERRORism. While in the preceding years Iraq and Syria had seen the worst levels of jihadist violence, by 2019 the epicenter of global jihadism had swung to the Sahel region of Africa.

There are two hot spots of violent conflict in West Africa. The first is the Sahel theater, which includes Mali, Burkina Faso, and western parts of Niger, and in which factions affiliated to al-Qaeda and Islamic State are operating. Jihadists in this area are further pushing southward into the equatorial states of Ghana, Côte d'Ivoire, Togo, and Benin. The second is in the Lake Chad Basin theater, in which Boko Haram in the form of Islamic State West Africa Province as well as splinter groups operate. Though distinct and geographically distant, there is potential for the two conflicts to converge, especially if a corridor is opened through northern Nigeria into southwestern Niger. While occasionally referencing events in the Lake Chad region, in this chapter we focus predominantly on the Sahel theater and will provide a background to the jihadist groups operating there, including their ideologies and strategies.

We are particularly interested in how jihadist groups relate to grievances identified in local communities, and the types of governance solutions that jihadists put forward. While we talk of VEOs as posing exogenous shocks to local communities, we also acknowledge that it is from local communities that jihadists seek to recruit new members. Jihadist groups often seek to establish their presence within communities, at times providing social services, acting as de facto authorities, and in some cases levying taxes or signing pacts in exchange for not targeting a given community.

We start the chapter by outlining recent shifts in the security landscape of the region before turning to an overview of most of the important jihadist factions—their core beliefs, goals, and actions—across Mali and Burkina Faso. JNIM, The Macina Liberation Front (affiliated to JNIM), Ansarul Islam (founded in Burkina Faso), and ISGS will form case studies that we examine. We will explain the ways in which these jihadist groups frame conflicts in the region and the extent to which they are successful in leveraging local grievances to advance their agendas. Jihadist organizations, and especially their propaganda offices, have become increasingly adept in drawing on issues with governance, especially around corruption, foreign influence, and what they believe to be the abandonment of local populations by central government in favor of partnerships with former colonial powers instead. As well as focusing on the national level, VEOs have also demonstrated an ability to identify and engage with grievances at the local level, in particular highlighting (perceived) injustices toward Fulani.

Overview of the Regional Security Landscape

Between 2019 and the writing of this book, a third of all deaths caused by terrorism have occurred in the Sahel, and the level of instability has increased exponentially. This violence is driven by jihadist groups that have the capacity to operate across nation-state borders between Mali, Burkina Faso, and Niger. Two broad jihadist organizations stand out for their lethality—Jama'at Nusrat al Islam w'al Muslimeen (JNIM) and Islamic State in the Greater Sahara (ISGS). JNIM (the name translates to the Group for the Support of Islam and Muslims) is an al-Qaeda–affiliated umbrella organization that brought together preexisting jihadist groups (discussed below) and was in 2022 the world's fastest-growing jihadist organization, measured by the increase in attacks and deaths (*Economist* 2022a). ISGS is an Islamic State–affiliated organization that has found increasing operational capacity in the region and stands out for its unyielding stance toward those who oppose its views.

Both organizations have carried out attacks in central Mali, northern and eastern Burkina Faso, and western Niger. In Mali 2,700 people were killed in the first six months of 2022, 40 percent more than in all of 2021 (*Economist* 2022a). Burkina Faso became the heart of the conflict in 2022, with violent events doubling when compared to 2021 (Nsaibia 2023). According to data from ACLED, May 2024 was the deadliest month in Burkina Faso since April 2023, with over 900 people reportedly killed. Casualties were a result of increased violence from JNIM, but also indiscriminate attacks from the armed forces (Serwat 2024). Ghana, long celebrated as a peaceful democracy, faces spillover as national borders routinely fail to contain jihadist activity. While Ghana has yet to suffer a direct attack, Burkina Faso shows how quickly the tide can turn. Tensions were heightened in February 2023, when, for the first time, attempts were made to blow up a bridge using explosives in northern Ghana, a region "where the government fears growing violent spillover" from jihadists in Burkina Faso (France 24 2023a). Ghana's northern frontier with Burkina Faso is an area with well-established smuggling routes, porous borders, and illegal gold mining—"a combination local officials and experts worry could benefit jihadists" (France 24 2023a).

The spread of violence to the littoral states of West Africa threatens regional stability, as well as US and allied interests. Violent events involving extremist groups in the region have doubled every year since 2015. What is further troubling is that jihadists have already moved into the littoral states, with at least sixteen attacks on Côte d'Ivoire in 2022 (*Economist* 2022b), and at least twenty-eight reports of violence in northern Benin attributed to JNIM or the Islamic State between November 2021 and September 2022, making it clear that jihadist cells have already entrenched in the country's northern regions (Brottem 2022).

Such fatalities reflect the rising tide of hostilities between jihadists and national and regional security forces, while approximately one-fifth of the battles were between "JNIM affiliates and ISGS over territory, revenues, and recruitment" (Brottem 2022). In addition to fatalities, the ongoing conflict in the Sahel has displaced some 1.7 million people, "including more than 170,000 refugees and 1.5 million internally displaced" (Africa Center for Strategic Studies 2021). Burkina Faso faced the brunt of this displacement, with roughly 1.1 million displaced. This militant violence has contributed to increased food insecurity—affecting more than 3 million in both Mali and Burkina Faso. Mali and Burkina Faso are struggling to contain the conflict within their own borders, and the impacts of insecurity have created a pool of grievances among the population, and especially in areas where violence is at its worst. It is these grievances that external actors, in this case jihadist groups, seek to exploit in order to undermine government legitimacy, and to bolster their own competing vision for the future of society.

Jihadist groups understand that to be effective in advancing their goals, their messaging has to be strategic and framed in ways that resonate with target audiences. To this end they have built elaborate media organizations that are tasked with constructing and disseminating their ideologies and publicizing their activities for maximum impact. Islamic State was particularly effective at this, having perfected the art of creating a complete media package and coordinating their messaging (at least for an international audience) through Al-Hayat media center (Pieri 2021a). JNIM also has its own dedicated media center—Az-Zallaqa—which releases statements, audio, and video messaging on a range of topics (discussed below).

Jihadist groups have become adept at weaponizing digital media to their advantage with the ability to utilize a broad range of technological services to deliver messages directly to their followers. Technology is improving the operational effectiveness of jihadists in the Sahel by helping them to better obscure contacts, plans, and coordination efforts. This can often be done through instant-chat services such as WhatsApp or Telegram, which allow end-to-end encryption, a function which makes it much more difficult for authorities to monitor what is being sent. One of the key things that technology has done is to flatten the intellectual battlefield. In the past, for a message to reach a broad audience, ideologues and movement leaders would have to write and publish pamphlets, books, and other written materials and distribute these. Taped sermons too would be distributed. But the distribution was, to an extent, limited. Now with social media, groups that understand how these tools work have the ability to wage guerrilla warfare of sorts, and to do so on their own terms without the need for large-scale budgets. Messaging can reach across the globe in a matter of seconds, with supporters sharing the message almost instantaneously. Devices (e.g., smart phones) can now also be encrypted as a whole, and when this is the case, the device can be locked down, rendering it useless, in particular to authorities who may want to access the data to build a better picture of an organization's motivations and actions.

Islamic State created digital resources that drew in recruits from around the world and allowed for their narrative to be presented in salient ways, accompanied by images, footage, and music (Winter 2015). Ansar Dine was among the first of the groups under the JNIM umbrella to adopt social media and messaging technologies to advance their narratives and agenda. Using Telegram, the group published messages that framed them as the "'good guys,' fighting off foreign oppression, including through releasing photographs such as ones of suicide bombers who carried out an attack on the Timbuktu Airport in 2018" (Vermeersch et al. 2020). As well as the desire to be seen in a positive light by local populations whom jihadists groups often depend on for support, whether direct or indirect, JNIM's media strategy has also focused on a number of themes, often tied to, or capitalizing upon, grievances expressed by local populations.

As will be seen in the second half of this chapter, issues around the carnage and devastation caused by foreign troops, corruption and mismanagement by national governments in the region (which are also seen as puppets of outside powers), Western values as promotors of societal decay and immorality, and the victimization of certain local identities all stand out in jihadist messaging. JNIM has attempted to distinguish itself from ISGS in their discourse primarily through presenting themselves as more pragmatic. JNIM's primary concern seems to center around local grievances as opposed to global jihad, which ISGS makes more of a point in stressing. Al-Qaeda successfully gained leverage in the Sahel through allowing local affiliates such as JNIM and its component member groups space to identify and leverage local grievances, recognizing the added value of coalescing power from the grassroots level. This is one of its key strengths. The other was its initial renunciation of mass casualties, thereby allowing it to present itself as more measured than Islamic State groups such as ISGS.

The Rise of VEOs in Mali and Burkina Faso

Jama'at Nusrat al Islam w'al Muslimeen

JNIM is without doubt one of the most significant jihadist organizations operating across Mali and Burkina Faso. It was established in March of 2017 and lauded by al-Qaeda's General Command, including

Abdelmalek Droukdel and Ayman al-Zawahiri, as a game changing moment for jihadism in the region (Zenn 2017). JNIM is not a unitary actor but rather an umbrella organization that brings together a number of preexisting Malian jihadist groups to create a more cohesive and lethal force in the region.

Included under the banner of JNIM are Ansar Dine, the Macina Liberation Front, al-Mourabitoun, and al-Qaeda in the Islamic Maghreb (AQIM). The formation of this alliance was significant because it brought together jihadist groups led by men who were from different ethnic backgrounds and geographic localities, and who may not have attempted to coordinate their activities in the past. It also allowed JNIM to present itself in a way that appeared to cut across the different ethnic communities in Mali as well as across grievances that stemmed from region-specific issues.

Ansar Dine, for example, is led by Iyad Ag Ghaly (b. 1954), an ethnic Tuareg of the Ifoghas tribe, whose group predominantly operates in the north of Mali. Ansar Dine was affiliated with AQIM and perpetrated attacks on both military and civilian targets in the north of Mali. Ag Ghaly was instrumental in the Islamist takeover of northern Mali in 2012, which sparked the French military intervention there in 2013. Ag Ghaly is seen as one of the most prominent jihadists in the region and took on the role of senior leader in JNIM. The Macina Liberation Front is led by Ahmadu Koufa, an ethnic Fulani who was born in central Mali in 1958 and whose group originated in the central region of Mali and has operational strongholds in Fulani areas. Despite various attempts on his life and claims by France in 2018 that it had killed Koufa in a military operation, video footage emerged showing him alive. Al-Mourabitoun's leader is al-Hasan al-Ansari, a Malian Tangara Arab who also serves as the deputy leader of JNIM (Zenn 2017). Al-Mourabitoun was once an offshoot of AQIM and led by the infamous Mokhtar Belmokhtar.

While ethnically diverse, and regionally dispersed, the constituent groups of JNIM came together in a shared ideology that envisages Mali and the broader region free from foreign troops and influence (primarily France and the United States) and the creation of a society based upon a Salafist interpretation of Islam. They view society as having fallen prey to moral degeneration and see a return to strict Islamic values as the solution to the ills of society. Where they have had the opportunity to impose their vision of society upon communities, Islamic law was instituted, and the morality of communities policed. This was the case when Ansar Dine seized control of territory in northern Mali in 2012 and moved swiftly to enforce Islamic dress codes, push the strict segregation of men and women, ban dancing and music, and implement strict punishments such as the severing of limbs or public floggings for crimes such as theft and adultery.

In addition to this, JNIM ideology distinguishes between a far enemy in the form of France and the United States, and a near enemy in the form of the governments of the region. The Malian government is seen as a corrupt and inept entity that has failed the population through seeking partnerships with the West rather than expanding religious laws. Because of this, JNIM seeks to topple the Malian government and champions itself as the protector of "true" Muslims in the country, as well as a guardian of specific ethnic groups such as the Tuareg in the north and the Fulani in the central regions.

As an official affiliate of al-Qaeda, JNIM's ideology aligns with its parent organization. All factions under the JNIM umbrella display intense antagonism toward the West, seeing the West as a vehicle for colonialism, immorality, and decadence. In addition to this, any government that actively collaborates with the West (e.g., in the form of counterterrorism operations) are viewed as "apostate" regimes that have lost legitimacy and are to be overthrown. In the West African context (and especially in Mali), "this translates into a fierce ideological opposition to the French Barkhane mission, MINUSMA, and government security forces" (Zimmerer 2019, 495). Indeed, this was evident in an audio message released by JNIM's Saudi spokesman, Abu Dujana Al-Qasimi, in January 2019, in which he framed the conflict in terms of a "battle between truth and falsehood" and "between the carriers of the Qur'an and the worshippers of cross," as well as "between the people of virtue and the followers of vice." Al-Qasimi continued to say that anyone who participates in the efforts of the "crusader armies" enters into a state of "infidelity and apostasy from the religion of Islam" (Jama'at Nasr al-Islam wal Muslimin 2019a).

JNIM funding sources are murky and difficult to verify because the organization operates in remote areas with weak state control. What is known, however, is that a significant portion of its funding came through kidnapping, extortion, and smuggling operations. Kidnapping for ransom has the capacity to generate significant revenue streams; often Western hostages in the Maghreb or Sahel are targeted, with JNIM threatening to kill them if appropriate ransom is not paid (Ortmann 2017). In 2018, for example, JNIM abducted and later killed four US soldiers from Niger. US and British hostages are, however, often avoided because those governments have a tough stance on negotiating with terrorists. In contrast, European hostages represent a valuable commodity on the kidnapping black market due to the perceived readiness of their governments to negotiate hostage releases (Jenkins 2018). *The New York Times* estimates that US$91.5 million were paid to JNIM between 2008 and 2013 (Callimachi 2014). One of the most prominent hostage release events happened in October 2020, in which two foreign nationals, including Sophie Petronin, were released. Petronin, a French aid worker, was kidnapped in 2016 and held captive by JNIM for four years. During that time JNIM released videos of her in which she entreated French president Emmanuel Macron to negotiate her release. It is speculated that 10 million euro (approximately US$10.7 million) were given to JNIM and 200 jihadists were released back to the group (J. Thompson 2021).

Macina Liberation Front

One of the most lethal groups to join JNIM was the Macina Liberation Front, founded in 2015 and primarily based in the Mopti region of Mali. The group is led by Ahmadu Koufa a one-time member of Ansar Dine who left after frustrations with what he saw as Ansar Dine's inability to address injustices faced by Fulani communities. The Macina Liberation Front was established, therefore, to specifically engage with grievances among ethnic Fulani in Mali's central region for purposes of recruitment, violent mobilization, and with an end goal of establishing a territory governed under Islamic law. The group draws both its name and inspiration from the historic Macina Empire, which was established through violent jihad by the Fulani Seku Ahmadu in the early nineteenth century. (See Chapter 2.) Koufa stresses the need to return to an Islamic form of governance based on the model of the Macina Empire as the only means through which to restore moral order and good governance in the region. Koufa places specific emphasis on Fulani identity and called for Fulani from "every place, in Senegal, in Mali, in Niger . . . to jihad in the path of God" (RFI 2018).

While accounts of the early days of the Macina Liberation Front are difficult to come by, Peter Chilson documented some of the narratives around its emergence, noting that Koufa first appeared in 1999 as a "penniless predator" in the Mopti region of Mali. It is there that he bullied villagers who feared being accused as bad Muslims "into giving him land for a madrassa and house" (Chilson 2019, 196). He actively recruited boys and young men who slept on the property, and who under his tutelage came to be convinced that the imposition of Islamic law was the only solution to the ills of society. Chilson also notes that Koufa presented himself as a knowledgeable Islamic scholar and used this to further his own ends. There were instances where Koufa would accuse "dissenters of blasphemy," even causing some village imams to flee, and another case where Koufa demanded to marry the thirteen-year-old daughter of a villager, condemned the father to hell for refusing to allow the marriage to proceed, and then did it anyway (Chilson 2019, 198). This highlights that even though Koufa may have built an organization around religious ideology, his purposes may have been much more much more worldly and with a political end game.

The Macina Liberation Front has a hierarchical command structure, though there is some degree of flexibility for decisions to be made locally. The movement splits its territory into administrative units, each called a *markaz* (center), with a military leader, a *shura* advisory council, and a *qadi* (judge) (International Crisis Group 2019). The leader of each *markaz* serves on the movement's central *shura* council, which is in turn led by Koufa himself, and where senior commanders receive reports on the actions taken within each *markaz* (International Crisis Group 2019). This organizational style was likely borrowed from the Tablighi Jamaat, an Islamic revivalist movement founded in 1926 in India, and which has gone on to become the largest Islamic missionary movement in the world (Pieri 2015). Tablighi Jamaat has been active in Mali since the 1980s, where it has established itself as one of the most prominent Islamic organizations in West Africa (Chauzal and van Damme 2015). While Tablighi Jamaat is not suspected of engaging in jihadist activity, the movement has served in the past to network through its activities Islamist leaders who went on to take key roles in jihadist organizations. Both Ahmadu Koufa and Iyad Ag Ghaly were active members in the early 2000s (Pieri 2021b). Both have since turned on the Tablighi Jamaat, arguing that it does not go far enough in helping to bring about an Islamic state.

Ansarul Islam

Ansarul Islam (Defenders of Islam) is a jihadist group that is native to northern Burkina Faso, and which finds greatest operational capacity around the province of Soum, which is directly adjacent to the Mopti region of central Mali, and where the community is heavily Fulani. The group was founded in 2016 by Ibrahim Dicko, a fundamentalist Fulani Muslim preacher who argues for the establishment of an Islamic state, or at least the establishment of territory governed under Islamic law in the Muslim parts of Burkina Faso. As with Ahmadu Koufa, Dicko gained inspiration from precolonial Islamic kingdoms that existed in the region and argues that a return to Islamic governance would solve many of the social and political ills faced by the Muslim population. His impetus was to reestablish the ancient Djelgoji kingdom, which though founded in the sixteenth century later fell under the fold of the Islamic Empire of Macina, and eventually disappeared with the coming of French colonialism. (See Chapter 2.)

Dicko seized upon this history and regularly invoked the role of the Fulani people as leaders in historical jihads that effectively reordered society and established Islamic kingdoms. In particular, he pointed to the Sokoto Caliphate and the Macina Empire, arguing that the Fulani of northern Burkina Faso had a long and proud history as well as directly relevant examples of how to act in order to bring about change in the contemporary period. Dicko outlined Ansarul Islam's goal as the desire to advance the "Fulani Struggle" to rebuild the ancient Macina Empire (Buchanan 2017). Dicko was especially clear in advancing the notion that the Fulani of northern Burkina Faso had been marginalized by their own government and that his group was fighting to restore dignity to a people that have faced enduring injustice from the modern "secular" state.

In this sense, Ansarul Islam shares a similar outlook to the Macina Liberation Front. Both Dicko and Koufa selectively draw on history and at times distort the historical record to fit within their own narrative and agenda for social change. Both leaders focus on exploiting grievances among the Fulani populations of the region, and repackaging history in a way that serves to mobilize them in violent ways.

Initially Dicko did not find support in Burkina Faso and as a result traveled to Mali to join the fight there. He returned to Burkina

Faso in 2016 during a state of emergency and a period in which there were instances of abuse of the population and community leaders by the security forces. This helped Dicko rally people around his movement. In December 2016, "Dicko and some 30-armed men attacked a military outpost in Nassoumbou, a village near the Malian border in Soum, killing 12 Burkinabé soldiers. This event is widely considered to be the birth—and first feat of arms—of Ansarul Islam" (Le Roux 2019).

In 2017 Ibrahim Dicko was killed in a French military operation. His brother Jafar Dicko took over the mantle of leadership in Ansarul Islam. Since then, Ansarul Islam has fractured, with a group of fighters that split from the group joining the Macina Liberation Front or ISGS, while other members remain loyal to Dicko (Le Roux 2019).

Islamic State in the Greater Sahara

The origins of the ISGS are somewhat convoluted and take place within a context dominated by al-Qaeda. The entity is often said to have begun with the merger of two other jihadist groups in 2013: "the Movement for Oneness and Jihad in West Africa (MUJAO) and the Masked Men Brigade, which created a third group, al-Mourabitoun" (J. Warner 2017). Al-Mourabitoun was led by Mokhtar Belmokhtar, a prominent jihadist, and operated without an official affiliation for its first two years. In May 2015, Adnan Abu Walid Sahraoui, a senior leader in al-Mourabitoun, broke with the movement and along with his Mali-based faction of fighters pledged allegiance to Islamic State's leader Abubakar al-Baghdadi. Islamic State did not acknowledge the pledge until October 2016, and it was not until April of 2019 that Islamic State central leadership formally accepted it (Rolbiecki et al. 2020). Once the pledge was accepted, the structure of the group changed, with Islamic State making the decision to fold the group into their already established Islamic State West Africa Province (ISWAP), formerly known as Boko Haram, which is based in northeastern Nigeria.

Given the geographic distance between the areas that ISGS and ISWAP operate in, the two groups should be viewed as quite distinct. It is true that both organizations subscribe to the same ideology of seeking to establish an Islamic state in their areas of operation and to rid their regions of any form of Western influence, but this is also true of many of the groups that fight under the banner of JNIM. For branding purposes ISGS draws on the notoriety of the Islamic State and its affiliate ISWAP, but it also likely has a high degree of autonomy in charting its own course. ISGS operates in a decentralized manner, with several cells that have a degree of independence but look to Adnan Sahraoui for direction.

Its first attack under the banner of ISWAP came on April 12, 2019, and quickly gained notoriety for the use of asymmetric tactics typical of insurgent groups, including roadside bombings, ambushes, and suicide attacks (Rolbiecki et al. 2020). As with JNIM, ISGS targets Western interests in the region, including Western tourists and aid workers, who are often used for large ransom payments.

Despite early predictions that JNIM and ISGS would turn against each other due to their differing affiliations, this did not initially happen. Indeed, the two organizations found ways to cooperate, though this was not formalized in any kind of pact. According to a report issued by the UN in 2018, cooperation between ISGS and JNIM was based on shared interests and centered around expanding the financial base of both organizations though criminal activities and kidnappings (United Nations 2018). By 2019 there was evidence of tactical cooperation, as demonstrated in a joint attack on security forces in Mali that included a military base involving hundreds of fighters and ensuring the death of dozens of soldiers. Following on from this, a joint claim of responsibility was issued in 2020 for several kidnappings in central Mali, and a joint attack on a Malian military convoy resulting in the death of twenty-eight soldiers (Reuters 2020).

This type of cooperation between al-Qaeda– and Islamic State–affiliated groups came to be known as the Sahelian exception in the global jihadist rivalries, but this situation started to change. By 2022 JNIM was openly calling for increased attacks against ISGS after more than forty JNIM members were killed in an operation executed by JNIM. The two groups reportedly increased hostility to each other due to a difference over ideology and tactics, with, for example, JNIM accusing ISGS of "indiscriminately killing civilians, while ISGS has accused JNIM of being too lenient toward their enemies" (Dahiru 2022). Another factor is likely competition for a limited number of recruits, resources, and territories. The situation has been further complicated with JNIM having taken a more open position toward negotiations with the Malian government, while ISGS saw this as an aberration and as a betrayal of the cause.

In March 2022, ISGS was recognized as its own independent province within Islamic State's broader franchise system and no longer under the administrative framework of ISWAP. The group changed its name to IS Sahel, and under this name expanded its activities into Benin, where it claimed two attacks in July 2022 (Nsaibia 2023).[1]

Jihadist Perspectives on the West

A central pillar of jihadist ideology is that the West is an immoral and decadent place that seeks to destroy Muslim societies through exporting hedonistic values, which they regard as ideological and structural forms of neocolonialism. Boko Haram was masterful in strategically framing this type of narrative, going so far as to become synonymous with the notion that "Western education is sinful" and that even Western ideals such as democracy, women's rights, and adherence to the constitution are tantamount to apostacy (Pieri 2019). Boko Haram is not unique in this regard, with the same beliefs advanced by JNIM (encompassing all its affiliate members) and ISGS.

The jihadist groups operating in the Sahel regard France as the archenemy of Muslims in the region, not only as a former colonial power, but also as an entity that jihadist leaders believe to be actively functioning to subjugate Islamic governance in the region today. The leaders of JNIM and ISGS see French activities in Mali and Burkina Faso today as exploitative, functioning to keep the region divided, and working to deprive populations from a return to Islamic forms of governance. Such sentiments are abundant in JNIM's publicly released statements. For example, in February 2020, JNIM's media office focused on France and its President Macron, who is accused of using Western systems of governance to destroy the region. JNIM warns of a soft form of neocolonialism that comes in the guise of friendship, but which ultimately seeks to continue French dominance. JNIM's statement puts forward the argument that "Macron has attempted to promote the end of the camouflaged system behind the françafrique system" and to replace it with "a softer system" of friendship and alliance, "which also bears more danger." The statement goes on to say that Macron styles himself as the "friend of the African peoples" and as the "the carrier of the fake torch to change the relationship between France and these countries, in order for him to continue the policy of looting, plundering, and occupying with soft gloves and ruthless hands" (Jama'at Nasr al-Islam wal Muslimin 2020a).

France is consistently cast as the ultimate enemy of the people in West Africa and highlighted as the most dangerous of neocolonial forces operating in the region. Indeed, France is so vilified by jihadist leaders, that one of the consistent demands that JNIM has made is that for any type of negotiations with national governments to proceed, France must withdraw from military activity in the region and end what JNIM calls "the racist, arrogant French Crusader occupation" (Jama'at Nasr al-Islam wal Muslimin 2020b). The hostility toward France is also echoed in statements released by ISGS, for example in March 2018, vowing "to the crusader French and those who serve them in their army, that we will not rest until we eliminate them from all of our lands." The statement goes on to "renew our call to our brothers in all parts of the world to support their brothers in West Africa to unite in the fight against the Crusaders and the tyrants" (Reuters 2018).

JNIM claims to have a policy of targeting troops and officials who are accused or suspected of conspiring with or working in partnership with French and international forces in the region. JNIM brands national governments as "colonially-installed" or "surrogate" regimes and accuses "presidents and prime ministers across the Sahel of granting their Western patrons unfettered access to local resources and of serving the interests of foreign powers to the detriment of their own citizens" (Bukart 2020). A similar stance is also taken by ISGS, which further sees the governments of the Sahel as shameful in their support of foreign forces in the region. In April 2020, ISGS released a statement claiming responsibility for an attack on a military facility in Tarint, a town in Mali, claiming that "the Mujahideen target the headquarters of the apostate Malian army." The statement went on to say that "the Crusaders and their allies, the tyrants of the region, will not rest until they destroy our religion and our land" (Al Jazeera 2020). To this end, jihadists seek to delegitimize the governments of the region through directly associating them with French neocolonialism, while also maintaining a near-and-far enemy distinction.

While France bears the brunt of jihadist ire, the United States also comes under attack in their discourse. Jihadist organizations, and especially JNIM, have been adept at tapping into resonant global narratives of grievance and amplifying them. This was especially clear in the aftermath of the mosque shootings in Christchurch, New

Zealand, in 2019, whereby a white supremacist gunman livestreamed his attack on social media platforms and posted a rambling manifesto filled with anti-immigrant and racist rhetoric. Though not an American, the ideological background of the gunman was not lost on JNIM, nor was the growing narrative around the West as having deep-seated issues with racism. In a joint statement released by al-Qaeda and JNIM to condemn the attack, the authors took the opportunity to magnify the United States as a leader of racist and Islamophobic practices. After describing the West as embedded in histories of "criminality" and "continued occupation of our lands," the statement proceeded to say that "we will never forget to take revenge for our martyrs from the Muslims, as long as we have a beating heart." The statement then turned to focus on the then president of the United States, Donald Trump, linking his presidency to the rise of the far right and white supremacist movements in the West (al-Qaeda in the Islamic Maghreb and Jama'at Nasr al-Islam wal Muslimin 2019):

> The arrival by Trump to the seat of power [in America], and the rise of Crusader right-wing populist movements and their ascension to power in many Western countries, whether in Europe, America, or elsewhere, is a visible part of the mountain of Western hatred against the Ummah of Islam. It exposes a small part of the plots and policies of the governments of these countries, and whatever attempts are made by our own people to flatter them and portray them as an example of civilization and progress, these actions are too bright to be hidden and obscured.

The fact that jihadist movements seized on the issue of racism is an interesting one and shows the ways in which they attempt to use events in the West to amplify the image of the West as mired in injustice. Beyond that, the narrative is used to shame the leaders of Sahelian governments, who are told that no matter how much they try to flatter the West as an example of progress and civilization, the record is consistent in showing animosity toward Muslims. The argument advanced by JNIM is that no matter how much national governments in the Sahel may try to highlight the positive aspects of their partnerships with the West, to the jihadists the consequences of such partnerships are always negative and rooted in systems of oppression.

Indeed, this type of message is echoed time and again. In one statement released on September 5, 2019, JNIM highlights engagement with the West as a distinct form of corruption. The argument explicates that if the government of Burkina Faso had focused its time and revenues on issues of governance instead of fighting as a "proxy for the French," then society would have had a much better chance at prospering. The statement is explicit in stating that rather than reliance on the French, Burkina Faso would have "been better off using its energies and resources to take its oppressed people out from the circle of poverty, hunger, and underdevelopment instead of fighting as a proxy for the French army." The statement goes on to say that through its actions in partnering with the French, the government of Burkina Faso is serving to "satisfy the greed of the thieving French politicians and the plundering companies operating across borders" (Jama'at Nasr al-Islam wal Muslimin 2019b).

JNIM is sharp in its focus of presenting Western governments as iniquitous and predatory. It is interesting to see how jihadist groups can switch their glare from Western activities in the region, to failures in domestic policy in Western countries. In a speech from November of 2018, a JNIM spokesman directly addressed his message to French protesters—the *gilet jaunes*—who at the time were protesting for economic and social justice in France. The JNIM spokesman highlighted that French people were suffering at the hands of their own government.

JNIM is strategic in using their messaging to stress to local populations that their government's cooperation with Western governments functions as a means for the exploitation of natural resources while also lining the pockets of corrupt politicians. In this way, JNIM links issues of corruption and Western neocolonialism together, discrediting both the West and West African governments through one narrative. In one statement from 2019, JNIM argued that they will continue to target troops from Burkina Faso, justifying this in terms of the Burkinabé government's failure to implement Islamic law. The statement makes clear that hostilities will continue for "as long as the Burkinabé government insists on usurping our freedom and our legitimate right to live in dignity under the shade of our Shariah, have control over our land, and have the final word on our resources and cultivating it to serve our people, far from the dictates of the occupation and the whims of transcontinental companies" (Jama'at Nasr al-Islam wal Muslimin 2019b). JNIM rejects Western principles and argues in the same statement that "it is high time for the governments of the Sahel called the G5 to reconsider their involvement with the occupier," and that they should look "with reason and wisdom to the interests of their people, which they abandoned between the Mujahedeen and the French occupation army, which would not have survived all these years were it not for the support of the armies of the Sahel region" (Jama'at Nasr al-Islam wal Muslimin 2019b).

As well as deep-seated hostility to foreign security personnel in the region, jihadist groups also take issue with humanitarian and aid workers. They link humanitarian work with the broader agenda of Western values and secularization, and as such want to see an end to all Western activity in the region. Indeed, ISGS made this point explicit when in November 2021, they claimed responsibility for attacking a convoy of humanitarian workers in Niger, explaining that "we targeted the convoy of the Crusaders and their agents, the apostate government, which seeks to secularize our society and spread corruption." The statement concluded by calling on all Muslims to come together in the region to "support us in our fight against the Crusaders and their agents, and to work towards establishing the rule of Allah in the land" (Reuters 2021).

The Leveraging of Fulani Identity

Jihadist organizations have been masters of picking up on local grievances, in amplifying these grievances, and in turn strategically framing their own narratives to resonate with local populations. Boko Haram in its early period was particularly effective in highlighting issues with corruption in Nigeria and arguing that the Muslim states of the northeast had been left behind by the federal government that had focused its investments in the south of the country (Pieri 2019). They also drew on historical narratives that presented the past as a golden age compared to the current state of affairs—for example, they have been effective in creating ethno-religious drivers of violence in the form of jihad, particularly through calling for a similar type of jihad as that enacted by Usman dan Fodio, but this time focused within the historic Kanuri lands of the former Kanem-Borno Empire (Pieri 2019; Pieri and Zenn 2016).

Across Mali and Burkina Faso, jihadist organizations such as JNIM, ISGS, and Ansarul Islam have also sought to exploit ethnic grievances, and particularly so among the Fulani. Ahmadu Koufa, leader of the Macina Liberation Front, has concentrated on highlighting injustices against contemporary Fulani communities in Mali, and in empowering those Fulani to take violent action as a means of rectifying the situation. Koufa uses modern technologies and social media platforms such as WhatsApp, Facebook, and Telegram to call for members of the Fulani community to revolt against the Malian government, the G5 Sahel countries, and France's Barkhane forces.

Koufa as with many other prominent jihadist leaders, does not recognize the validity of modern nation-states in the Sahel, instead pushing an irredentist narrative based on what the governance structure of the region looked like in precolonial times. Here he was able to draw upon the Macina Empire as an example of what contemporary governance should look like, and in turn promised that his group would work to erase nation-states whose borders the French and British drew over a century ago and to replace them with an Islamic caliphate modeled on the nineteenth-century Fulani jihadis. Koufa declared that Mali is a false state that embraces false gods. His famous words were "Mali est mort . . . Allahu Akbar [Mali is dead . . . God is great]" (Chilson 2019, 193). Peter Chilson found that sympathy for Koufa's movement was growing, and especially because he promised disadvantaged Fulani that jihad would offer them a pathway to power that is blessed by God. Chilson observed Fulani men gathering to listen to Koufa and nod their heads in agreement and concluded that to a group that feels marginalized, or at least victimized, it is not too difficult to see why Koufa's narrative is appealing (Chilson 2019).

Narratives surrounding injustices to the Fulani are not straightforward and are often intertwined with other grievances, such as government corruption or malevolent actions by Western military intervention. In a statement released by JNIM in February 2020, the movement highlighted French injustices toward the Fulani, specifically in the form of a military operation in early February in which forty-eight Fulani tribesmen were killed. JNIM decried the situation that the Fulani were in and refered to France as a "perpetrator of massacres . . . the occupier, the plunderer, and the blackmailer." To hammer home the message, JNIM argued that because "Macron entered upon such heinous crime against the Muslim Fulani tribes and all the Muslim villages that reject the injustice of tyrants and the occupation by the invaders, [it] is proof of the failure of his satanic alliance to achieve the military victory promised by his predecessor [President] Hollande" (Jama'at Nasr al-Islam wal Muslimin 2020a). JNIM further stressed that in this instance it was the Fulani who were being targeted and through this hoped that the Fulani would support the goals of JNIM.

The narrative that the Fulani are being directly targeted as a population is a consistent theme of jihadist discourse in the region. In another example, a JNIM statement from March 2019 claimed that the movement carried out a raid on the G5 Sahel base in Doura in which JNIM killed approximately thirty soldiers, and which is said to have been led by Koufa himself, as retaliation against injustices to the Fulani. In this case, it is not only the actions of the French that are called out, but also the Malian government and militiamen that support the government in their military alliance with France and other international partners. JNIM was explicit that the raid "comes in response to the heinous crimes committed by the forces of the formal Bamako government, and the militiamen that support it, against our Fulani people" and also pointed out that for all the West's focus on ethics, there has been a "shameful silence of the region and world, and complicity with the French occupation forces and their crusader allies" (Jama'at Nasr al-Islam wal Muslimin 2019c).

Ansarul Islam also focuses on amplifying grievances of Fulani populations in Burkina Faso. Its former leader Ibrahim Dicko was passionate in saying that the government of Mali had abandoned the Fulani people while also turning its back on the dictates of Islam. He would specifically highlight the poverty and suffering faced by Fulani populations at the hands of the government and the government's alignment with Western powers. Highlighting grievances, however, is one thing, but jihadist movements are able to use such grievances in recruiting and mobilizing some Fulani to their cause. Dicko was masterful in providing action-oriented solutions to grievances as a means to inspire people to action. In particular he would claim that the time is ripe for Fulani Muslims to take matters into their own hands and refashion society in a way that would preserve traditional practices, reject Western influence, and create compassion and justice (Reuters 2019).

For all its talk about reviving Islamic states and kingdoms, JNIM has not formally annexed any territory. This may be because it has learned the lesson that in doing so international attention and perhaps further military intervention could be focused on the group, or because it does not want the responsibility of providing services that come along with governance. Instead, their focus is on controlling economic sites such as markets. Their strategy is to seize key infrastructure—that is, roads and bridges—and to set up checkpoints, thus controlling access and flow of goods into any given market. Populations in turn become dependent on cooperating with jihadists. General Dagvin Anderson, while in position as commander for US Special Operations Command Africa, noted that jihadist groups operating in Mali and Burkina Faso invite people to come back to their homes and say, '"all you have to do is accept sharia law; you're welcome back,' which is, when you look at it, a brilliant strategy. Now they're forcing those people to make a mental shift and acceptance of that extremist governance in order to return home" (J. Warner 2020). Once home, people are required to follow regulations enacted by JNIM or ISGS.

Troop Withdrawal, Afghanistan, and Potential for Negotiations

Both JNIM and ISGS have given ultimatums to national governments in the region stating that peace will only be possible once foreign actors have withdrawn from the region and Islamic forms of governance are implemented. ISGS has been resolute in rejecting any type of negotiations with national governments in West Africa, instead demanding that any type of peace is first predicated on foreign troops leaving the country, followed by the institution of Islamic governance. JNIM, however, has been more flexible and has publicly claimed that it is willing to negotiate with the government of Mali, but only once certain conditions have been met—for example, the vacating of French and other foreign military forces from Mali. Even though JNIM is an umbrella organization, the decision over whether it would agree to negotiate or not was deferred to its senior leader, Iyad Ag Ghaly. This decision was controversial and highlighted some fissures within JNIM, as some elements were less enthused about entering into negotiations with the government of Mali. To this end, some fighters from the Macina Liberation Front faction defected to ISGS in 2019, claiming that they were disgruntled with Koufa's openness to negotiate with the government of Mali, and in his deferring to Ag Ghaly's decision on the matter.

While both JNIM and ISGS were both initially resolute on wanting to avoid negotiations with the government of Mali, this started to change, at least for JNIM, in 2019 and early 2020. This was at the same time that the Taliban was negotiating with the United States as part of a deal that would see the eventual withdrawal of US troops from Afghanistan. The US withdrawal from Afghanistan in the summer of 2021, effectively leaving the Taliban in a position to take power, resonated with jihadists across the world, and especially with JNIM's leaders. The Taliban's success showed that negotiations could ensue in a positive outcome for jihadists. Ag Ghaly was quick to recognize the significance of the moment and lost no time in sending a congratulatory message to the Taliban; he felt buoyed that JNIM could follow a similar strategy in Mali. A key takeaway for JNIM leaders was that as well as being skilled insurgents, part of the Taliban's success rested on a willingness to negotiate and demand a withdrawal of US troops. With regard to the situation in Mali, the narrative around the evacuation of French and other foreign military personnel as a precondition for any form of negotiations with the government of Mali started to appear in JNIM's discourse in 2020 and intensified through 2021 and 2022.

In March 2020, for example, JNIM issued a statement arguing that the Malian government should "either take a historical stand and take the side of its people and request the occupation forces to depart . . . or it continues the policy of submitting to the will of the corrupt politicians of the Elysée Palace and the delusions of French President Macron" (Jama'at Nasr al-Islam wal Muslimin 2020c). JNIM's position is that if the Malian government continues to ally with France, then all that can be achieved is the reestablishment of "the miserable Franco-Afrique system while preserving its essence bases on discrimination and theft." For JNIM, "in order to enter into direct negotiations with the mujahideen under the command of Sheikh Iyad Ghaly" the "exit of the occupier is a prerequisite" (Jama'at Nasr al-Islam wal Muslimin 2020c).

JNIM's statement reiterated that in their opinion the war waged by the West "against the Mujahideen and its attempt to prevent them from establishing a state governed by the Shari'a of Allah is a losing war." After expanding on this and noting that Western leaders have to "forget their dreams of expansion and occupation," the statement proceeded to focus on the situation in Afghanistan. It notes that "here is America today, the largest force on earth, with all its material and military capabilities that exceed the power of your country multi-fold in terms of equipment, and after nearly two decades of its invasion of Afghanistan, it is seeking to negotiate with the Mujahideen, to leave in humiliation after tasting woes at the hands of heroes" (Jama'at Nasr al-Islam wal Muslimin 2020a). This indicates that from JNIM's perspective, even in an asymmetric conflict with a major western power, jihadists can still win, and that inspiration should be drawn from the events that unfolded in Afghanistan.

It is not just French forces that JNIM and ISGS take issue with, but all foreign troops. The UN-led Multidimensional Integrated Stabilization Mission in Mali (MINUSMA), established and deployed in 2013, has also come under attack. JNIM demanded its exit from the region and stated that they would not be willing to enter negotiations, and indeed would continue violent operations against MINUSMA, until it withdraws. This was evidenced in a statement from February 2021 where JNIM claimed that "operations against MINUSMA take place almost daily and the number of dead is much more than is being tallied." The statement went on to warn that, "while the commanders of these armies . . . maintain their positions and well-being, their soldiers meet inevitable death from our land mines and booby-traps in the arid plains and deserts of Mali" (Jama'at Nusrat al-Islam wal Muslimeen 2021).

At the same time that JNIM was starting to show interest in engaging with the government of Mali, Mali's then president, Ibrahim Boubacar Keïta (2013–2020), also changed his stance from one of hostility toward negotiating to one of greater openness to the idea. In February 2020, Keïta also looked to the context of negotiations between the Taliban and the United States (which had yet to sour) and said that he would start the process of contacting JNIM leaders about negotiations. Amid the increasing likelihood of negotiations between the Malian government and JNIM, President Keïta's government fell as a result of a coup in 2020 before any formal negotiations could take place. The transition period was tempestuous, with the interim administration itself being ousted in 2021. A new period was ushered in with governance enacted through a military junta lead by Colonel Assimi Goïta. Despite these changes, a level of commitment to dialogue with JNIM remained in place, alongside a military strategy to eradicate jihadist groups.

Ultimately, negotiations between JNIM and the different Malian administrations did not amount to much, yet in a twist of events, JNIM was to see the fulfilment of their desire of French troops vacating the region. This was not so much as a result of repeated demands by JNIM and ISGS for regional governments to oust foreign troops as a basis for starting a process of negations, but rather as a result of a series of coups that fundamentally changed the nature of national governments along with their relationship to France and other Western powers. As already stated, in Mali there were coups in 2020 and 2021, and Burkina Faso saw two coups in 2022 (January and September) in which military juntas were established. It was following these coups in Mali and Burkina Faso that relations with France soured as the generals sought more aggressive methods in their approaches to counterterrorism efforts, and as a result deepened their relationships with Wagner Group mercenaries, which were likely seen as more ruthless than European forces.

In 2022, President Macron announced that France would withdraw the entirety of its forces from Mali before the end of that year. This meant that all 2,400 French troops in Mali, out of the total 4,300 stationed in the Sahel, would leave (though some of these would be transferred to Niger) (King 2023). A year later, in February 2023, France announced that it would vacate its troops from Burkina Faso after the government there spoke of Russia as their preferred choice for fighting jihadists (France 24 2023b). France's last major base of operations in the region remained in Niger until that country succumbed to a coup in 2023, after which its military leaders urged France to withdraw its troops from Niger. This process was completed in December 2023. At the same time, the UN MINUSMA forces were also asked to leave Mali in 2023, and this process was completed at the end of December 2023.

Such withdrawals from the region came as a shock and clearly altered the regional balance of power. After a long history of military involvement in the region, the departure of France alongside other Western forces will have the most striking impact. While Wagner Group mercenaries might try to fill this gap, it is yet unclear as to the type of endurance or effectiveness these forces will have. While jihadist discourse rarely mentions Russian or Chinese activities in the region, this could now start to change as Russian-affiliated Wagner mercenaries start to have more confrontations with jihadist groups. A rare statement from JNIM in April 2022 highlighted that the issue of Russian military activity, especially in the form of Wagner Group operations, is on the organization's radar. The statement not only acknowledges, but also highlights in yellow coloring (but in italics here), that "Allah granted upon his Mujahideen the capture of a soldier from the *Russian Wagner forces* in the mountainous region in the state of Segu." The statement then went on to call Wagner group mercenaries "those criminal forces" and gave details of Wagner Group activity in the region, claiming that they "participated with Malian forces in air landing operations of the Mora village market" and also clashed with jihadists in the same location. JNIM's statement claims that Wagner Group forces besieged Mora for five days, killing "hundreds of defenseless innocents." It is also claimed that fighters from JNIM were able to repel a further assault "which the mercenary armed forces undertook above the mountains of Banjagra" and where JNIM "looted some of the mercenaries' weapons" (Jama'at Nusrat al-Islam wal Muslimeen 2022).

Conclusion

JNIM and ISGS have established themselves as the two dominant jihadist organizations in the Sahel with ample capacity to operate within and across nation-state borders in the region. The security landscape in West Africa, however, is clearly more complex, with a range of actors from insurgent groups, civilian militias, and vigilante groups, to banditry, and lower levels of crime that serve to lessen the control that nation-states have over their territories. It is in these types of spaces that VEOs such as JNIM and ISGS can exert a level of control over the population and resources. Understanding the ways in which jihadists operate regionally, how they frame their messages, and how they seek to recruit and mobilize individuals into violent action is of crucial importance. Through examining jihadists' discourse, key themes and issues that jihadists prioritize emerge clearly and show how such organizations draw upon local grievances to amplify their own agendas. Understanding the trajectories of JNIM and ISGS is particularly important, not only as a means to gaining insights into their motivations for violence, but also as a way to develop strategies that may lead to a disengagement from violence.

Though JNIM and ISGS operate as two distinct and increasingly competing organizations in the Sahel, what is evident from discourse put out by both is that they are united in their vision of the West. For them, the West and Western values are foundational to the ills of the region. The West, therefore, is the main reason why jihadist leaders claim to be fighting in the region and for calling others to violent action. They want Western powers to leave, taking with them what jihadist leaders believe to be corrupt practices (in the form of sponsoring servile national governments in the region), as well as seeing an end to the exploitation of resources. Both JNIM and ISGS present the West as a vehicle for moral decline that functions to dilute Islamic influences in the region. In essence the West is a far enemy that has become a near enemy through military action in the Sahel. National governments are seen as a close second enemy, and this is often predicated on national governments' collaboration with Western powers, their failure to implement Islamic forms of governance, and large levels of corruption and mismanagement of resources that are visible to all.

That local communities and individuals are very important to the direction and longevity of any given insurgency is a given. Understanding popular grievances and attempting to address those grievances is one way to gain leverage or support in communities, and jihadist groups have demonstrated an ability to do this. Talking about Islamist governance in a vacuum is unlikely to get a jihadist group far, but presenting Islamic governance as the solution to local grievances could have the capacity to boost recruitment and galvanize action. It is also evident that jihadist groups have sought to exploit issues around identity and ethnicity. The Macina Liberation Front and Ansarul Islam, for example, have recruited Fulani communities in Mopti and parts of northern Burkina Faso, arguing that Fulani once had a glorious past governing themselves through Islamic kingdoms in the region, while they are now left out and even targeted by their respective states. The perceived link between the Fulani and jihadist groups such as Macina Liberation Front and Ansarul Islam contributed to reaction from some local populations in the form of the creation of vigilante justice groups. In Burkina Faso, these were predominantly formed among Mossi communities, who have gone on to pursue criminals and bandits, as well as "jihadists," often inflicting violent punishments, and sometimes attacking innocent people (Le Roux 2019).

Yet, it should also be noted that despite attempts by jihadists to mobilize Fulani into violent action and in spite of the constant framing of issues by jihadists as ones in which Fulani are discriminated against, cooperation with extremist groups "is often out of fear of reprisal rather than conviction" (Cissé 2020). Indeed, survey results carried out for this study, and which are discussed in Chapter 5, indicate that a majority of respondents in the region did not believe jihadist discourse regarding the role that jihadists play in fighting corruption and poor governance, with most respondents stating that they did not believe that VEOs in the region were successful in their goals. It has been argued that many traditional chiefs and ordinary Fulani have "not been convinced by militant Islamists groups' goals. Rather, Fulani leaders have for the most part distanced themselves from the ideology of militant Islamists who call for a return to Islamic theocracy" (Cissé 2020). Chapter 5 turns to the data collected as part of our survey and examines how local communities and governance structures respond to the threat of VEOs.

Note

1. For the sake of consistency, this book will continue to refer to IS Sahel as ISGS.

5

Local Resilience in the Face of Violence

MALI AND BURKINA FASO HAVE BEEN DESTABILIZED BY REGULAR MILITANT activities of jihadist VEOs, with insecurity occasionally expanding to the littoral states of West Africa. Yet, the blame for violence cannot be pinned solely on jihadists, with poor governance and indiscriminate military action also adding to the dynamics of regional instability. It is because of issues such as corruption, nepotism, injustice, and feelings of disenfranchisement by populations that groups such as JNIM and ISGS are able to make inroads, promising alternate forms of governance based on Islam, which they argue will usher in more equitable forms of justice. They also make assurances to elevate the status of marginalized groups and, in some cases, promise to restore stolen grazing land in areas where local government and courts struggle to function. While it is true that competition between jihadist groups in Mali and Burkina Faso have made the region increasingly difficult to govern, issues with governance were present long before such groups emerged on the scene. It is poor governance that made it easier for towns to be attacked and taken over, and government corruption and ineptitude that made efforts to vanquish jihadists largely ineffective. Supplies into areas where jihadists have a strong presence often need a military escort, "which may or may not be available. Jihadists block roads and plant bombs on bridges. All this gums up trade and makes remote areas even poorer. The government's inability to beat the jihadists infuriates nearly everyone" (*Economist* 2023e). Burkina Faso suffered two coups in 2022. Mali suffered a coup in 2020 and 2021. Countries experiencing economic growth and expanding good governance into the hinterlands rarely experience these kind of disruptions (Herbst 2000; N. Singh 2014).

Research on the Boko Haram conflict in the Lake Chad Basin shows that grievances are central to how populations perceive governmental institutions, both at national and local levels. In addition to this, grievances also affect recruitment and mobilization of recruits into violent action—or at least the level of support jihadists might receive (Delia Deckard and Pieri 2017; Pieri 2019). There is some variation between the types of grievances expressed in Mali, Burkina Faso, and Ghana, but corruption, economic mismanagement, ethnic disparities, and religious complaints all factor into the level of legitimacy that a population accords the state or local government.

Literature on the ramifications of corruption for economic growth is extensive (e.g., Mo 2001; Gyimah-Brempong 2002), as, too, for democracy and the health of democratic institutions (e.g., Rothstein and Uslaner 2005; Gerring and Thacker 2004). Less explored are the ways in which corruption can work to reduce government legitimacy and empower jihadists (or any type of violent extremism). The extent to which public knowledge of corruption in the governance process undermines the legitimacy of government is important to consider, especially for its wide-ranging implications (Heidenheimer 1970, 485). In this chapter the extent to which corruption is a significant grievance (either in reality, or as perceived by those surveyed) in Mali, Burkina Faso, and Ghana is examined along with other sets of grievances.

Corruption has implications for democracy, as well as for the health of governance more broadly. Rothstein and Uslaner (2005) argue that corruption undermines social trust, which in turn functions to weaken civil society and democratic processes that are built upon it. Corruption is widely believed to occur because people are only concerned with their individual best interests and, to the extent that this is the case, democratic self-governance is impossible. Theoretically, long-standing and known corruption in a democracy should not be possible because citizens will vote out corrupt leaders (Delia Deckard and Pieri 2017). When this truism proves false, it weakens trust in government, and as voters find themselves unable to eradicate corruption, they may question their collective control of the state and devalue its institutions.

Although some political institutional arrangements may foster corruption more than others, the presence of corruption serves to universally delegitimize the authority of all forms of democratic states (Gerring and Thacker 2004). Corruption also empowers nonstate actors, such as religious and ethno-tribal leaders, who are powerful enough to intervene on behalf of people and garner widespread loyalty (Onapajo et al. 2012). Essentially, high levels of corruption reduce the government's ability to function as a state that enhances welfare and encourages citizens to seek that welfare in forms of nonstate authority.

This chapter recognizes that there is a relationship between governance and grievance, and indeed that both governance and grievance have an impact on security in the region and the capacity of jihadist groups to operate in any given locality. In this chapter, grievances are measured through asking what survey respondents across sites in Mali, Burkina Faso, and Ghana view as top concerns for "people like me." By leaving responses to this question open-ended, participants were given the freedom to comment upon the issues they were most concerned about without the researchers pushing preconceived notions. Open-ended questions were followed by a series of closed-ended questions asking survey respondents to rank grievances (e.g., corruption, security, lack of employment, lack of infrastructure, declining morals, etc.) as a means of observing how they order grievances relationally. Through triangulating grievance data across multiple formats, the chapter will compare results across Mali, Burkina Faso, and Ghana.

Understanding Governance and Corruption in West Africa

Governance in West Africa is not static, and indeed, governments in the region are building upon reforms made in the early 1990s. The African Development Bank notes that good governance needs to rest on "(1) effective states, (2) mobilized civil societies, and (3) an efficient private sector. The key elements of good governance then, are accountability, transparency, combating corruption, citizen participation, and an enabling legal framework" (African Development Bank 2000). Across West Africa, the rise of jihadist groups such as JNIM, ISGS, Ansarul Islam, and Boko Haram have threatened national security and put both external and domestic pressure on state governments to defeat these movements. Attempts have thus far predominantly taken a military approach with the goal of tactically defeating the movements. Following a military approach means that governments in the region have failed to view jihadist groups as having sprung from complex social forces that require systemic, organized redress from the government, nor that grievances serve to sustain such movements (Delia Deckard and Pieri 2017). Instead, states for the most part have limited their response to coercive means.

A military approach seems to have failed (e.g., Boko Haram is now over two decades old, while JNIM and ISGS have expanded their activities in West Africa and show no signs of decline), while also creating negative externalities. The militarization of the West African states, and the sometimes brutally indiscriminate approach taken in areas where jihadists operate, have alienated citizens while laying bare governmental ineptitude. It is unsurprising to find that military brutality is a grievance expressed by some communities, and when such instances do happen, it is equally unsurprising to see jihadists in the region amplifying this grievance in their strategic narratives. Indeed, jihadists seem to be quite masterful in picking up on grievances expressed by local communities and rearticulating these as part of their own message that seeks to undermine government and governance institutions through the emphasizing of state corruption, negligence, and brutality.

Recommendations for how to accomplish the goal of eradicating jihadists in the region have moved beyond traditional security plans and include the idea that West African states must deliver public goods more equitably, strengthen democratic institutions, and reform the policing of citizens, especially in areas where jihadists are gaining traction. These recommendations exhort states to minimize the discontent from which jihadists are presumed to spring (or at least manage it to further their own agendas), thus weakening support and ultimately undermining the jihadists (Comolli 2015).

In Mali, for example, there are numerous grievances that arise from poor governance. These are particularly pronounced among the young, who form a third of the country's workforce. According to some figures, unemployment among young people has reached "almost 15 percent, up [in 2020] from 7 percent eight years ago before Keïta took office. The country's poverty rate has increased from 45 percent in 2013 to almost 50 percent" (Obaji 2020a). In addition to this, the insecurity crisis in the country displaced more people in 2019 than at any other time in its recent history.

Burkina Faso's Sahel Region where Ibrahim Dicko launched Ansarul Islam (a jihadist group native to Burkina Faso and which stresses injustices against the Fulani population), "scored just 2.7 on the United Nations Human Development Index compared with 6 for the area around the capital, Ouagadougou. About 40 percent of its children are stunted by malnutrition, against only 6 percent in the capital" (Cocks 2019). A key issue is that the northern portions of Burkina Faso are disconnected from the capital. Indeed, as with the northern parts of Nigeria, populations report feeling disenfranchised from national government processes and feel a greater affinity with those of the same ethnic background who live across a border than with those of a different ethnicity living in a different part of their own country (Pieri 2019). It is not uncommon for those living in the north of Burkina Faso to complain that the few interactions they have with the state tend to be predatory: "Bureaucrats demand money to issue title deeds for houses, then never provide the papers; gendarmes charge up to $40 to take down a complaint; there are mysterious taxes and extortion at police roadblocks" (Cocks 2019).

The issue of corruption is unavoidable in any discussion of governance in West Africa, though some states fare worse than others. Defining corruption as "behavior which deviates from the normal duties of public role because of private-regarding (family, close private clique), pecuniary or status gains" (Nye 1967, 417), corruption may be the central function of some states in the region (Osoba 1996). Transparency International's Corruption Perceptions Index measures the extent to which corruption is considered a problem. In 2022, Mali ranks 137 of 180 countries in terms of the perception of corruption in government and government dealings, Burkina Faso ranks 77, and Ghana ranks 72 (Transparency International 2022).

In a Global Corruption Barometer survey conducted in 2019, in Mali 60 percent of respondents thought that corruption had increased in the past twelve months. In addition to this, 21 percent of public service users reported paying a bribe in the past twelve months. In Burkina Faso the situation seems to be more positive, with 22 percent of those surveyed indicating that they thought corruption had increased and 16 percent of public service users paying a bribe over the past twelve months. In Ghana, 33 percent of respondents said that they thought corruption had increased in the past year, and 33 percent of public service users reported paying a bribe over the same period (Transparency International 2021).

Ghana is an example where the government has undertaken reforms since the early 1990s, including "the design and adoption of a new democratic constitution, which places emphasis on the separation of powers with checks and balances to transform its political system" (Mbaku 2020). Because of this, Ghana became a leader in the institutionalization of democratic rule in the region, and this was illustrated "by the quick acceptance of defeat by incumbent President John D. Mahama during the 2016 elections" (Mbaku 2020).

The issue of corruption in some West African states has escalated beyond the economic sphere and into the movement of bureaucratized state functions into the realm of private decisionmaking. With regards to the police force, extrajudicial killings have become more frequent and further serve to weaken the state's legitimacy. In 2020, for example, a UN MINUSMA report stated that approximately 150 people were extrajudicially killed by Malian security forces. The report found "an increase in serious human rights violations attributable to the Malian security forces" and added that Malian security forces were responsible for 94 such killings over the three-month period between April and June 2020. The report further noted 50 extrajudicial killings in May by Burkinabé troops in the village of Boulkessi and settlements close to the Malian border. The claim is that Burkinabé forces targeted numerous terrorist elements in central Mali but at the same time also carried out "reprisal operations against civilian populations" they believed to be supporting militants (MINUSMA 2020).

Historically and in other places, extrajudicial killings occur entirely outside of the state apparatus by vigilante groups or criminal elements. That the police and military forces of some West African states have incorporated extrajudicial killings into their purview, without allowing those accused or suspected of crime to first be tried in a court of law, is not only concerning, but also playing into the discourse of jihadists who capitalize on these killings for recruitment purposes. In Nigeria, for example, the extrajudicial killing of Mohammad Yusuf, Boko Haram's leader from its inception to 2009, strengthened and emboldened Boko Haram and its supporters. In fact, the extrajudicial execution of Yusuf is considered the main catalyst in Boko Haram's radicalization (Pieri 2019).

Extrajudicial killings more generally have led to a reality in which Malians and Burkinabé may be deprived of life without legal recourse, leading to more widespread, and terror-driven, distrust of the state. Though not themselves corruption, "these types of killings may feed into a larger picture of a state overwhelmed by private interests and of public bureaucracies overtaken by individual decision-makers" (Delia Deckard and Pieri 2017, 373). State illegitimacy in Mali and Burkina Faso could hamper the state's ability to contain the threat and growth of jihadists. Ethno-religious, political, and economic violence are commonplace across Mali and also in parts of Burkina Faso, with the state unable to control most of the ensuing bloodshed. But the crises across both countries have become symbolic not just because of high casualty numbers, but because of the links to Islamic extremism and in particular to the broader context and association with al-Qaeda, in the local form of JNIM, and Islamic State, in the local form of ISGS. This compounds the pressure on governments to overcome the movements—to retain their monopolies on "the legitimate use of force" and remain coherent nation-states.

Survey Data from Mali, Burkina Faso, and Ghana

Grievances, real or perceived, factor into how citizens regard the legitimacy of the state, and as such knowing the extent to which citizens have grievances of governance can help us understand why some local areas prove more resilient in the face of exogenous shocks such as jihadist violence or great power competition. The data we gathered in local communities across parts of Mali, Burkina Faso, and Ghana highlight the overarching concerns of local populations, gauge levels of life satisfaction, and measure perceptions of safety, government effectiveness, and community cohesion.

A striking finding is that people who live in Burkina Faso are far more likely to have lower levels of satisfaction than those who live in Mali or Ghana across almost all factors that they were questioned on. Given the proliferation of jihadist activity in Burkina Faso, and the state's inability to effectively combat the situation, what emerges is a population that has a keen awareness of a society that is in a state of flux and with a high degree of civic fragility. The level of dissatisfaction that is shown over security, income, health, and conditions of dwellings help create an atmosphere in which government legitimacy is weakened. It is also an atmosphere that jihadist groups seek to exploit, both through increasing their operational activities in the region, and through propaganda activity that consistently emphasizes the failures of the state and its institutions.

Life Satisfaction

A key indicator of how content people are with their given situation in life and the extent to which they may have grievances is that of overall life satisfaction. Simply put, this indicator allows individuals to state on a sliding scale (very satisfied through to very dissatisfied) their level of life satisfaction. When asked about overall life satisfaction (see Figure 5.1), those in Ghana were far more likely to report that they were very satisfied or satisfied (70 percent) when compared to those in Mali (56 percent) and those in Burkina Faso (34 percent). Individuals in Burkina Faso were most likely to report higher levels of overall life dissatisfaction, with almost half falling into this category.

Overall life satisfaction is often impacted by a range of other indicators—for example, the extent to which an individual is content with their health, security, housing, finances, and education. In Burkina Faso we found that respondents reported lower levels of life satisfaction, which was often linked to concerns over security. While in Ghana three-fifths of respondents noted that they were satisfied with their level of security, and in Mali just over half said that they were satisfied, in Burkina Faso only one-third of those we surveyed

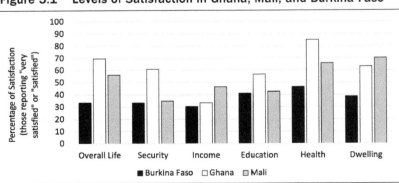

Figure 5.1 Levels of Satisfaction in Ghana, Mali, and Burkina Faso

were satisfied with their level of security. Half of all our respondents in Burkina Faso reported that they were either very dissatisfied or dissatisfied with their overall level of security.

As well as feeling pessimistic about their security, individuals from Burkina Faso were also more dissatisfied with their household income than those living in Mali or Ghana. Less than a third of Burkinabé stated that they were satisfied with their household income, while in Mali and Ghana almost half of all respondents said that they were satisfied with household income. Respondents from Burkina Faso were also more pessimistic about their overall health and most pessimistic about their dwelling conditions. Almost half of those surveyed in Burkina Faso said they were satisfied with their health, a much lower number than in Ghana where three-quarters reported being satisfied, or when compared to Mali where just over two-thirds reported being satisfied. When it came to satisfaction over housing, only two-fifths of those surveyed in Burkina Faso reported being satisfied, while in Ghana two-thirds were satisfied and in Mali over two-thirds were satisfied. The findings from Mali stand out as being more positive than expected, especially when compared to Burkina Faso. Given that Mali has faced insecurity for a significantly longer period of time, it may be that communities have made some form of adjustment to turmoil, whereas the decline in Burkina Faso was more recent to the time of the survey, and as such, feelings may have been much more raw.

Perceptions of the Police

A factor that is important to good governance is the level of confidence that a population has in law enforcement to attend the scene of a reported crime promptly and to deal with the situation in a just and equitable way. This is an issue that many African countries struggle with. Police corruption has consistently been highlighted as one of the most pressing and egregious issues across Africa, and public perceptions of the police are found to be very low indeed. According to one prominent report (Appiah et al. 2020), the police are seen in the following way:

> [One of the] most corrupt among eight key government and societal institutions. Almost half of respondents say "most" or "all" of the police in their country are corrupt, far outstripping the proportion

who perceive widespread corruption among members of Parliament (38 percent), tax officials (35 percent), judges and magistrates (35 percent), and Presidency officials (35 percent). Fewer than half (45 percent) say they trust the police "somewhat" or "a lot," making them less trusted than presidents and their staff (50 percent), traditional leaders (57 percent), and religious leaders (68 percent).

Given such overall negative perceptions of the police, our own survey aimed to test how true this was across areas of Mali, Burkina Faso, and Ghana. To do this we asked respondents to tell us how likely they would be to contact the police in their localities if a crime had been committed. In addition to this, we asked them to tell us how satisfied they are with how police were performing/executing their duties.

When asked to select from a list of who they would first call in the instance of theft, it was not surprising to see that across the three countries (and dozens of local areas) most of our respondents did not select the police as their first choice. To give an example, when presented with the hypothetical situation of having to imagine who they would call if money was stolen from them, about one-quarter of Malians said that they would first deal with the situation themselves, another quarter would first turn to the police, and almost another quarter said that they would first turn to the village chief. The remaining respondents had more diffuse solutions. In Burkina Faso, those saying that they would first go to the police was the highest among the three countries, with two-fifths of respondents selecting this option. In Ghana, about a quarter said that they would first turn to the police, while just over half indicated that they would first turn to their village chief.

This indicates that across the three countries, confidence in the police for resolving small crimes is low, with most relying on themselves or on local actors such as the village chief to solve the issue. When it comes to the more serious crime of armed robbery, a higher proportion of our respondents claimed that they would be willing to contact the police as their first option, though this still did not form a majority of respondents across each of the three countries. The highest number of respondents who said that they would first turn to the police in case of robbery were in Ghana (almost half), followed by Burkina Faso (two-fifths), while in Mali only just over a quarter said that they would turn to the police. In Mali, the highest proportion of respondents (about a third) said that they would first turn to the local chief. The implication of these findings is that confidence in the police is at low levels across the three countries and is an area where more accountability is likely needed.

In addition to these two hypothetical scenarios, we asked our respondents to estimate how much time it would take for their local police to respond to a burglary on an average day. Our Ghanaian respondents were the most optimistic, with just over half of them estimating a response time of thirty minutes or less. Our respondents in Burkina Faso were not far behind those in Ghana, with approximately half of respondents saying that police would respond within thirty minutes. In Mali, however, two-fifths of our respondents indicated that a police service either did not exist, or that if it did, they would not call. In Ghana, for the sake of comparison, only 3 percent of respondents selected this option.

Perceptions of the police as corrupt or brutal have fueled protests in countries such as Nigeria, South Africa, and Ghana. In Ghana, for example, thousands of people gathered in the streets of the capital Accra in early July 2021 to protest police violence after police killed two people in the south of the country. One protestor was reported as saying: "They are killing our people, that's why we are protesting. The police system is weak. The police is [sic] filled with tyrants and vigilante groups, of which they have been killing our people" (Asala 2021). Failure to reform the police or to hold them accountable weakens overall perceptions of governance in a state and increases grievances against the state.

Local Governance Versus National Governance

It is well established that across parts of West Africa, national governments have low levels of legitimacy among the population. Government, however, is a broad construct and is made up of numerous different actors that function across different levels of society. To test the level of legitimacy that government actors have, our survey respondents were asked to select which they were most likely to turn to in a given (hypothetical) situation (e.g., concerns over public infrastructure, access to health care, theft). In each case our respondents also had the option to select between different levels of government or to select alternatives such as family, friends, and themselves. The higher the number of respondents willing to turn to formal government actors, the more legitimacy they have. This gives an indication of the extent to which perceptions of government and particular grievances may have impacted the way in which populations regard the ability of government to provide certain services.

Results from across the three countries indicate that Malians are mostly likely to try and deal with issues themselves before turning to others, while Ghanaians are most likely to turn to government, especially at the local level. Across the three countries, representatives of local forms of government including mayors, chiefs, and local assembly persons were generally perceived in a positive light when compared to government actors at the national level. Local-level officials were usually the first port of call that our respondents would turn to in matters involving land concerns, stolen money, concerns over water, education, roads, and flooding. This finding resonates with previous research on Burkina Faso, which found that when it comes to formal institutions of local governance, "in the minds of Burkinabè, the mayor and municipal council are front and center" (Ariotti and Fridy 2020, 45).

In Ghana almost all our respondents said that they would first approach either the local chief or local assembly person for concerns regarding water. Both of those options were also popular in Mali and Burkina Faso. When it came to the question of concerns over teachers, almost all Malian respondents said that they would first seek the help of the local mayor or chief to deal with the issue. In Burkina Faso two-thirds of respondents indicated that they would turn to the mayor or local chief to deal with problematic teachers, and in Ghana over three-quarters of respondents selected the same options. Respondents across the three countries also expressed that they would turn to local-level officials to deal with road concerns. This was highest in Burkina Faso, where over three-quarters of respondents selected that option, followed by just over a quarter in Ghana and about two-thirds in Mali. A similar picture also emerged when we asked our respondents who they would first contact with concerns over flooding. In both Burkina Faso and Ghana, over three-quarters of the respondents said that they would first turn to a local official, while in Mali about two-thirds said that they would. In Ghana some respondents had so much trust in local authorities that one-half even claimed that they would first go to their local chief in an instance of or concern over marital infidelity, including when another villager was flirting with their spouse.

When asked who they would turn to for concerns over school fees, local government featured less prominently. In Mali approximately half of respondents said that they would try to deal with the issue themselves first, while in Burkina Faso two-fifths said that they would first turn to family to help with school fees. In Ghana respondents answered differently, with many indicating that they would turn to government. One-quarter of our Ghanaian respondents said that they would turn to a local assembly member, and one-fifth said that they would go to their member of parliament. Only a small fraction of those in Ghana said that they would first try and solve the issue themselves, though about a quarter said that they would turn to family first.

These types of responses demonstrate that local governance across Mali, Burkina Faso, and Ghana is robust and does not lack legitimacy to the extent that affects government at the national level. This may be because people are able to directly see the actions and consequences of decisions taken at the local level. Where our respondents had the option to select members of parliament or civil servants to help resolve their issues, they rarely did—though this could also be because some of the concerns asked about may have been perceived as more local than national-level issues. This was most striking in Mali, where just over 10 percent said that they would first approach a civil servant over concerns relating to teachers, while in Burkina Faso and Ghana no one selected this option. When it came to concerns over jobs, just 10 percent of Ghanaians said they would first contact a member of parliament, whereas in Mali and Burkina Faso no one selected this option. In Ghana 18 percent of respondents said that they would turn to a member of parliament with concerns over school fees, and 9 percent said that they would contact a member of parliament for concerns over medicine.

Ghanaians are most open to engaging with national-level government representatives, while in Mali and Burkina Faso there is greater hesitancy. One factor that may explain this is the relative stability of the Ghanaian state, whereas the governments in Mali and Burkina Faso are besieged with concerns over security and have often had to take extreme measures to combat jihadists, sometimes with negative impacts on citizens themselves.

Corruption and Ethnic and Religious Identities

As argued throughout this chapter, perceptions of corruption are instrumental in determining government legitimacy and can also correlate with the level of success a jihadist group has in a given area. We were interested to see how our respondents across Mali, Burkina Faso, and Ghana perceived corruption both in their localities and nationally, as well as the impact that corruption has on them personally. (See Figure 5.2.)

We asked participants to respond to the following prompt: "My country is too corrupt for people like me to get ahead in life." Across all three countries, respondents felt that their countries were too corrupt. It was our respondents in Mali that were most concerned about corruption, with approximately half strongly agreeing with the claim, and with another two-fifths agreeing with the claim. Only a very small fraction of respondents in Mali disagreed that the country was too corrupt. While not as emphatic as in Mali, our respondents in Burkina Faso also thought their country was too corrupt for people like them to get ahead in life, with one-quarter strongly agreeing with the claim and almost half agreeing. In Ghana just over one-fifth of our respondents strongly agreed, and just over half agreed with the claim. This indicates that for most respondents across the three countries, corruption is a serious issue that they believe has hampered their own success in their respective country. Once individuals feel that they are not able to get ahead, that no matter what they try corruption will hold them back, it creates an atmosphere in which those same individuals start to feel disenfranchised and despondent.

At the local level it is unsurprising that Mopti, the region of Mali where jihadist violence has been among the highest in West Africa, respondents overwhelmingly perceived corruption to be one of the most pressing problems to face them personally. Almost every single respondent across every village in Mopti strongly agreed or agreed that corruption in Mali had stopped them from getting further ahead in life. This finding is so stark that it indicates a level of perceived corruption that is damaging to the legitimacy of the national government and is also likely contributing to the operational success of jihadist movements in the region such as the Macina Liberation Front that seek to exploit grievances over corruption to recruit and mobilize those who join the movement to violence. In Burkina Faso, there was a little more variance across the different towns that our

Figure 5.2 Survey on Corruption

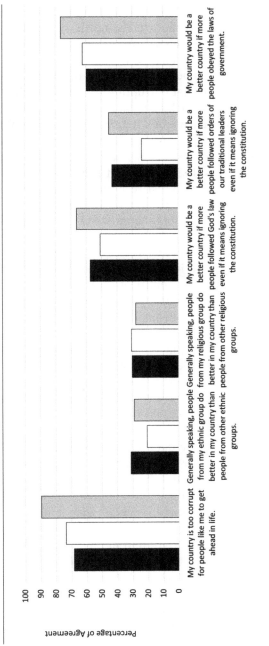

respondents came from, though with the majority still viewing the country as significantly corrupt. In the north of the country, in the town of Korizena, for example, almost all respondents agreed with the statement that Burkina Faso was too corrupt for them to get ahead in life, while in the neighboring town of Yacouta, three-fifths of respondents disagreed that corruption was holding them back. In some towns in the south, such as Gonce, Guiaro, and Toanga, many respondents sat on the fence when it came to the issue of corruption in the country. The picture in Burkina Faso is more complex than that of Mali, and governance mechanisms at the local level could indeed explain such differences. In Ghana, apart from the towns of Pelungu and Natinga in Upper East, most respondents believed that Ghana was too corrupt for them to succeed in. In particular, the towns of Nangodi, Kulungugu, and Bolgatanga stand out for a particularly strong sentiment in this direction.

In addition to asking whether their country was too corrupt for our respondents to succeed in, we also wanted to explore any differentiation based on the ethnic identification of each respondent, and to gauge whether some ethnic groups feel better integrated into the country. To do this, we asked respondents to state their level of agreement with the following statement: "Generally speaking, people from my ethnic group do better in my country than people from other ethnic groups." As expected, there was some variance to the way people responded across the three countries (see Figure 5.2), with more people in Mali and Ghana disagreeing with the statement than in Burkina Faso. In Mali and Ghana just over half of those surveyed disagreed with the statement, while in Burkina Faso two-fifths disagreed.

Digging deeper into the data, it appears that most respondents from each ethnic group were more likely to disagree that people from their own ethnic group do better than those from other ethnic groups. Only two groups stand out for regarding members of their own ethnic group as doing comparatively better than others—these were members of the Kassena (a smaller ethnic group primarily situated in northern Ghana), where just over half agreed that they fared better, and members of the Dogon (an ethnic group predominantly situated in the central plains of Mali, where they form about 8 percent of the population of Mali) in which approximately half of respondents agreed with the question. All respondents who identified as Busani (an ethnic group that straddles the border between Burkina Faso and Ghana) felt that they did not do as well as members of other ethnic groups. Over 70 percent of Bozo (a small ethnic group in Mali's Mopti region) and Nabit (predominantly in northern Ghana) respondents disagreed with the statement, and approximately 60 percent of Fulani (located in Mopti for the purposes of this survey as well as some parts of southeastern Burkina Faso) and Songhai (located in the Mopti region of Mali) disagreed. There was a little more variance with Mossi (the largest ethnic group in Burkina Faso) respondents, in which approximately a third of respondents agreed, a third disagreed, and a third neither agreed nor disagreed.

In order to gauge the ways respondents felt toward different layers of their identities, they were asked to rate the extent to which they felt connected to their family, neighborhood, ethnic group, and country. One of the strongest, yet not particularly surprising, results to emerge is that most respondents across all three countries felt most connected to their family, then their friends, followed by their neighborhoods and ethnic groups, and least of all with their country. Indeed, over four-fifths of our respondents across the three countries said that they felt very connected to family, two-thirds said that they felt strongly connected to their neighborhood, one-third said they were strongly connected to their region, and only about one-quarter said that they felt strongly connected to their country. Because of this, it seems that for most respondents the most important level of identification is with the most local level of governance/support systems.

Differing Forms of Governance

We also sought to understand the extent to which alternative models of governance may have some traction among the population, and the level of legitimacy such forms of governance might have when compared to the constitution of each country. To gauge the extent to which there may be any friction between constitutional governance and a desire for more religious forms of governance (see Figure 5.2), one question asked participants to indicate their level of agreement with the following statement: "My country would be a better country if more people followed God's law even if it means ignoring the constitution." Across all three countries, over half of respondents agreed with the statement indicating a prominent belief in each country is that they would be a better place if people followed religious dictates even if it meant ignoring the constitution. This suggests that messages put out by jihadist groups promising governance based on religious models might have some traction among populations; however, what is not clear is the extent of how formal such governance should be. It is unclear, for example, whether governance based on "God's law" should come in the form of a completely revitalized system based on the Islamic caliphates and empire of the past, or whether a few new laws need to be enacted, or whether individuals should enact new patterns of behavior based on religious teachings in their own lives. Respondents in Mali were most likely to agree with the statement, with two-thirds either strongly agreed or agreed; in Burkina Faso three-fifths strongly agreed or agreed; and in Ghana just over half strongly agreed or agreed.

A follow-up question (see Figure 5.2) sought to gauge the level of trust respondents had in traditional leaders through asking them the extent to which they agreed with the following question: "My country would be a better country if more people followed the orders of our traditional leaders even if it means ignoring the constitution." There was some level of disparity between the three countries. In Mali respondents were evenly split, with 45 percent saying that they broadly agreed with the statement, and 45 percent saying they broadly disagreed. In Burkina Faso almost 44 percent broadly agreed, while 30 percent broadly disagreed. In Ghana slightly more than half of respondents broadly disagreed with the statement.

Perhaps the most significant finding was that across all three countries, most respondents were firm in their opinion that their country would be a better place if more people obeyed the laws of the government. In Mali 76.5 percent of respondents agreed with this statement, while in Burkina Faso 59.7 percent agreed, and in Ghana the percent was 62.4. While existing laws may not be perfect, the results indicate that for the most part respondents are supportive of existing laws and processes of governance and would like to see the system working as it should. Alternative forms of governance gain additional appeal when the existing system is seen to have broken down or to have failed to benefit the majority of citizens.

Perceptions of Security

Security is fundamental to the functioning of any community and can range from something as simple as having the confidence to go out for a walk in one's neighborhood, to feeling physically protected from the onslaught of terrorist attacks. Perceptions of how secure a community feels (see Figure 5.3) often mirror the extent to which those same individuals have confidence in their systems of governance, for without security little else is possible. Across all three countries most respondents reported feeling safe when walking alone in their community during the daytime. When the question was switched to ask whether individuals feel safe walking alone in their community at nighttime, results changed. In Mali just over three-fifths of respondents said that they did not feel safe, while most people in Ghana reported feeling safe to walk alone. Across all three countries, respondents felt safe from violence when alone in their own home but with some degree of variance—for example, just over half of respondents in Burkina Faso felt safe at home, while in Ghana just over four-fifths felt safe at home. When asked whether they avoid certain routes or regard certain areas of their communities as dangerous, almost all of our Malian respondents agreed with this, while in Burkina Faso just over half agreed, and in Ghana fewer still. This signals that respondents from Mali felt greatest insecurity in their own communities and could be in part because communities surveyed in Mali were in the volatile Mopti region of the country. Given the rise of instability in Burkina Faso since we completed our survey, these types of results are likely reflected there too now.

Across all three countries (see Figure 5.3) respondents claimed that they felt their communities were overall peaceful. Having said this, respondents in Mali were least likely to agree that their community was peaceful (just over half), with Burkina Faso fairing a little better (just over two-thirds), and Ghana the most positive (over four-fifths). Drilling deeper, the survey asked respondents to rate the occurrence of violence in their own communities. In Mali the majority of respondents stated that their community is marked by the repeated occurrence of violence, while in Burkina Faso and in Ghana the majority said that their communities did not have reoccurring forms of violence. In the case of Burkina Faso, this is likely to have changed since the completion of our survey as violence started to spike alongside the general spread of political instability across the country in 2022.

To assess whether violence has increased over time, respondents were asked to note whether they thought that violence had increased significantly over the past two years (see Figure 5.4). Again here,

Figure 5.3 Perceptions of Security

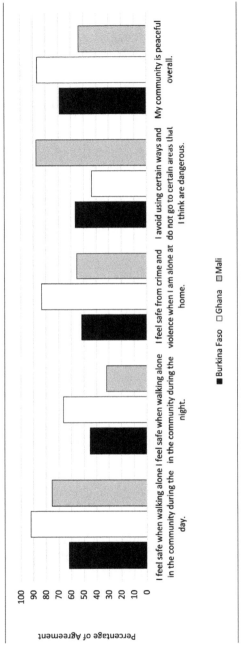

107

Figure 5.4 Perceptions of Violence

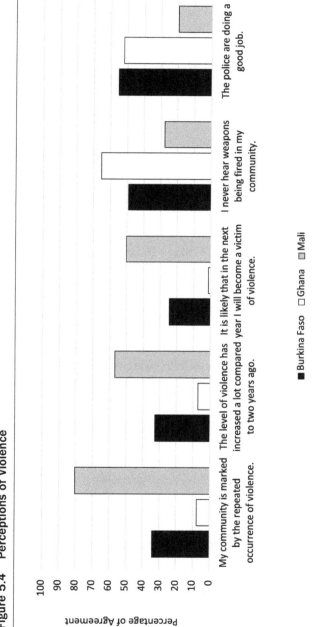

there was discrepancy between Mali and the other two countries. In Mali, a majority responded to say that violence had increased in the past two years, while in Burkina Faso and Ghana respondents said that violence had not increased. In addition to this, the survey sought to gain a sense of perceptions of security in the future through linking this with likelihood of future violence through asking respondents if they thought that they would become victims of violence within the next year (see Figure 5.4). In Mali almost half of respondents believed that they would be victims of violence within twelve months, whereas in Burkina Faso, and especially in Ghana, respondents were more likely to report that they did not see themselves as future victims of violence. Despite Malians consistently reporting higher levels of insecurity in their communities, the majority of Malian respondents said that they did not hear weapons being fired in their communities, while almost half of our Burkinabé respondents said that they did, and even more (almost two-thirds) said that they did in Ghana. This again, is likely to have changed in Burkina Faso since our survey was conducted.

To close out questions on security, respondents were asked whether they thought the police were doing a good job (see Figure 5.4). The results of this seem to mirror the broader patterns of insecurity from the survey. In areas where security was highest—this is in Ghana—most respondents said that the police were doing a good job. Where perceptions of security were at their lowest—Mali—less than 20 percent of respondents thought that the police were doing a good job.[1]

Perceptions of Terrorism and VEOs

Trying to understand peoples' perceptions of jihadist activity in the region, including even basic aspects such as whether they have heard of a certain jihadist group, is a difficult task. In a region that not only has an active jihadist presence, but also has many communities seeing the realities of casualties of terrorism on a regular basis, it is not surprising that many respondents were hesitant to engage with us on questions of jihadist groups and their activities.

Of those who did respond, the majority across all three countries said that they had not heard of what we considered to be the most prominent terrorist groups in the region, including JNIM, ISGS, and

Boko Haram. The most recognizable group to our respondents was Boko Haram, while groups operating within the borders of their own countries had low levels of recognition. Less than one-third of Malian respondents said that they had heard of JNIM, and approximately one-third said that they had heard of ISGS. In Burkina Faso less than a quarter of those who responded to the question said that they had heard of JNIM, and far fewer said that they had heard of ISGS. Given the complex security environment, and fear of jihadist retribution in the region, it is not surprising that respondents may not have felt comfortable engaging on questions relating to jihadist activities, even if they had heard of the specific jihadist groups that they were asked about.

Perhaps the more interesting set of results on the topic pertained to the questions that asked respondents to comment on the key reasons for why they thought people join groups like JNIM and ISGS. All the respondents who answered the question in Ghana (where there has not yet been any large-scale jihadist attack) thought that the main reason someone would join JNIM was for spiritual reasons, while in Burkina Faso (which has recently seen the brunt of jihadist violence) only a third of respondents selected that option, and even fewer still in Mali, with less than 10 percent claiming that someone would join JNIM for spiritual reasons. In Mali, where respondents may have been most familiar with JNIM as a jihadist organization during the time of our survey (due to JNIM having been formed there as well as being a strategic area of operations), responses were more nuanced. Most Malian respondents thought that the primary reason as to why people would join JNIM was for financial reasons or because joining the group served as a means of "employment."

When it came to the question of why people would join ISGS, responses from the three countries were varied. As with the case of JNIM, it was predominantly our Ghanaian respondents (about two-fifths) that were most likely to believe that people primarily join for spiritual reasons. Almost two-fifths of our Burkinabé respondents believed that someone would join ISGS for primarily spiritual reasons, and as with JNIM, the lowest rate for those who believed this was in Mali, with just one-fifth saying so. The majority of our Malian respondents believed that the primary reason one would join ISGS related to employment and finances, while only about a quarter of Burkinabé and Ghanaian respondents selected this option. For both JNIM and ISGS there were small numbers of people who though that primary reasons could also include fighting Western influence, or as a way to help their community, or as a means to avenge the death of a loved one, or to be seen as a strong person.

While responses to this part of the survey were low, the findings are important because the perception among those closest to jihadist activity is that people are more motivated in joining out of financial gain or for employment purposes as opposed to purely ideological or religious motivations. This is significant not only for understanding how and why people are recruited into violent extremism, but also for finding more innovative ways in which to counter violent extremism. The findings also present a more complex picture of jihadist movements in the communities in which they operate, not just as religiously ideological organizations, but as ones that have a more instrumental approach, including the provision of jobs and in some cases security and community services. The finding indicates that in cases where people have a stake within their communities and some level of prosperity, the pull of joining a VEO might be more muted.

In addition to perceptions of why people would join jihadist groups, respondents were also asked to state what they believed to be the main goals of JNIM and ISGS. Understanding how populations perceive the goals of jihadist groups can provide additional insight into how jihadists actually operate in and around communities irrespective of the types of ideology that a group might publicly claim. In addition to this, it is interesting to note the extent to which the stated objectives of jihadists match with the ways in which they are perceived, and arguably where there is a higher level of congruence between the two, the more effective a group might be in its strategy.

Across the three countries our respondents had some variance in how they defined jihadists' key objectives. Starting with JNIM, the strongest and most unified response came from our respondents in Ghana, all of whom said that the organization's primary goal was to promote its own beliefs. This does not necessarily tell us what those beliefs are, but it does indicate that Ghanaians take at face value that JNIM is following its own publicly stated objectives. In Burkina Faso, about half of our respondents believed this to be the main goal of JNIM, while in Mali only two-fifths of our respondents agreed. Malian respondents identified other objectives (or perhaps what can be seen as more specific objectives) for JNIM, with a further quarter believing that JNIM's primary objective is to overthrow the government, and a smaller proportion saying that it was to provide spiritual leadership. Indeed, just over 10 percent of respondents in Mali and Burkina Faso saw JNIM as providing some form of spiritual leadership. This undermines the belief that local populations look to jihadist groups for moral or religious guidance, even though this is an aspect that jihadist groups themselves might try to emphasize.

Given the immense emphasis that JNIM places on highlighting government corruption in its strategic narratives, it is significant that not a single respondent across the three countries felt that the primary goal of JNIM was to combat corruption. This is especially interesting because JNIM has frequently promised that if they were allowed to take power and change the governance structures of communities, things would be different—that there would be an end to corruption, that justice would be equitable, and that people would be able to get ahead in life. It appears that our respondents are not convinced of this, or at least did not believe this to be JNIM's primary objective.

When it came to the main goal of ISGS, most respondents in Burkina Faso thought that it was to promote its beliefs, while in Mali and Ghana results were more distributed across a range of different responses. In Ghana, for example, one-third of respondents said that the main goal of ISGS was to fight the West, with just over 16 percent of respondents stating that the main goal was to provide financial resources or jobs, promote its beliefs, provide spiritual leadership, and to fight government corruption, respectively. In Mali almost 40 percent saw the main goal of ISGS as promoting its beliefs, with smaller numbers saying that it was to overthrow the government, and to fight the West.

Respondents were also asked to state how successful they though JNIM and ISGS had been in reaching their objectives. Of those who responded to these questions, the majority thought that both groups had failed to reach their objectives. Over two-thirds of respondents in Burkina Faso felt that JNIM was failing, while in Mali just under two-thirds thought that JNIM was failing, and in Ghana responders were equally divided on the question. With regard to ISGS, two-thirds of Malians thought the group was not achieving its goals, a figure that was roughly reflected among respondents in Burkina Faso and Ghana, too.

Because of the low response rate on these questions, the reliability of results remains in question. Despite this, what was clear from the results is that in areas where jihadist groups have a greater operational capacity, reasons for why people join and objectives of groups are more nuanced. This demonstrates that reasons for recruitment and mobilization can be quite complex, ranging from individuals having a belief in the ideology of the group, to more likely seeing jihadists as a source of employment or financial gain in a region where unemployment is high and household incomes are low.

Across all three countries most respondents said that their governments had some level of efficacy in combating terrorism. Respondents in Mali were most pessimistic, and respondents in Ghana were most optimistic. Given that Mali, at the time of our survey, had experienced most instability from jihadist violence and Ghana the least, the results are less than surprising.

Population Perspectives on the West

There is no doubt that jihadist groups across the spectrum in the Sahel work hard to present the West (and especially France and the United States) as corrupt and exploitative powers that want to extend their occupation of Muslim lands and keep Muslim populations in positions of servility. This type of narrative is seen across a majority of the jihadist propaganda ecosystem and over the past several decades has come to be a standard grievance expressed by jihadists globally (see Chapter 4). Jihadists, however, not only shape popular sentiment but also amplify what already exists. The argument here is not that people in the Sahel are opposed to the West per se, but rather that Western values are for the most part seen as having the capacity to engender moral decay, which in turn is seen as fundamentally weakening the foundations of local communities. It is unlikely that most people at the local level across Mali, Burkina Faso, and northern Ghana have much experience of Western activity or interaction with Westerners in their own villages, but despite this, jihadists have managed to profoundly shape the narrative, conflating problems and grievances with national governments in the Sahel to the continued interactions of those governments with the West.

To gauge the extent to which populations across Mali, Burkina Faso, and Ghana agree with such sentiments, we sought to gain an insight into population perceptions of the West. Our survey respondents were asked to state the degree to which they agreed with the following statement: "When Western countries try to influence my country, they lower moral standards." With just a few exceptions (see Figure 5.5), a significant majority of respondents across Mali, Burkina Faso, and Ghana agreed with that statement. Some villages had a far higher degree of agreement than others, showing intraregional variance. In Mali a majority from all villages surveyed agreed with the statement, with the highest proportion of those agreeing located in Sofara, where 91 percent were in strong agreement with the statement. In Burkina Faso the results were more varied at the village level, with some villages like Korizena in northeastern Burkina Faso having a high proportion (86 percent) of respondents that strongly agreed with the statement. Some Burkinabé villages, for example Nobili in Centre-Sud, had unanimous disagreement with the statement. In Ghana results were more dispersed between the strongly agree to strongly disagree categories, with respondents in the village of Amongorebisi most likely to disagree with the statement and respondents in the village of Nangodi most likely to agree.

On the whole it would appear that jihadists in the region have a narrative on the West that at least in part resonates with what many local populations believe. The implications for this are important, especially in an age of increasing great power competition in the region, and in a context where different powers may try to access or

Figure 5.5 Population Perspectives on the West

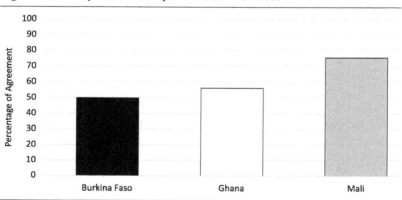

Note: Respondents were asked about agreement with the statement, "When Western countries try to influence my country, they lower moral standards."

leverage communities for conflict resolution, provision of aid, or in some cases resource extraction. The impact of great power competition on communities across Mali, Burkina Faso, and Ghana will be the focus of Chapters 6 and 7.

Conclusion

Governance is a complicated business in West Africa, with formal states in the region lacking legitimacy among large swaths of the population. This situation can be compounded by instability and insecurity, and certainly through corruption. Jihadist groups work hard to exploit and amplify grievances that further undermine state legitimacy.

The ways in which communities respond to failures in governance vary. For example, in Mali a high degree of "self-help" was expressed by our respondents, where many stated that they would try and solve a problem themselves first before turning to others. It is not clear if this is due to a distinct libertarian attitude in Mali or rather that individuals know that government will not address issues even when petitioned to do so. Despite national governments being perceived in negative ways by large portions of the population, governance across those countries is not completely failing. The survey showed that populations still turn to a range of officials for help, and these tend to be at the local level. Even at the local level, there is a degree of variety, with some types of officials proving more popular than others. Because of this, it becomes increasingly important for those outside of the region (and who wish to act in the region) to understand and differentiate between different governance actors, as well as understand the kinds of reactions that associating with certain levels of government can illicit.

What is most important is that many of our respondents across Mali, Burkina Faso, and Ghana stated that they believed their countries would be better places if more people followed the laws of the land. This opinion was more popular than those who believed that following the laws of God would improve the country. Because of this, it is important to find ways in which to bolster legal frameworks and ensure that the frameworks in place are followed. Indeed, in order to promote good governance that makes the most impact on communities, local government should be funded as mandated, so that they have the resources for community projects.

These public works projects "also fall within the issue areas formal local governments are charged with tackling the world over" (Ariotti and Fridy 2020, 47).

Corruption, unsurprisingly, is perhaps the biggest issue facing good governance across Mali, Burkina Faso, and Ghana, with significant numbers of respondents stating that corruption in their country has personally held them back from success. Corruption is also perhaps the most pressing grievance that jihadists highlight in their narratives, knowing that such discourse will resonate with local communities. So ingrained is corruption that almost no respondents believed that even jihadists who focus so much on highlighting corruption could do much to solve the issue. Combating corruption is not an easy task and requires a whole of government approach. The suggestion here is not that all state institutions across the three countries fail to enact their civic roles, but rather that corruption is so widespread that many citizens view this as the key threat facing their countries.

It is further clear that corruption exacerbates a myriad of factors that leads to deepening perceptions of the illegitimacy of the three country states. Traditionally, recommendations here have focused on trying to convince states to professionalize—making their civil service a fair and just bureaucracy accountable to the needs of the populace; having independent military and police agencies that work to protect citizens irrespective of their social position, ethnic affiliation, or ability to pay; and creating a general accountability to the needs of national citizens, rather than a commitment to self-enrichment (Delia Deckard and Pieri 2017, 382). While such attempts are indeed admirable, they have failed. What we argue is that Western governments should reconsider how development assistance is structured and the degree to which providing such assistance through national bureaucracies is the most effective way. In many instances, developing relationships with local governance actors could yield better results. At the same time, governments should be encouraged to address real concerns that citizens have, and these concerns often relate to structural issues within the functioning of the state that are often difficult to deal with—for example, perceived views that one ethnic group is favored more than another by decisionmakers, or that economic investment is greater in one part of the country compared to another, or that certain communities have been left out of the political process.

Such recommendations also relate to the argument advanced by Comolli with regard to eradicating jihadists in the region. This is a debate that has shifted beyond solely traditional security concerns and needs to include the idea that West African states have to deliver public goods more equitably, bolster democratic institutions, and reform the policing of citizens, especially in areas where jihadist groups have gained (or will gain) traction (Comolli 2015). These recommendations exhort states to minimize the discontent from which jihadists are presumed to spring, thus weakening support and ultimately undermining them. As is discussed in more detail in ensuing chapters, great powers can amplify and diminish support for local power structures by activities that go far beyond traditional discussions of security.

Note

1. For a more robust discussion of perceptions of policing, see the discussion earlier in this chapter.

6
Enter Great Power Competition

GREAT POWER ADVERSARIES MOST OFTEN COMPETE DELIBERATELY BELOW THE threshold of intensity likely to escalate to conventional war. As the post–Cold War world fades into its replacement, we expect to see an increase in these subwar competitive behaviors (Blankenship and Denison 2019; Haffa 2018; Medeiros 2019). Greater emphasis on understanding the relationship between weaker states and the rise of revisionist powers such as China and Russia, the response of former colonial powers, and a reimagined US superpower is necessary. Africa is fast becoming a primary arena for great power competition. How are these global powers engaging with the slice of Africa under investigation in this book? How do these engagements compare with those of their rivals? This chapter uses available data to answer these questions. Chapter 7 follows with an exploration of the impact of these engagements.

Africans are no strangers to international influence. Chapter 3 documents the waves of great power competition that swept across the geographical region yet to become the independent states of Mali, Burkina Faso, and Ghana during the precolonial, colonial, and independence eras. Exertions of force by outside actors are generally viewed at the national level with scant attention paid to how these great power actors impact communities differently within a country. In addition to regional differences, great powers may vary the nature of their interactions with African partners by sector. Though a comprehensive rundown of all potential activities existing under the umbrella concept of "great power competition" is impossible—activities can range from promoting cultural activities to dropping bombs—there are some relatively well documented and regionally varied modes we explore here: military relations, development assistance, and extractive industries.

In this chapter, we explore these three spheres of great power competition sequentially beginning with arms trading and military-to-military coordination, moving to bilateral development assistance, and concluding with an exploration of extractive industries. The research focus is on the activities of China and the United States as the two most prominent poles of contemporary great power competition, though also considered are the activities of major (e.g., Russia, the European Union, and the United Kingdom), Middle Eastern (e.g., Turkey and Saudi Arabia) and regional (e.g., Nigeria) powers who often complement and compete with the efforts of these dominant poles (Jones et al. 2020).

Where evidence of competition is clear, the fact is noted. In a period of great power competition, virtually any activity can be viewed as part of a larger geostrategic competition (Nexon 2021). Where evidence is unclear and/or underdocumented, a description of the activities from as neutral a vantage point as possible is presented. Descriptions of activities begin at the West Africa regional level before moving quickly to country-level descriptions in Mali, Burkina Faso, and Ghana. The focus concludes on the four subnational units where survey data is collected: Mopti, Sahel, Centre-Sud, and Upper East. These descriptions operationalize independent variables by pointing out areas under investigation where certain activities are happening at considerable scale and areas where they likely are not. Subsequent chapters explore whether these activities shape the types of grievances citizens have and explore the way they organize their local problem-solving institutions.

Military Relations

Because of the clandestine nature of many military-to-military arrangements, much of what goes on in this realm is hidden. In relying on public reporting, the portion of the iceberg revealed above the waterline may be dwarfed by what lurks below the water's surface. Countries also differ in how they advertise their presence militarily. Coordination that may be well-advertised in one case may be handled covertly in another. This unevenness makes it likely that countries whose military relations are less transparent will be relatively underreported. These caveats do not, however, negate the utility of the exercise. Clear patterns in relationships emerge in the analysis. These patterns may be diminished or made more nuanced with more data, but it is unlikely that they will be negated.

United States

In terms of shared military exercises and status of forces agreements, the United States and its Western allies are at the forefront in the region. As of 2019, Mali, Burkina Faso, and Ghana were included in the twenty-six African states that have acquisition and cross-servicing agreements with the United States. These agreements promote interoperability, readiness, and effectiveness between the countries' militaries (United States Africa Command 2019, P-AI-7). United States Africa Command (AFRICOM) reports enduring cooperative security locations in Accra, Ghana, and Ouagadougou, Burkina Faso. Mali hosts a nonenduring footprint in Bamako and has hosted nonenduring footprints in the north (Turse 2020).

Brown University's Costs of War project sites training and/or assistance for counterterrorism in all three countries (Savell 2021). Military exercises, like AFRICOM's Flintlock, African Lion, and Western Express, involve regular military-to-military exchanges between US troops and their Malian, Burkinabé, and Ghanaian counterparts (Waddington 2013). This training is so pervasive that at least three former military heads of state in Burkina Faso (Lieutenant Colonel Isaac Zida took a course on counterterrorism at MacDill Air Force Base in Tampa and both Lieutenant Colonel Paul-Henri Damiba and General Gilbert Diendéré were prominent Flintlock attendees) and two in Mali (Captain Amadou Sanogo learned English in Texas, did trainings in Georgia and Arizona, and was fond of wearing a US Marine Corps pin on his uniform, and Colonel Assimi Goïta took part in MacDill Air Force Base trainings and Flintlock) took part in these exercises of US-based training programs sponsored by the US Department of Defense (Turse 2023; Whitehouse 2012).

In coordination with the United Nations and West African allies in the global war on terror, the US military has been involved in significant operational assessment and what political and military leaders often characterize as "indirect military intervention" wherein billions of dollars "training, equipping, deploying and sustaining African intervention forces" are allocated but US forces are kept largely out of harm's way (Burgess 2018, 5). This policy stands in stark contrast to direct military activities of allies where large numbers of troops and equipment are stationed in theater to conduct conventional warfare. On the ground, things are not so clear-cut. US troops were involved in repelling a daytime raid by al-Qaeda affiliates at UN Super Camp near Timbuktu in April 2018 (Rempfer 2020). Barely half a year earlier four US soldiers (Sergeant First Class Jeremiah Johnson, Staff Sergeant Bryan Black, Staff Sergeant Dustin Wright, and Sergeant LaDavid Johnson) and five members of a Nigerien troop (Bagué Soumana, Abdoul Rachid Yerimah, Yacouba Issoufou, and Goubé Mahamadou Issaka) were killed in an ambush in western Niger (N. Singh 2021). These noteworthy examples point to a liberal usage of "section 127e" in the region, where special operations forces are broadly empowered to support with boots on the ground and mission management allies combating terrorism at home (United States House of Representatives 2016; W. Morgan 2018).

China

China's boots-on-the-ground coordination with the three countries under intense study here is relatively small compared to that presented by the United States. China's military strategic interests in Africa diminish the further one gets from the Indian Ocean economic sphere, where its Belt and Road Initiative infrastructural project becomes more peripheral (Dahir 2019; Nantulya 2019). There is no West African equivalent to the overseas base China recently established in Obock, Djibouti, and smaller enduring cooperative security locations are not currently part of the People's Liberation Army's blueprint (Baldor 2021; Neethling 2020).[1] Under President Xi Jinping, China has been ramping up military personal visits in Africa and elsewhere, and China has dramatically boosted both its financial and personnel contributions to UN peacekeeping missions. In 2020 China became one of the top ten countries in terms of contributions of troops and police to UN missions. Though the commitment has not yet surpassed 500 troops at any given time, since 2013 China has taken an active role in the UN Multidimensional Integrated Stabilization Mission in Mali (MINUSMA) (K. W. Allen et al. 2017; Cabestan 2018; Gowan 2020).

Where China has been more significantly involved in the region is in arms exports. Though a bit player in Mali and having shunned Burkina Faso until 2018 due to its recognition of Taiwan (Blanchard 2018; Kironska and Dramane 2022), China supplied Ghana with more than 40 percent of its registered arms transfers over the period 2001 to 2021 in terms of trend-indicator value (TIV).[2] Figure 6.1 shows graphically how these arms exports compare across importers and exporters. During this period the Ghanaian government received from the Chinese nine 122mm multiple rocket launchers, four K-8 trainer aircraft, four Type 062 gunboats, 86 WZ-523 armored personnel carriers, four AS565 Panther helicopters, and 100 FN-6 portable surface to air missiles (SIPRI 2023a).

Other Major International Actors

France, in particular, takes an active role in its former colonies (Chivvis 2016). Under the auspices of Operation Barkhane, France committed 3,000 troops to fighting terrorism in the Sahel in 2014. By 2020 this commitment had increased to 5,100 troops (Kajjo and Toure 2021; Kelly 2020). Bowing to domestic political pressures in France and increasingly frosty receptions in host countries, Operation Barkhane was officially shut down by the French government in late 2022. Mali requested that French troops depart the country in early 2022. Burkina Faso followed Mali's lead in early 2023. Estimates in 2023 were that roughly 3,000 French troops remained in the region operating primarily from Niger, Chad, and Côte d'Ivoire (Macaulay and Winter 2023; Maclean et al. 2023). Niger subsequently asked France to leave, and the Macron government put forward a plan to reduce the French footprint in West and Central Africa to 600 troops (Radio France 24 2024). The reduction of French troops in West Africa continued into 2025, with the government of Côte d'Ivoire asking French troops to leave in January of that year, and the government of Senegal asking all foreign troops to vacate the country at the end of the year. This also came at a time when the government of Chad was establishing control over French bases in the country.

Along with Germany and the European Union, France was the major technical and financial partner of the G5 Sahel (De Riviere 2022; Ministère de l'Europe et des Affaires étrangères 2020). Five francophone countries (Burkina Faso, Chad, Mali, Mauritania, and Niger) agreed to pool their counterterrorism efforts into G5 Sahel in

Figure 6.1 Trend-Indicator Value (TIV) of Arms Imports, 2001–2021

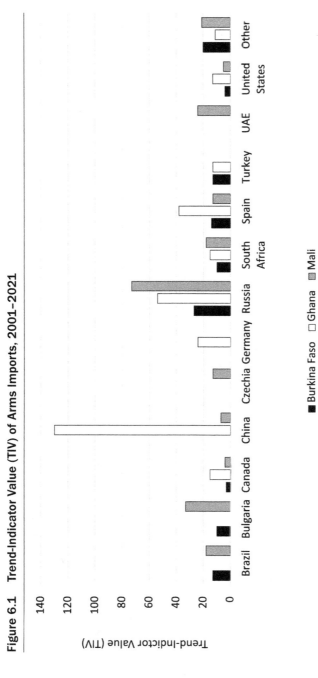

Note: Stockholm International Peace Research Institute (2023a).

2017. The combined G5 Sahel and French forces totaled more than 10,000 well-equipped troops at one point, was the second largest international military engagement in the region, and was at the forefront of Europe's renewed interest in regional security (Gegout 2018). Fewer joint operations than originally anticipated, a deteriorating security situation, and Mali's abrupt withdrawal in 2022 left the future of this effort in grave doubt (AfricaNews and Agence France-Presse 2022). The organization was further diminished with the announced withdrawal of Burkina Faso and Niger in 2024, again further highlighting the shifting sands of regional security dynamics.

The largest recent international military contingent in the region was coordinated by the United Nations. Established in 2013 to stabilize areas of Mali's north after a Tuareg rebellion, the UN MINUSMA consisted of more than 15,000 uniformed personnel at the start of 2023, drawn primarily from other African countries and Bangladesh, with a smattering of troops from around the world (United Nations Peacekeeping 2023). This mission was dubbed the "most dangerous" in UN history after Tuareg secessionists were replaced by operatives from al-Qaeda and the Islamic State looking to establish a foothold in the weakly governed areas around the Sahara (Sieff 2017). At the beginning of 2023, more than 300 peacekeepers had lost their lives to the operation as irregular warfare tactics honed in the Middle East made their way to sub-Saharan Africa (Stepansky 2020). Then, much to the surprise of a UN body preparing to follow the secretary general's recommendations to renew the MINUSMA mandate for 2023–2024, Mali's transitional minister of foreign affairs called on July 16 for the "withdrawal without delay of MINUSMA." The wishes of the Malian government were endorsed by the Security Council a few weeks later as the UN agreed to terminate the MINUSMA mandate effective June 30, 2023, with the remainder of the year to be used to transfer tasks and oversee an orderly withdrawal (Security Council Report 2023).

Though post–Cold War Russia has historically had only a small footprint on the continent, there are indicators of expanding interests (Adibe 2019; Mackinnon 2020). The numbers are small in absolute terms, but over the past decade Russia has sold more weapons to Mali and Burkina Faso than any other country (see Figure 6.1). In Ghana, Russian arms follow only Chinese arms in terms of volume (Kondratenko 2020). When Mali's president Ibrahim Boubacar Keïta was overthrown in August 2020, there was widespread speculation that either Russia or Turkey was behind the coup (Muvunyi 2020; Tastekin 2020). Very little publicly available evidence to support this speculation was proffered at the time, but the smoke pointed to the fact that both Russia and Turkey would welcome opportunities to undermine France and increase influence in the region (Paquette 2020).

Anti-French sentiment was not only high in Mali at the time but spilling out into the streets in wide-scale protests. The military government followed public sentiment, turning its back on France and many of its European allies, as well as regional West African bodies condemning the coup and eventually the UN (Elischer 2022). Filling the vacuum was the Russian private military company known as the Wagner Group. Able to boast victories over Islamic State in Iraq and Syria in Syria and touting anticolonial bonafides from the Cold War era, the paramilitary organization tightly wound up with the Russian state entered Mali quietly in late 2021. A few months later Russian Foreign Minister Sergey Lavrov acknowledged Wagner Group's presence and lauded it as an opportunity for a Russian contractor to help West Africans win their protracted war on terrorism. Though best reports suggest the secretive organization has never had more than 1,000 troops on the ground, Wagner forces regularly participate in counterterrorist operations alongside Malian forces and have been implicated in psychological operations in support of the current regime. There are credible press reports of Wagner Group operatives occupying former French and UN bases, abusing ethnically Fulani civilians, and illegally trafficking in gold from Mali to support operations in Ukraine (Pokalova 2023, 14–16; J. Thompson et al. 2022).

It is useful to note that Wagner Group does not operate as a unitary organization, but rather as a "network of firms with links to the Russian state that operate under contracts with foreign governments" and in ways that allow the Russian state to engage in "foreign adventures with scant accountability" (*Economist* 2023d). With regard to Sahelian Africa, Wagner Group pursues a three-pronged strategy (military, economic, and political) that varies depending on each specific state that it has dealings in. The military pillar is perhaps the most striking one in Mali and Burkina Faso (and potentially Niger too), as those states have increasingly looked to non-Western partners for security solutions. In addition, Wagner functions to propagate anti-Western messages in the Sahel while also providing an alternative external "support system" to those states, with the promise of filling some of the vacuum that will come from French and Western withdrawals from the region. Following the death of Wagner Group's chairman Yevgeny Prigozhin in a plane crash in August 2023, it is unclear whether Russia will seek to nationalize some of the activities that the mercenary groups have been involved with. This was best evidenced in news that the Kremlin had scrambled to "reassure the countries that host Wagner of its continued commitment to the missions, whether under the group's banner or not" (*Economist* 2023d).

Official Development Assistance

Compared to military engagements, overseas development assistance is more transparent and easier to compare across providers. While it can be difficult to definitively determine which projects were funded by foreign assistance and where in a country they are situated, there is decent data on total flows budgeted for transfer from the major development assistance donors to recipients. There is something of an apples to oranges issue of comparing assistance from Organisation of Economic Co-operation and Development (OECD) countries like the United States and non-OECD countries like China.[3] OECD members report their official development assistance totals in a regular forum known as the Development Assistance Committee (DAC). Because most of the major international donors are members, several large states that are not members of the OECD follow DAC reporting guidelines to be consistent (OECD 2019). The biggest outlier donor nation is China. This means it both reports its data differently than the large Western donors and has its own definition of what constitutes official development assistance (Sears 2019).

United States

Figure 6.2 shows US overseas development assistance (ODA) given bilaterally to Mali, Burkina Faso, and Ghana for the decades covering 2001 through 2021. US assistance is color coded light gray. ODA is a technical concept that includes most of a reporting country's development assistance. ODA is not inclusive of all foreign

Figure 6.2 Official Development Assistance, 2001–2021

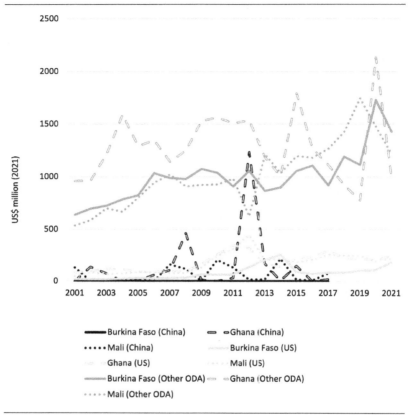

Source: Custer et al. (2021), Dreher et al. (2022), US Department of State and USAID (2023), and OECD (2023a).

Note: Aid represented is in millions of constant US dollars (2021) and is identified as overseas development assistance (ODA), or in the case of China ODA-like. US and other ODA figures are official. Chinese data represents ODA-like flow class assistance recommended by AidData for aggregation. Data availability ceases after 2017. Chinese ODA-like assistance is multiplied by 1.12 to bring it from 2017 to 2021 dollars.

assistance, but the two largest excluded areas are military assistance and peacekeeping, which are covered above (OECD 2023b).

Though there are countries in the world more giving on a per capita basis, the United States is the single biggest donor of ODA in total dollars, so all of these figures are substantial proportions of these three countries' foreign assistance inputs (Sachs 2005). Over the twenty-one-year period depicted, Ghana averaged just over $180 million a year, Mali just over $175 million, and Burkina Faso just over $80 million. These funds become substantial portions of all three countries' public expenditures. If we look at 2019, the last pre-Covid-19 budget, this level of US assistance would make up between 2 and 7 percent of each of the three country's budgets (World Bank 2023a).

Another way to parse this data is to look at the three countries in question and compare them to their African neighbors. To perform this analysis, it makes no sense to compare total development assistance given the disparate nature of the countries' population sizes. In terms of aid per capita, the United States has been most generous with Mali, averaging about $10.50 per person over the period 2001–2021. This reached a high of nearly $27 in 2012 when the country faced the Tuareg rebellion in its north and which transformed into the current jihadist conflict. Over the same period, Burkina Faso averaged only $4.50 per capita in US ODA. In only 2013 and 2014 did this figure reach double digits. Ghana, which is about 150 percent the population of either Mali or Burkina Faso and is a substantially wealthier country, came between these two figures at $6.75 per person. The years 2011 through 2013 were their only double-digit years. Sub-Saharan Africa as a whole averaged around $7.90 per person in aid over the 2001–2021 period.

The story told by these per capita numbers is one of relative consistency. This consistency can be witnessed across years, countries, and sectors. Compared to other sub-Saharan Africans, Burkinabé received slightly less US assistance in nineteen out of twenty-one years. Malians received slightly more than average in eighteen of twenty-one years. Ghanaians were between the two. These discrepancies from the median are relatively small, however. On average Mali received about $75 million more per year than would be expected assuming a standard sub-Saharan African aid formula. Ghana received around $20 million less than expected, and Burkina Faso around $65 million less than expected. In terms of the purpose of the foreign assistance, in all three countries health and economic development are in the top three categories of assistance provided. In Burkina Faso and Mali the third top-three category was humanitarian assistance. In Ghana it was program support (US Department of State and USAID 2023). Another story this data tells is one of these three country's positions in US geostrategic thinking. Were one of these countries significantly below the continental averages, it would be reasonable to assume the state was being punished. Were one of these countries significantly above continental averages, it would be reasonable to assume the state holds the keys to some vital national interest. The fact that neither of these scenarios is revealed by the data suggests these three countries are typical sub-Saharan African countries in terms of US interest (Early and Jadoon 2019).

One of the big challenges with US ODA assistance data is its location. With publicly available data there is no reliable way to pinpoint regional disbursements to see whether Mopti in Mali, Sahel and Centre-Sud in Burkina Faso, and Upper East in Ghana were disproportionately favored or burdened by aid disbursements in comparison to national averages. Given that one of USAID's focuses is poverty alleviation in all three countries and the nature of these regions, however, there is reason to believe they are receiving their fair share of development assistance. Mopti, Sahel, and Upper East are among the poorest in their respective countries. Centre-Sud is the outlier, being in line with typical Burkinabé development statistics (Global Data Lab 2023).

China

In approximately 2011 China became the largest supplier of foreign development assistance, and Africa has been a major recipient. Of these facts, one can be fairly certain. This equivocating language is intentional. Chinese aid, unlike aid from Western donors, largely exists outside of the ODA definition. It also happens outside the DAC accounting and reporting framework, meaning there is no convenient aggregator of the volume, structure, or recipients of Chinese foreign assistance. The data available comes from the AidData project using the Tracking Underreported Financial Flows (TUFF) methodology. This approach compiles and triangulates news reports, official statements from Chinese government agencies, reports from recipient countries, and field reports from scholars and nongovernmental organizations to reverse engineer a picture of Chinese foreign aid that resembles in structure that reported by most other major international donors (Dreher et al. 2021, 3). Because this data collection technique is laborious, it is not reported in real time or with a slight delay. Years available go from 2000 to 2017.

China's contemporary significance as an international donor is apparent even with suboptimal data. Between 2001 and 2017, estimates of Chinese ODA-like aid to sub-Saharan Africa are nearly $50 billion. Over that same period, US official figures show just over double that number (Custer et al. 2021; Dreher et al. 2022; US Department of State and USAID 2023). If we look at ODA-like flows of aid (see Figure 6.2) for the three focus countries, it is clear that during years with available data Chinese aid was less than that offered by the United States over the same period. If we add to these amounts assistance that is not comparable to ODA, however (see Figure 6.3), Chinese aid begins to dwarf US assistance in Ghana. In Africa, this non-ODA-like aid was six times as much over the period 2001 to 2017 as ODA comparable aid.

In the Chinese loans chart in Figure 6.3, each country is represented by a column that depicts total loan amount over the period 2000–2020 as well as the sectors funded with the loan. Burkina Faso received $160 million for information and communication technology (ICT). It was the only sector funded by the Chinese.

Figure 6.3 Chinese Loans (2000–2020) by Country and Sector

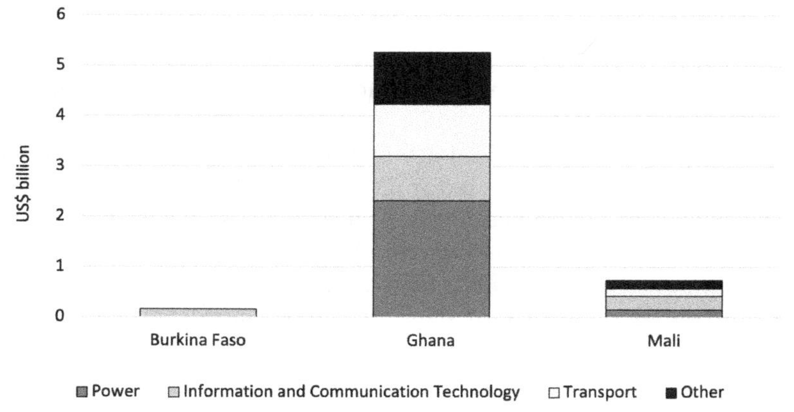

Source: Boston University Global Development Policy Center (2022).

Note: Data presented is in billions of US dollars and is in current dollar amounts at the time of the loan. Defense, water, agriculture, education, industry, unallocated, government, and business are the sectors lumped into "Other." They each represent a much smaller component of Chinese loans to the three countries displayed than the sectors depicted individually.

This sector was the modal sector of loan for Mali as well, though they totaled nearly three-quarters of a billion dollars spread across four sectors. African publics have been clamoring for more and better access to cellular and internet technology, Chinese companies are anxious for new markets, and the Chinese government sees the industry as one of potential geostrategic interest (R. Wang et al. 2020). For Ghana ICT is third behind the power and transport sectors. Ghana also received more than $5 billion in loans from China over the period. As is detailed in the next section on natural resource extraction, unlike in Burkina Faso and Mali where Chinese companies have relatively few investments, Ghana is a major target for Chinese investment.

These results fit a well-reported, though contested by the Chinese state, pattern. Chinese non-ODA aid often comes in the forms of infrastructure loans backed by natural resources as collateral (Acker and Brautigam 2021; P. Morgan and Zheng 2019; Zajontz 2022). Between 2000 and 2019, Chinese banks loaned $153 billion to African public sector borrowers (China Africa Research Initiative 2021). These loans are laden with confidentiality clauses, leaving publics in the lending and borrowing countries largely ignorant of their terms. What is known is that most have clauses to deal with high-risk borrowers. This means borrowing countries must put up natural resources as collateral, maintain escrow accounts for repayments, and exclude debt from any future restructuring arrangements (Usman 2021). It would be unfair, however, to ladle all of Africa's debt problems onto China's plate. As of 2020, Ghana was roughly $50 billion in debt. Burkina Faso and Mali were approximately $8 billion in debt. Data depicted in Figure 6.3 represents loans over time, some of which have likely been paid back. Even if we consider a worst-case scenario where all the debt is outstanding and has compounded over the years at market rates, it would not account for the majority of these countries' current debt burdens (A. Singh 2020).

Other Major International Actors

Outside of the United States and China, the biggest sources of foreign assistance to Africa are other countries that contribute to ODA. The largest of these are Germany, the United Kingdom, France, and Japan who make up almost 60 percent of ODA once the US total is subtracted (OECD 2023a). Since the vast majority of other major international actors cooperate with ODA, the patterns represented in Figure 6.2 (non-US ODA is depicted in the darker gray) give a reasonable approximation of what non-US and non-China foreign aid in Burkina Faso, Ghana, and Mali looks like. Because these data are ODA, they present a comparison of like to like with US foreign assistance and like to proxy with Chinese foreign assistance.

For the non-US ODA funds, the average sub-Saharan African country received around $38 per citizen for the decade stretching from 2001 to 2021. European countries, which dominate the non-US ODA, reduced aid to Ghana as it moved from low-income to lower middle-income status in 2011 (Hou and Kennan 2013). Though Ghana averaged $11 per person over sub-Saharan expectations for the period in question, figures were much closer to the continental average for the latter half of the time period. With Burkina Faso and Mali facing deteriorating security situations over the decade, they moved in the opposite direction (Gegout 2018, 246). They began the decade receiving more support per citizen than the median and showed a general upward trend over the period averaging $22 and $24 over expectations.

One area of international finance that can blend into development assistance is debt. Presumably governments like those of Ghana, Burkina Faso, and Mali take on debt burdens, at least ostensibly, to provide for the public good. Of the three countries under close inspection, Ghana is by far the most debt burdened. The country is wealthier than its northern neighbors and with that comes more access to international financial markets. A close look at the providers of loans making such high levels of public debt possible (by most estimates between 80 and 90 percent of gross domestic product in 2023) reveals other international development players that often receive less attention than bilateral donors (Ministry of Finance 2022). In 2021 approximately half of Ghana's public debt was external in nature. Of this external debt, a third was owed to multilateral lenders, like the Bretton Woods institutions and African Development Bank, and around 5 percent was owed to bilateral lenders from across the globe. Commercial banks owned 10 percent of the debt, and international capital markets a whopping 40 percent. These latter lenders are not directly beholden to a country or group of countries but rather a multinational group of shareholders (Calderón and Zeufack 2020).

Natural Resource Extraction

Though natural resources were a peripheral zone of great power competition during the Cold War, the most active area of interaction between the United States and China is economic (Valkenier 1980). Sometimes this interaction is liberal and cooperative. Figures 6.4, 6.5, and 6.6 show the relationships between Burkina Faso, Ghana, and Mali and China and the United States in terms of imports and exports. All figures are listed in percentages of total imports or exports from 2001 to 2021. In all three countries, consumer goods are the modal import category. The top import product in Burkina Faso and Mali is petroleum. Ghana, with its own petroleum supply, has vehicles as its top import products. China is a bigger player than the United States in all three countries, being the first source of imports for Ghana over the period in question and in the top four for Burkina Faso and Mali after only former metropole France and regional neighbors the landlocked countries are reliant on for international trade. But the United States is a substantial partner, ranging from number three in Ghana to number twelve in Burkina Faso and Mali (World Bank 2023b).

Though there have been suggestions that trade will become increasingly mercantilist as great power competition between the

Figure 6.4 Imports and Exports from 2001 to 2021: Burkina Faso

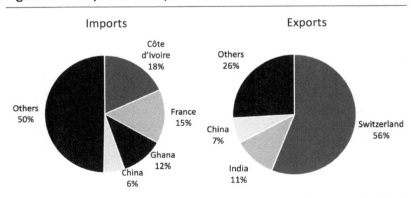

Source: United Nations Department of Economic and Social Affairs (2023).
Note: Countries named represent at least 5 percent of trade. All other countries are lumped into "Others."

Figure 6.5   Imports and Exports from 2001 to 2021: Ghana

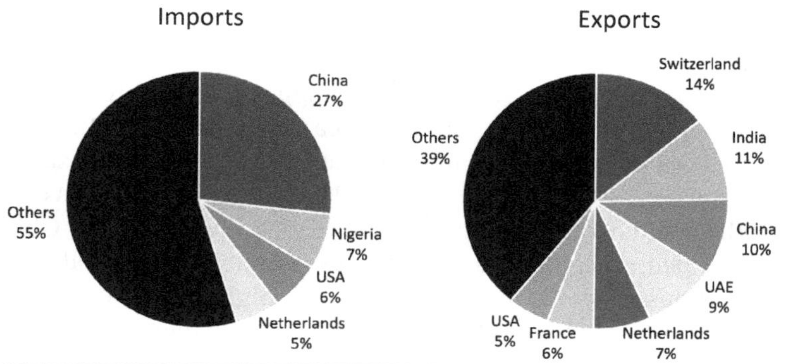

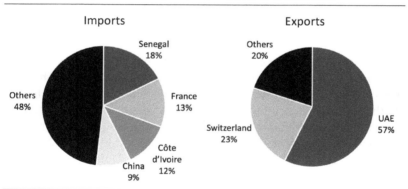

Source: United Nations Department of Economic and Social Affairs (2023).
Note: Countries named represent at least 5 percent of trade. All other countries are lumped into "Others."

Figure 6.6   Imports and Exports from 2001 to 2021: Mali

Source: United Nations Department of Economic and Social Affairs (2023).
Note: Countries named represent at least 5 percent of trade. All other countries are lumped into "Others."

United States and China heats up, nearly all of this conversation revolves around control of export commodities in a host country, not imports (Collins and O'Brien 2022; Lake 2018; Ziegler and Menon 2014). At least when it comes to products sold in West Africa, the relationship with both the United States and China seems less like great power competition and more traditional liberalism, with companies located in China and the United States trying to outcompete a global assortment of rivals for Africa's growing base of consumers (Kassim 2015).

Where claims of imperialism and suggestions of great power competition more often arise are in Africa's raw material export sectors.[4] Western countries have long coveted these resources to supply their manufacturing industries. Natural resources were a driver of colonialism and neocolonialism (Boahen 1987; Langan 2018). China has developed a healthy appetite for these materials as it takes on larger portions of global manufacturing (Brautigam 2009; Cheru and Obi 2010). In the three countries and four regions explored here, gold is the elephant in the room. In 2023, Ghana, Mali, and Burkina Faso were first, second, and third on the continent in terms of gold production and sixth, eleventh, and twelfth in the world (World Gold Council 2023). Gold is the top export in each country, and there are active industrial and informal mining operations in Ghana's Upper East, Burkina's Centre-Sud and Sahel, and Mali's Mopti regions (World Bank 2023b).

United States

In Burkina Faso, Ghana, and Mali, Newmont in Ghana is the only US-based gold producer to crack the top-five largest firms. The Colorado-based company has sites in Ahafo and Akyem in Ghana's south, but no presence in the north of the country. Newmont reports extracting nearly 900,000 ounces of gold from these two mines annually, which at current gold prices yields just shy of US$2 billion (Newmont 2022). Though headquartered in the United States, Newmont is publicly traded on the New York Stock Exchange and has a multinational management and ownership structure.

China

In Mali, Burkina Faso, and Ghana, there is a long tradition of gold prospecting that predates colonialism (Botchway 1995; Nixon et al. 2011). It was when the Europeans began to industrialize the process, however, that many West Africans began to adopt a hybrid approach that combined some of the chemically intensive techniques of industrial gold mining with labor intensive and low capital digging and sifting techniques well suited to a disaggregated system of artisanal mining. This approach came to be known as *galamsey* in Ghana and *orpaillage* in the francophone countries (Grätz 2004; Ofosu-Mensah 2011). Around 2005, large numbers of Chinese nationals began migrating to Ghana to join the hunt for gold, but they lacked the large pockets of the multinational gold conglomerates. Over the next decade, it is estimated that around 50,000 Chinese miners came to Ghana to illegally prospect alongside their local counterparts (Huifeng 2013). This illicit mining was met with mixed reactions. Much of the public grumbled about the large numbers of foreigners among them polluting the environment and exporting most of the profits. The Ghanaian government would occasionally threaten a crackdown on this illegal mining, but for the most part these threats were empty (Asante 2017; Boafo et al. 2019; Crawford and Botchwey 2017; G. Hilson et al. 2014).

Over time, some of these small-scale illicit mining operations gave way to more substantial corporate operators looking to increase scale and legitimize production. The largest of these is Shaanxi Mining Company in Talensi District in Ghana's Upper East Region. Small-scale mining concessions can be legally granted to Ghanaians. There was, however, a loophole in Ghana's 2006 Minerals and Mining Act (Government of Ghana 2006). Foreigners could not apply for a small-scale gold mining license, but foreign-owned companies could negotiate arrangements with local rights holders to supply mining equipment in exchange for a percentage of the profits. While this loophole was closed in 2015, the policy shift is not retroactive, thereby grandfathering in Shaanxi. The company's reported cut of profits is 93 percent to the local concession holder's 7 percent. There have been widespread reports of safety and environmental violations at the mine (Antwi-Boateng and Akudugu 2020; van de Camp 2016; Crawford et al. 2017). It was temporarily closed numerous times only to be reopened months later. Seven miners were killed by smoke inhalation in April 2017; a cleaner was killed by equipment in October 2018; and thirteen miners died in a blast in January 2019 (Associated Press 2019). Two large Chinese gold mining companies backed by state financing further legitimized Chinese gold mining in Ghana in 2020 with the purchase of assets from large multinational companies. Chifeng Jilong Gold Mining purchased the Australian-owned Resolute mine in Bibiani, and Shandong Gold Mining purchased Australian Cardinal Resources assets in Namdini (Reid and Wu 2021).

This path from small-scale illicit mining to large-scale legally sanctioned mine purchases is one that has been blocked to Chinese nationals in Burkina Faso and Mali. Though there were almost certainly Chinese miners who explored the idea of extracting gold from the widespread and rich deposits of gold to the north, China's "go out policy" took a while to ramp up in West Africa (Grimm 2014, 996). By the time artisanal miners from China began to enter Ghana in large numbers, there were already serious security threats developing in northern Mali (Zounmenou 2013). Since then the terrorist threat has expanded in Mali and trickled down into Burkina Faso (Campbell 2019). Because artisanal mining is labor intensive and Chinese mines tend to be very dependent on foreign (i.e., Chinese) labor, security threats put a significant damper on a firm's ability to staff an operation (Wegenast et al. 2019). Because these mines start small, they lack the resources multinationals employ to provide their own security bubble for equipment and their largely local workforce (Coulibaly 2021).

Other Major International Actors

Though ownership of mines and volume of production rapidly changes, in 2020 anglophone allies of the United States dominated large-scale gold production in the region. AngloGold Ashanti (South Africa), Gold Fields (South Africa), Gold Star (Canada), and Kinross (Canada) joined Newmont in Ghana's list of top-five mining companies. In Burkina, Iam Gold (Canada) is the dominant player, with Endeavor (Cayman Islands), SEMAFO (Canada), and Roxgold (Canada) joining them in the top five. For Mali the five biggest producers are Barrick (Canada), B2Gold (Canada), Resolute (Australia), AngloGold Ashanti (South Africa), and Hummingbird (United Kingdom). All these mining companies have multinational management and are publicly traded on the New York, Toronto, or Australian stock exchanges (Extractive Industries Transparency Initiative 2023).

Like the US-based Newmont, these publicly traded multinational mining companies face criticism for negative social and environmental impacts. There has been a big push by headquarter countries and investors to mitigate these impacts through corporate social responsibility (CSR) programs (Government of Canada 2009). While there is a great deal of variance across companies in terms of the level of resources dedicated to CSR (Selmier 2015; Selmier and

Newenham-Kahindi 2021), on aggregate it has been difficult to detect positive social and environmental impacts. Study after study testing the connection between CSR policies and community-level development indicators finds null results when comparing sites hosting CSR and non-CSR large extraction corporations (Ackah-Baidoo 2012; A. Hilson et al. 2019; Kumi et al. 2020; Pan et al. 2014).

The one exception to the publicly traded rule is Nordgold, which operates the significant Bissa-Bouly mines in Burkina Faso. Nordgold is a Russian firm that spun off from Alexei Mordashov's Severstal (Engels 2020, 486–488). Nordgold used to operate a mine further north in Burkina Faso but closed it in 2022 citing conflict in the region (Reuters 2022). They have been actively exploring new sites in the south (Reuters 2023). In 2020 Nordgold was looking to move into Ghana and showed a strong interest in the sale of Cardinal's (Australia) Namdini assets in Upper East Region. Those assets neighbored the Chinese-run Shaanxi site. After a nine-month bidding war and several hostile takeover attempts, Shandong (China) managed to acquire more than half the Cardinal shares but at a great price. In April 2020 shares of Cardinal could be had for less than 40 cents. By December the price was more than 1 dollar a share (B. Thompson 2020). Though a direct connection between Nordgold's ambitions in the region and Russian foreign policy is impossible to document, it does fit into a pattern of increasing Russian interest in Africa (Locherer 2020).

Turning Narratives into Variables

In terms of military relations, development assistance, and natural resource extraction, there is wide variance for both China and the United States with regard to Mali, Burkina Faso, and Ghana. Looking to measure the impact of these great power activities, this variance is a necessary ingredient. The variance does not, however, stop at international borders. While there are no corners of these three countries that have been shaded from international impacts, there are places within each that are more deeply impacted than others. In order to operationalize the variables for the impact of great power competition, we identify sites in Mopti, Sahel, Centre-Sud, and Upper East that have hosted military exercises and outposts, substantial per capita ODA-like flows, and international gold mines.

The substance of great power competition is a fluid topic. A gold mine owned by Australia one day can be owned by China the next; a coup can replace a president aligned closely to France with a colonel willing to try an alliance with Russia; a deteriorating security situation can prompt increased assistance from different international donors looking to work in the area of internally displace people. All of these hypotheticals happened in at least one of the three countries under close inspection in the first half of the 2020s. Because great power competition is as much a current event as a history topic, we focus on the state of affairs in early 2021 when data for our survey was being collected in the field. Though the narrative of events presented above goes through submission of manuscript, it is this early 2021 period, and the years immediately preceding, that best reflects the events respondents were experiencing as they reflected on great power competition in their communities.

US troops are, or have been in recent years, in Ghana's north and Burkina's south partaking in training exercises. In terms of more sustained engagement, as part of the regional war on terror US troops operate in a training and support capacity in the Sahel and Mopti regions of Burkina Faso and Mali, respectively (Mednick 2019). Reports of troop numbers range in the several hundreds but not several thousands. France served a much more central role along with troops from African neighbors, though this situation has changed in the wake of surveying. Hundreds of Chinese troops are cycled in and out of Mali as part of the UN contingent. There was substantial speculation of Russian involvement in Mali over the survey period that was later confirmed (Ramani 2020a).

Neither the United States nor China openly reports foreign assistance at the subnational level. China does not use the ODA reporting system, which makes it a challenge to construct a complete dataset of foreign aid. The projects it does publicize, however, tend to be specific—for instance, a dam here or a road there. This specificity makes it possible to geolocate much of the available data. In Ghana's Upper East Region, there are a handful of records for basic ICT extension and infrastructure. Because of data limitations, this data is dated, but it suggests that China's assistance finds its way into the research area. In Burkina Faso and Mali, the same cannot be said. There has been almost no Chinese foreign assistance in Burkina Faso and none in Centre-Sud or Sahel. In Mali there has been Chinese assistance, but it rarely name-checks the Mopti Region, and when it does it is in a list of sites (Patterson 2018).

The United States provides more consistent data on the amount of ODA given to foreign countries. USAID reports on the sector and implementing agency of funded projects. It does not, however, provide location data for projects. Most projects are general and country-wide in scope. They focus on things like nonviolent conflict management, broad-based economic growth, and improved health-care delivery and are designed to support host country government objectives (USAID 2014b, 19). All the regions under consideration in this book are rural and poor and either implicitly or explicitly targeted by USAID documents as beneficiaries (USAID 2014a, 2019). Therefore, a reasonable assumption is that USAID projects are situated in all regions under close consideration here. Other OECD aid, dominated by EU members, mirrors that given by the United States.

China's mineral extraction footprint in the regions explored here is present in only Ghana's Upper East. Here it is significant, with an existing medium-scale extraction exercise in Gbane that has been operating for more than a decade. In 2020 this mine was joined by a neighboring Chinese large-scale mine when Shandong Mining Company bought Australian Cardinal's shares of the Namdini site (Boafo et al. 2019). Though the United States has no American-owned mines operating in the regions investigated here, Canadians operate the largest mine in Burkina Faso at Essakane in the Sahel Region (Engler 2015). Due in part to security concerns, gold deposits in Mali's north have been left to artisanal miners, with industrial-scale mining relegated to the south and west of the country.

Table 6.1 summarizes these activities and the countries associated with them for Upper East, Centre-Sud, Sahel, and Mopti. It is a bit of a blunt instrument, but data on great power competition is limited and often veiled by the countries participating. If development assistance, military relations, and/or mineral extraction have positive or negative impacts on perceived grievances or local governance, the rules of most similar system design will help isolate these impacts. That is to say, if similar places where an international power is active return results dissimilar to those where they are not active, a relationship between the great power competition activity and the outcome being measured is supported by the data. This data is triangulated with more fine-tuned analysis. In each of the four regions, there are between ten and twelve survey sites. Some are closer to mining

Table 6.1 Summary of Great Power Presence in Research Sites

	Development Assistance	Military Relations	Natural Resource Extraction
Upper East (Ghana)	China European Union United States		China
Centre-Sud (Burkina Faso)	European Union United States		
Sahel (Burkina Faso)	European Union United States	African Union France United States	Canada
Mopti (Mali)	European Union United States	African Union France United Nations Russia United States	

operations than others. Some are closer to staging areas for foreign troops than others. Some are closer to development projects than others. If the impact of great power competition is stronger closer to these activities than farther within a region, the results bolster findings at the regional level. Chapter 7 delves deeper into the impacts of international actors on local dynamics and governance, as well as the ways in which populations view external great power actors.

Notes

1. For years there have been public rumblings that China is interested in a naval base on the Atlantic coast of Africa, though nothing has been formalized at time of publication. Even if a Chinese base were established in Atlantic-facing Africa, the Chinese military footprint on the continent would remain extremely small in comparison to the US presence (van Staden 2022).

2. The TIV is a value measurement meant to assist in the comparison of different weapons systems. The Stockholm International Peace Research Institute (SIPRI 2023b) defines TIV as "the known unit production costs of a core set of weapons and is intended to represent the transfer of military resources rather than the financial value of the transfer. Weapons for which a production cost is not known are compared with core weapons based on: size and performance characteristics (weight, speed, range and payload); type of electronics, loading or unloading arrangements, engine, tracks or wheels, armament and materials; and the year in which the weapon was produced. A weapon that has been in service in another armed force is given a value 40 per cent of that of a new weapon. A

used weapon that has been significantly refurbished or modified by the supplier before delivery is given a value of 66 per cent of that of a new weapon."

3. The complete membership of the OECD includes Australia, Austria, Belgium, Canada, Chile, Colombia, Czech Republic, Denmark, Estonia, Finland, France, Germany, Greece, Hungary, Iceland, Ireland, Israel, Italy, Japan, Latvia, Lithuania, Luxembourg, Mexico, Netherlands, New Zealand, Norway, Poland, Portugal, Slovakia, Slovenia, South Korea, Spain, Sweden, Switzerland, Turkey, United Kingdom, and United States.

4. Western imperialism has been a significant talking point in recruitment efforts by VEOs in the region, as detailed in preceding chapters.

7

International Actors, Local Dynamics

ACROSS GHANA, BURKINA FASO, AND MALI, CONSIDERABLE OVERLAP EXISTS IN how great power competition impacts the local populations. There are also some significant differences that correlate with the level, type, and proximity of this competition. The same observation applies to localities. Even communities separated by dozens of kilometers may experience their role in great power competition in significantly different ways. We begin this chapter by comparing and contrasting the countries in terms of how they view powerful international actors across multiple dimensions. The analysis then turns to individual-level differences. How do people's personal experiences with international actors and proximity to international activity impact their grievances with powerful international actors and perceptions of great power competition? We further explore the relationship between great power competition and governance. This exploration commences with an examination of community cohesion and a cognitive map of governance in the communities under investigation. It concludes with an analysis of the correlation between great power competition and sense of community and governance.

Perceived Nature of Great Power Competitors

Figure 7.1 displays respondents' perceptions of the most important global military power. The United States was name-checked by the plurality of our respondents across Ghana, Burkina Faso, and Mali.

Figure 7.1 Which Country Do You Think Is the Most Important Military Power in the World?

[Bar chart showing percentage of respondents from Burkina Faso, Ghana, and Mali identifying the United States, Russia, China, European Union, Other, or No answer as the most important military power in the world.]

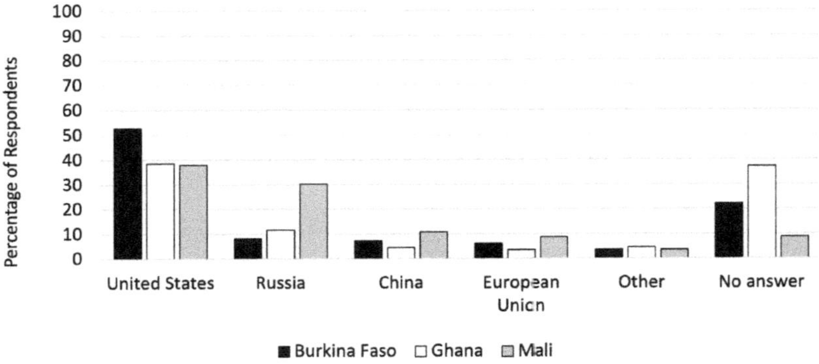

Note: States not identified by at least 3 percent of respondents in at least one country are placed into the "Other" category.

In Burkina Faso just over half of respondents identified the United States as the most important global military power, and just under 40 percent of Ghanaian respondents perceived of the United States in this way. In Burkina Faso and in Ghana, the second most popular answer pales in comparison. Russia, China, and the European Union hover in the 5 to 10 percent range plus or minus a few percentage points. Mali is the exception to the rule. While the United States is considered the most important global military power at a rate similar to those seen in Ghana and Burkina Faso, Russia is a close second in Mali with just under one-third of respondents identifying Russia as the most important global military power. Though the extent of Russian involvement in Mali was still poorly understood in early 2021 when our survey was collected, there was widespread speculation of Russian involvement in the 2020 Malian coup, and the years since have added a great deal of support to this speculation (Elischer 2022; Obaji 2020b, 2021).

Economic power, as Figure 7.2 demonstrates, is also something the plurality of respondents assigned a number one spot to the United States. Across the three countries under study, the United States was noted as the most important economic power in the world by between a third and half of respondents. China comes in second,

Figure 7.2 Which Country Do You Think Is the Most Important Economic Power in the World?

[Bar chart showing percentage of respondents from Burkina Faso, Ghana, and Mali identifying the United States, China, European Union, Japan, Russia, Other, or No answer as the most important economic power in the world.]

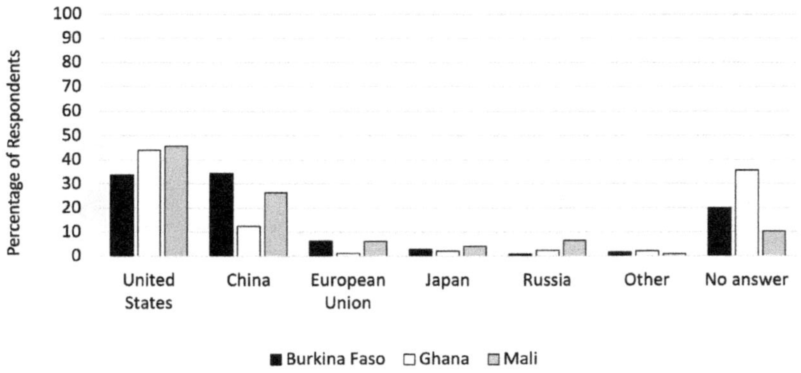

Note: States not identified by at least 3 percent of respondents in at least one country are placed into the "Other" category.

again for all three countries. There is some variance in the proportion of respondents who identify China as the second most important global economy, however. It is interesting and important to note that the countries line up inversely to the involvement of China in their national economies. Ghana has the most Chinese nationals living within its borders (estimates place the figure at around 30,000), signed onto the Belt and Road Initiative before the other two countries, and is a bigger trading partner with China (Debrah and Asante 2019). Burkina Faso fought Chinese economic ties longer and harder than most African countries, going so far as to host an embassy for the Republic of China (Taiwan) until 2018 (Blanchard 2018b). Yet the countries stacked China up from more important (Burkina Faso) to less important (Ghana), with Mali falling in the middle. Perhaps this is circumstantial evidence of a rising tide of anti-Chinese sentiment in countries that have experienced more significant economic ties with China (Sibiri 2021). In other words, people may be withholding positive evaluations based on negative experiences.

Military and economic power are attributes without inherent positive or negative connotations. Just because one is powerful, does not mean one is well liked. Figure 7.3 depicts a characteristic that is less neutral. Intensified narratives around anti-Black racism rose as a

Figure 7.3 Racism Is a Problem in the World. Which Place Have You Heard Is Most Racist Against Africans Like You?

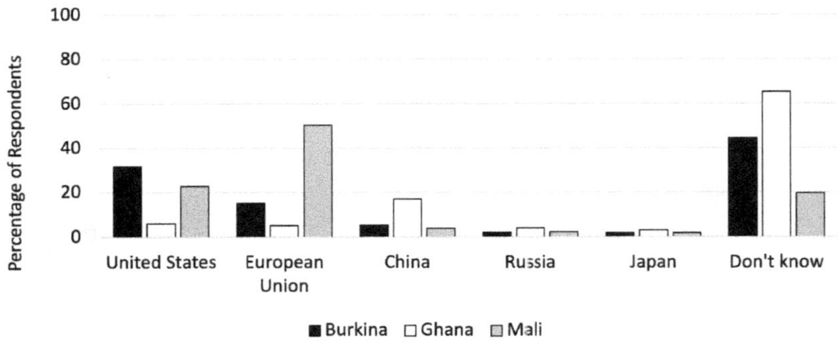

[Bar chart showing percentage of respondents from Burkina, Ghana, and Mali identifying United States, European Union, China, Russia, Japan, or Don't know as most racist.]

■ Burkina ☐ Ghana ▣ Mali

Note: States not identified by at least 3 percent of respondents in at least one country are placed into the "Other" category.

global problem in the first decades of the twenty-first century (Blain 2020). Though pan-Africanism's reach outside of the continent has ebbed and flowed over the decades, the murder of George Floyd, an African American man, in the US city of Minneapolis in 2020 pushed African Union leaders to condemn global anti-Black racism and propelled the issue of global racially charged violence against the African diaspora into the headlines of newspapers across the continent (Adi 2018; Kagumire 2020). Indeed, even jihadist groups in the region were quick to recognize the salience of anti-Black racism and sought to exploit these narratives, releasing communiques highlighting the supposedly racist nature of the US and Western nations, and leveraging that as further evidence as to why Western powers should vacate the region.

When asked about which country is most racist against "Africans like them," the United States fares poorest in the two francophone countries of Burkina Faso and Mali (see Figure 7.3). Outside of "don't know" responses, the United States is the modal category in Burkina Faso at just over 30 percent of respondents. In Mali, the United States was identified by a little more than 20 percent of respondents, making it the modal response for the country, but it is the European Union, likely driven by France as explained later, that tops the list overall as being most racist by just over half of respondents across the three countries. The one anglophone country of the three, Ghana, is the outlier. The majority of respondents in Ghana did not identify a country as most racist, but for those who did it was China that received the plurality of responses, having been identified as most racist by just over one in six respondents. Though stories of Chinese treatment of Africans and people of recent African decent are not as widespread, there is fodder available for the narrative (Castillo 2020; Wang 2021). Much of this was amplified during the Covid-19 pandemic, with reports in some Chinese cities of Africans being singled out for forced coronavirus testing and of some landlords evicting "African residents, forcing many to sleep on the street, and hotels, shops, and restaurants refused African customers," while other foreign groups were generally not subjected to similar treatment (Human Rights Watch 2020).

Responses displayed in Figure 7.4 likely incorporate some of the perceptions contained in Figures 7.1–7.3. Respondents were asked where they would like to travel if, in a hypothetical situation, they possessed a visa to any country in the world. Remittances rival foreign direct investment and overseas development assistance as a source of financial support to residents in the three countries under study (Ratha et al. 2019). People leaving for work abroad to support a family is a regular occurrence that most residents in the region know about personally. For all three countries studied here, the United States was the modal choice, with between a quarter and half of respondents identifying it as their preferred destination. This finding suggests the "American Dream," at least the West African version of it, remains alive and well (Abramitzky et al. 2021). The only other two countries that rise above 10 percent of responses in at least one country are Saudi Arabia and France for Burkina Faso and Mali. Both countries are majority Muslim, with Hajj and Umrah visas likely accounting for Saudi Arabia's showing. Though France is sometimes viewed in a negative light as a former colonial power in the region, as a destination for Malians and Burkinabé it presents a relatively high-wage work destination without the language barrier present in the United States (Adama 2009; D. Thomas 2006).

Perceived Impact of Great Power Competitors

Though the previous figures give a good idea of the general nature of multifaceted perceptions of great power competition in the region,

148

Figure 7.4 Of the Countries I Asked About, If You Were Given a Visa to Visit One of Them, Which Would You Choose?

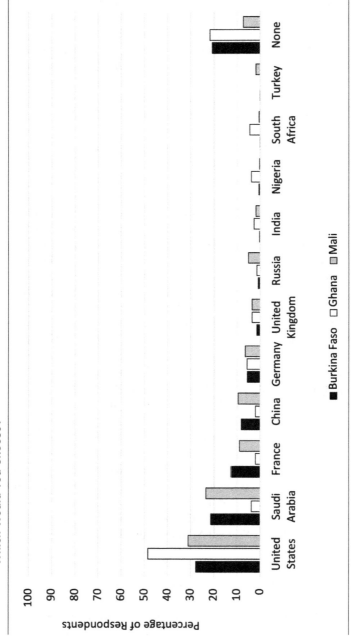

Note: States not identified by at least 3 percent of respondents in at least one country are placed into the "Other" category.

Figures 7.5 and 7.6 showcase the implications of these natures for local populations. They deal with perceived magnitude (Figure 7.5) and direction (Figure 7.6) of a foreign power's impact on the respondent's home country. In other words, how much do these countries shape life in Ghana, Burkina Faso, or Mali? Secondly, is this impact generally good, bad, or indifferent?

As far as magnitude of impact, hands down the most likely answer in the two francophone countries is France. Nearly 70 percent of Burkinabé and slightly more than 80 percent of Malians identify their former colonizer as the foreign power that continues to influence the fate of their respective countries. This is not surprising given that the countries use currencies pegged to the euro via the French franc; have French companies dominating several notable sectors of their economy (e.g., Total in energy, Air France in aviation, and Orange in telecom); and were reliant on French forces to coordinate and bolster their responses to regional terrorism at the time of the survey (Korkmaz 2019). No other strategic competitor rises to even 10 percent of responses. As residents in an anglophone country, not a single Ghanaian respondent identified France as the country that most impacts theirs. With approximately two-thirds of responses, the United States is the country that replaces it as most

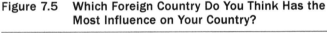

Figure 7.5 Which Foreign Country Do You Think Has the Most Influence on Your Country?

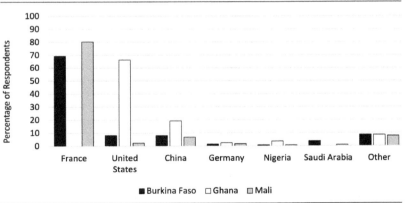

Note: States not identified by at least 3 percent of respondents in at least one country are placed into the "Other" category.

Figure 7.6 Do You Think These Countries Have a Mostly Positive, Mostly Negative, or Neutral Impact on Your Country?

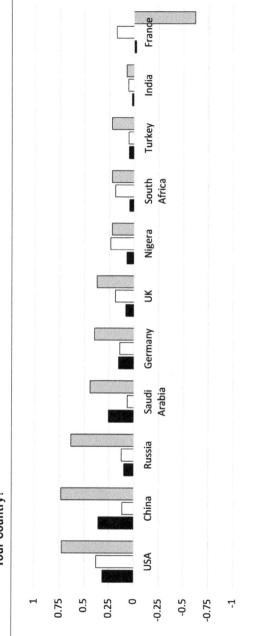

Note: Scores displayed are averages for each country. If a respondent answers mostly positive their response is coded 1. If a respondent answers mostly negative their response is coded −1. Neutral responses are coded 0.

impactful in the eyes of Ghanaians. Since Ghana's transition to democratic governance in the early 1990s, it has been viewed favorably by US officials for its relative economic prosperity, good record on human rights, peaceful status quo, and ability to maintain said democracy. To reward these perceived accomplishments, US presidents Bill Clinton, George W. Bush, and Barack Obama made official state visits to Ghana. During the first Trump administration, First Lady Melania Trump made a visit, and Vice President Kamala Harris made the trek on behalf of the Biden administration (Dahir 2018). With just shy of 20 percent of Ghanaian responses, however, China provides a more significant challenge to the United States in Ghana than to France in Burkina Faso and Mali. This status is no doubt related to China's substantial Belt and Road Initiative and private enterprise projects in the country (Han and Webber 2020).

Figure 7.6 shows where these impacts are perceived to be positive and where they are perceived to be negative. Respondents were given a list of countries and asked if they believe they have a positive, negative, or neutral impact on their country. For the purposes of this figure, neutral and "don't know" responses are coded 0, positive responses are coded 1, and negative responses are coded −1. For Ghanaians, all countries listed elicited, on average, positive responses. The United States drew the most positive responses, followed by Nigeria and South Africa, though no country strays too far from the neutral center line. Burkina Faso is similar in that respondents' views crowd the center line. Their relative ranking is, however, different. China and the US are neck and neck for top spot followed by Saudi Arabia. France does trend slightly negative for Burkinabé respondents but not overwhelmingly so. Mali is where there is the most movement, and it comes largely in the form of fewer nonresponses. Perhaps the opinionated nature of Malians has something to do with MINUSMA and the internationalization of the conflict in the north, where surveys for this study were collected. There are lots of international actors around for people to base their opinions on (Charbonneau 2017). Malians rank US and Chinese intervention very high. They also recognize positively Russian, Saudi, German, British, Turkish, Nigerian, South African, and Indian involvement. France, on the other hand, suffers mightily in Malian perceptions. Jihadist discourse in the northern and central parts of the country have consistently presented France as the enemy of the Malian people, while colonial-era resentment and hard feelings associated simultaneously with violations of sovereignty and failure to provide security have left lots of lingering grievances (Guichaoua 2020).

Behavior of Great Power Competitors and Perceptions

The impact of lived experience on perceptions of great power competitors is an understudied phenomenon. While one might anticipate certain reactions based on one's own circumstances, it is easy to imagine a situation where someone in a different set of circumstances might react differently. In this section we explore the relationship between lived experience and perceptions using the dependent variables (magnitude and direction of strategic competitors' impact) described above. The focus is on the United States, China, and France as these are the three countries consistently identified as important across multiple countries under study. For the independent variables, the experience of having met a foreign national and the proximity of great power competition to one's home site are used.

Figure 7.7 displays respondents' answers to the following question: Have you personally met anyone who is a citizen of these countries? Countries provided to respondents in a list included China, France, Germany, India, Nigeria, Russia, Saudi Arabia, South Africa, United Kingdom, and the United States. This is not a random assortment. Rather, this list includes major trading partners and regional and international powers. Overall, Malians have met a more diverse sampling of internationals than their neighbors. The region in which surveying was conducted was in MINUSMA operating zones, which could explain this phenomenon. France is mentioned by more Burkinabé and Malians than any other country provided, likely due to French military operations in the two countries under Operation Barkhane and G5 Sahel operations during the time of surveying as well as the shared language, colonial relationship, and relative ease of transport between countries. For Ghanaians, the group most respondents identified as having met is Nigerians, citizens of the largest anglophone country in the region. Francophone respondents identified Nigeria slightly lower but still in great numbers, with just shy of one in three Burkinabé and Malians answering in the affirmative to having personally met a Nigerian.

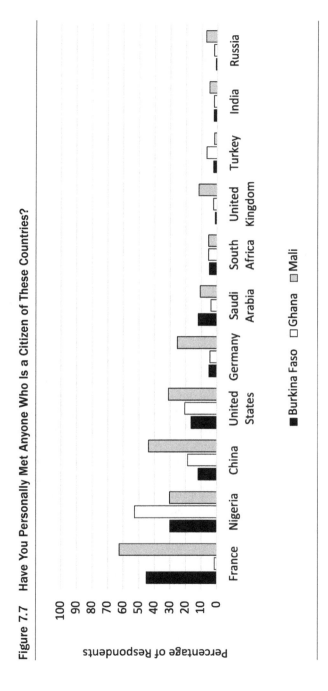

Figure 7.7 Have You Personally Met Anyone Who Is a Citizen of These Countries?

The United States and China are next in the table, with between a fourth and a fifth of respondents having met a national. The three countries stack up identically with regard to both the United States and China. More Malians have had personal contact, followed by Ghanaians, and lastly the Burkinabé have had the fewest contacts. In no country did fewer than 10 percent of respondents report having personally met an American and a Chinese, indicating either high levels of foreign nationals in the three countries, the United States and China as travel destinations for nationals, or some mixture of both.

Whether or not a respondent met someone from a great power as the independent variable is supplemented with variables about the activities of foreign actors around sampling sites. Survey enumerators were asked if an international mine or troop encampment are located within 5 kilometers (approximately 3 miles) of where they live. If they answered in the affirmative, they were asked for the site location to confirm and whether there was any additional information about the nationality of the people occupying the mine or encampment. As gold mines are the mostly publicly traded companies, confirming their location and existence was quite simple. They are identified here as either Western (run by Canada or Australia) or Chinese. Those sites with a mine are scored 1, those without 0. Foreign troop encampments are more difficult to confirm. Though some are visible using publicly available satellite imagery, their occupants tend not to advertise their existence. In the regions under study here, military encampments are generally small and not intended to be permanent, with the exception of MINUSMA sites in Mopti. Though active at the time of surveying, these sites are currently being vacated under the orders of Mali's new ruling junta. Because of the ambiguity over what constitutes a military site, these sites are classified here only as "foreign troops." Those with a foreign troop encampment are scored 1, those without 0. Since Chinese and Western aid agencies do not geo-locate their assistance, this measure is the bluntest of the lot. It is a per capita average of the yearly overseas development assistance figures provided in Chapter 6. For the United States this equates to $4.52 (Burkina Faso), $6.76 (Ghana), and $10.48 (Mali). For China the figures are $0 (Burkina Faso), $5.63 (Ghana), and $4.38 (Mali).

Table 7.1 shows these dependent variables as columns in a correlation table. It adds the dependent variables to the independent variables as rows. The advantage to duplicating the dependent variables in the table is so one can see the impact of perceptions and rat-

Table 7.1 Predicting Respondents' Perceptions of Strategic Competitors

	US most influence	US rating	France most influence	French rating	China most influence	China rating
US most influence		−.138**	−.261**	−.137**	−.071**	−.047
US rating	−.138**		−.225**	−.026	−.000	−.487**
France most influence	−.261**	−.225**		−.311**	−.226**	−.319**
French rating	−.137**	−.026	−.311**		−.010	−.074**
China most influence	−.071**	−.000	−.226**	−.010		−.086**
Chinese rating	−.047	−.487**	−.319**	−.074**	−.086**	
Western gold mine	−.011	−.035	−.043	−.068*	−.013	−.107**
Chinese gold mine	−.169**	−.021	−.234**	−.077**	−.041	−.159**
Foreign troops	−.021	−.070**	−.077**	−.020	−.096**	−.115**
US development	−.058*	−.288**	−.206**	−.357**	−.010	−.255**
Chinese development	−.088**	−.166**	−.205**	−.084**	−.009	−.002
Met American	−.154**	−.210**	−.091**	−.000	−.030	−.141**
Met Chinese	−.101**	−.215**	−.073**	−.076**	−.064*	−.165**
Met French	−.070**	−.130**	−.315**	−.147**	−.058*	−.233**

Note: **p < 0.01, *p < 0.05.

ings of one great power competitor on the other. A negative sign before the number denotes a negative relationship. Absence of a sign denotes a positive relationship. Significance is denoted with asterisks. The number assigned in each box is percentage of variance in the dependent variable explained by the independent variable. Numbers approaching 1 suggest a very strong correlation. Numbers approaching 0 suggest a very weak correlation.

Given the fact that the "most influence" question allows respondents to identify a single country, it is not surprising that the US, French, and Chinese "most influence" variables are negatively correlated with each other and are significant. What is interesting is the impact of influence on ratings. For the United States and China, respondents who identified them as having the greatest influence on their country ranked these countries more highly than those who identified a different country as the most influential. For France, this relationship is reversed. Respondents who think France is the foreign power with the greatest influence on their country rate France lower than those who think France's influence is less. The stressed postcolonial relationship between France and its former colonies seems the likely culprit.

In terms of interaction, there is a negative relationship, a null relationship, and a positive relationship. The negative relationship is between respondents' rankings of France and China. The impact is not huge, but it is significant. People who like France's impact on their country are less likely to like China's impact and vice versa. The null relationship is between respondents' rankings of France and the United States. Though the two countries are viewed as allies in general and in the region's war on terror specifically, respondents' ratings of these two countries are unconnected. The two countries, which are often assumed to be rivals, are intertwined the most in respondents' minds when it comes to impacts. Half the rating of Chinese involvement is explained by the rating of the United States and vice versa, and this relationship is positive. Respondents who view Chinese influence as positive are likely to view US influence as positive. Respondents who view Chinese influence as negative are likely to view US influence as negative. Though it is speculative, perhaps this relationship has to do with respondents' perceptions of international power. The United States and China are two powerful international actors. If respondents are prone to view international power positively, perhaps they upgrade both. If they are prone to view international power as negative, they would downgrade both.

Gold mines operated by Western companies have a different influence than those operated by Chinese companies. Western mines have a positive or null impact on respondent ratings of the United States and France. While the mines in the region are run by Canadian and Australian-based companies, they are widely multinational in nature and ownership interests are spread throughout the globe. Chinese mines, on the other hand, significantly and negatively impact perceptions of Chinese influence. Chinese mines have a reputation as being environmentally destructive and employing relatively few host-country nationals (Antwi-Boateng and Akudugu 2020; Lu et al. 2020; Wegenast et al. 2019). Perhaps this reputation, whether real or perceived, is what is driving these results.

Overseas development assistance is assumed to promote positive feelings. In the case of US assistance, the hypothesized relationship is supported by the data. Respondents in countries that received more US development assistance tend to feel more positively toward the United States than respondents in countries that received less. Chinese aid has a null impact in the sample. People feel the same toward China regardless of their level of assistance. Chinese aid has a reputation for being more quid pro quo oriented (a framework often referred to as *resource-for-infrastructure*) than official ODA aid from OECD countries (Tsikudo 2021). The data here suggest this type of aid may not be as effective in winning hearts and minds. Partnerships for development, as Cheru and Obi explain, may be interpreted as benevolent at the onset but when the bills come due and promises appear shallow can be reinterpreted by disappointed publics as neocolonialism by invitation (Cheru and Obi 2010).

Foreign nationals can leave positive or negative impressions. For the Americans and Chinese these interactions appear generally more positive than negative. Respondents who identify having personally met an American or a Chinese are more inclined to see that country as the most influential and to have positive perceptions of the relationship. The opposite relationship holds for France. Along with the relationship between French influence and ratings, this evidence points to the challenging relationship between residents of what was once referred to as "Françafrique" and its former metropole (Mallet et al. 2020).

Impact of Great Powers on Community and Governance

One can feel deeply attached to the community in which one lives. Conversely, one can feel isolated and indifferent and dream of living elsewhere. The difference between these two hypotheticals is the individual's sense of community, which has been defined as "a feeling that members have of belonging, a feeling that members matter to one another and to the group, and a shared faith that members' needs will be met through their commitment together" (McMillan and Chavis 1986, 9). This concept is traditionally measured via four facets: reinforcement of needs, membership, influence, and shared emotional connection. Individuals who feel their community reinforces their needs, includes them, influences them, and shares an emotional connection rank high on the sense of community index.

Figure 7.8 displays the sense of community for respondents in Mali, Burkina Faso, and Ghana. For each item respondents were given a statement and asked to place themselves on a five-point scale from strongly disagree (1) to strongly agree (5). The statement for reinforcement of needs reads: "I think my community is a good place for me to live." For membership the statement is: "I can recognize most of the people who live in my community." Influence's statement is: "I care about what people in my community think of my actions." Shared emotional connection is measured by responses to the statement: "It is very important for me to live in this community."

As national borders are not the only way to define community, Figure 7.9 displays the same sense of community measures for the three largest ethnic groups in the sample. These ethnolinguistic groups include Fulani (18.2 percent), Mossi (16.8 percent), and Gurune (17.8 percent). Though each of these three ethnolinguistic groups crosses international and internal borders, respondents identifying as Fulani predominate in the Mali and northern Burkina Faso portions of the sample, Mossi form the plurality of the Burkina Faso sample and are part of both the northern and southern country samples, and Gurune form the majority of the Ghanaian sample but exist into southern Burkina as well.

What stands out in these displays are two things: generally high marks and similarities across countries and ethnic groups. The generally high marks for sense of community are not entirely surprising.

Figure 7.8 Sense of Community Index by Country

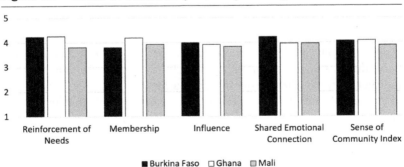

Note: Responses to statements about community were given on a five-point scale (1 being strongly disagree, and 5 being strongly agree).

Figure 7.9 Sense of Community Index by Ethnicity

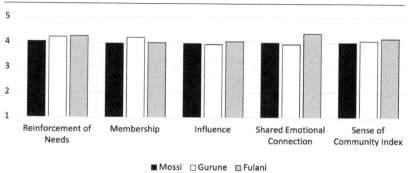

Note: Responses to statements about community were given on a five-point scale (1 being strongly disagree, and 5 being strongly agree).

The communities where respondents live are mostly rural or smaller regional towns. No capital cities or large metropolises are surveyed here. These conditions, all things being equal, tend to generate higher sense of community index scores (Prezza and Costantini 1998). On a scale from strongly disagree to strongly agree, the average across facets of sense of community is agree. Similarities across countries and ethnic groups are useful for the present analysis. It is not as if Malians have substantially less sense of community than Ghanaians or Burkinabé. The same can be said about Fulani, Mossi, and Gurune speakers. Therefore, differences are likely driven by community conditions and not the national or ethnic situation. Within countries and ethnic groups, however, there is substantial variance. The expectation would therefore be for individuals with a greater sense of community to be more actively engaged in their community governance than those with a reduced sense of community (Anderson 2009, 2010; Anderson and Fridy 2022).

If sense of community measures one's investment in the local context and engagement with neighbors, it does not tell us much about what avenues this community-mindedness has to impact community governance. This is where the cognitive map of community governance becomes relevant (Myers and Fridy 2017; Fridy and Myers 2019). Respondents were given twelve hypothetical situations—here is a problem, who would you engage with in order to solve it? Problems fit into three categories: public goods, personal welfare, and law and order. An example of a public goods question is, "If your community needs water, who do you think is the best person to take your concerns to?" For personal welfare, an example is, "If you or a family member need help finding a job, who do you think is the best person to take your concerns to?" A law and order example is, "If you believe someone has stolen money from you, who do you think is the best person to take your concerns to?"

These open-ended questions give respondents twelve opportunities to identify an important governance provider in their community. Figure 7.10 displays the percentage of times respondents from each country identified various providers. Figure 7.11 does the same for the three largest ethnic groups in the sample. There is some variance in the responses across countries and ethnic groups. Ghanaians go to traditional leaders slightly more, Malians to friends, and Burkinabé to family. These differences, however, are rather subtle and only by a few points. The most substantial difference concerns formalized local government. In the two francophone countries, people look to the executive or mayor. In Ghana, respondents are more likely to identify the local assembly. Not unexpectedly, Fulani and Mossi (who predominate in the two francophone countries) and Gurune (who were the dominant group in the Ghanaian sample) followed the pattern set by their countries. Across all three countries and ethnic groups, there is individual-level variance in the nature of the governance providers.

If one looks at only those governance providers identified at least 5 percent of the time in at least one country, there is traditional leadership, local governance, civil servants, representatives in the national government, nongovernmental organizations, and friends and family. For these providers, Figure 7.12 displays how well the average Ghanaian, Burkinabé, and Malian in the sample evaluates them. Figure 7.13 repeats the theme with identical information for Fulani, Mossi, and Gurune members of the sample. Possible answers range from excellent (5) to poor (1). The pattern developed in Figure 7.8 of slight differences from country to country persist, but overwhelming similarities across countries repeat here. With few exceptions, national and ethnic averages congregate between good (4) and average (3). There is variance within countries and ethnicities. For each of these providers, the standard deviation hovers around 1.

When sense of community, cognitive mapping of local governance, and evaluation of governance are considered across national and ethnic boundaries, differences are evident but the scope of these

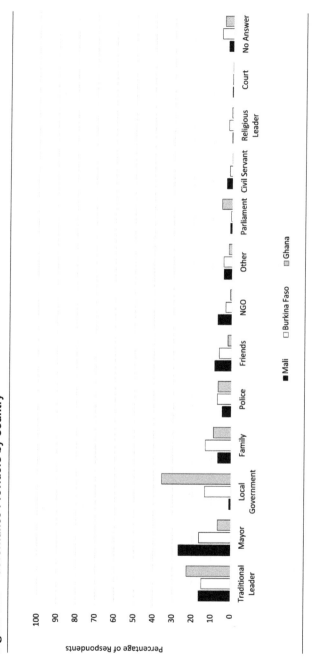

Figure 7.10 Governance Providers by Country

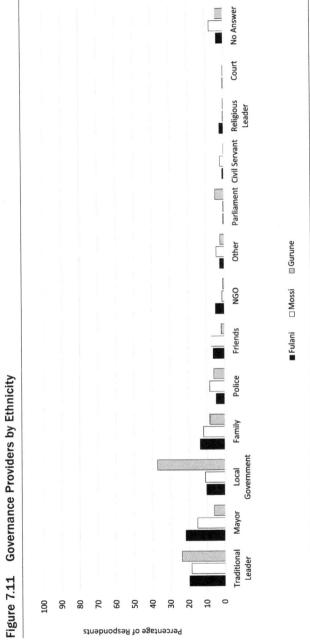

Figure 7.11 Governance Providers by Ethnicity

International Actors, Local Dynamics 163

Figure 7.12 Evaluations of Governance Providers by Country

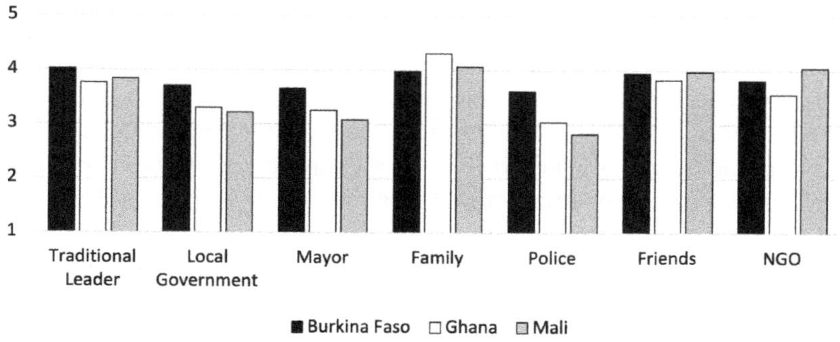

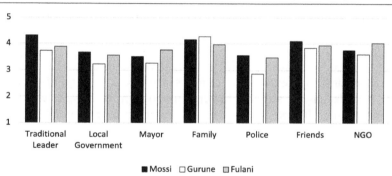

Note: Evaluations of governance providers were given on a five-point scale (1 being poor, and 5 being excellent).

Figure 7.13 Evaluations of Governance Providers by Ethnicity

Note: Evaluations of governance providers were given on a five-point scale (1 being poor, and 5 being excellent).

differences is not dramatic. Due to these similarities, any meaningful relationships between a causal variable and these outcome variables must be caused by an identity below the nation or ethnic group. Likely culprits include the individual or community, which are often intertwined in more communalistic societies in rural parts of West Africa (Friesen et al. 2022).

Independent variables that address an aspect of great power competition are again constructed in three distinct ways. With the "met" variables, survey respondents reported whether they had ever personally met an American, Chinese, or French person. The two gold variables and the troop variable are constructed based on enumerator feedback. At each site where interviews were conducted, the survey enumerator was asked if there is a Chinese gold mine, a Western gold mine, or an encampment of foreign troops within 5 kilometers of the site. If the answer to these questions is affirmative, these variables are coded 1. Otherwise, they are coded 0. For the two overseas development assistance variables the average foreign assistance per citizen is given. Since foreign assistance is impossible to geolocate, these figures are based on country-level data.

To show how these proxies for great power competition impact sense of community for residents in Ghana, Burkina Faso, and Mali, a correlation table is displayed in Table 7.2. Patterns here are not stark. There are some points of significance, but they do not hold together in a theoretically coherent way. The largest and most significant positive finding is between Western mines and sense of community. This suggests the 143 Burkinabé around Western mines feel slightly happier within their communities than the rest of the sample. The largest and most significant negative finding is between US overseas development assistance and sense of community. Malians in the sample have a slightly lower sense of community index score than their neighbors. They also received about $4 more of US ODA than Ghanaians and $6 more than Burkinabé. Would Western devel-

Table 7.2 Predicting Respondents' Sense of Community Index

	Sense of Community Index
Western gold mine	−.120**
Chinese gold mine	−.006
Foreign troops	−.075**
United States development	−.130**
Chinese development	−.049
Met American	−.021
Met Chinese	−.030
Met French	−.070*

Note: **p < 0.01, *p < 0.05.

opment assistance and private mining operations operate in opposite directions? While such a relationship is not unimaginable, a theory supporting an affirmative answer to this question is not obvious. Given the relatively small correlations and mixed signs across measurements for Chinese and French interactions, the safest way to handle this data is as a push. The data does not support a strong connection between great power competition and sense of community.

When it comes to evaluations of governance providers, a clearer pattern emerges from the noise (see Table 7.3). US ODA shows a negative correlation with perceptions of local governance providers for all but the most informal options (family, friends, and nongovernmental organizations). This result suggests either US support is going to areas with relatively unpopular governance structures or causing this lack of popularity. Foreign troops, Western mines, and met American, however, show no similar correlation with governance. A reasonable hypothesis would link these modes of foreign involvement. For variables linked to Chinese great power competition, there is more consistency. Negative relationships abound between Chinese mines, Chinese development assistance, and met Chinese on the one hand, and evaluations of traditional leaders, local government, mayors, police, and the legislature on the other as reliable. There is a negative relationship across all three modes of Chinese intervention and across all three sources of formal local governance, one traditional informal source, and the local member of the national parliament. This consistency is striking and presents one small piece of evidence against the developmental model presented in defense of Sino-African bilateral relations (Ergano and Rao 2019). Evidence presented here suggests a correlation between the Chinese presence and the hollowing out of respect for local governance providers. This finding supports the warning that not all interventions will bear positive fruit.

Great Powers Impact on Local Communities in the Global South

Measuring the impact of great power competition on communities is challenging. The stuff of great power competition has too many facets to tackle in a single work. The globe is interconnected, with the cultural, military, and economic impact of powerful nations taking an incalculable number of forms and reaching into far-flung corners

Table 7.3 Predicting Respondents' Evaluations of Governance Providers

	Traditional leader	Local government	Mayor	Family	Police	Friends	Non-governmental organization	Legislature
Western gold mine	-.013	-.072*	-.000	-.024	-.043	-.068*	-.027	-.051
Chinese gold mine	-.064*	-.133**	-.112**	-.046	-.131**	-.033	-.078**	-.030
Foreign troops	-.046	-.081**	-.060*	-.027	-.113**	-.030	-.078**	-.011
US development	-.088**	-.212**	-.236**	-.053	-.302**	-.018	-.122**	-.264**
Chinese development	-.128**	-.220**	-.227**	-.156**	-.296**	-.041	-.020	-.097**
Met American	-.015	-.045	-.072*	-.058*	-.001	-.051	-.035	-.074*
Met Chinese	-.029	-.052	-.089**	-.055*	-.130**	-.064*	-.053	-.145**
Met French	-.023	-.034	-.052	-.145**	-.027	-.006	-.044	-.187**

Note: **p < 0.01, *p < 0.05.

often in unexpected ways. Only 45 percent of respondents in the samples from Ghana, Burkina Faso, and Mali have access to electricity in their household. Nearly 30 percent of respondents, however, report knowing who Beyoncé is and have an opinion about her influence on the world.[1] The spheres of extractive industry, overseas development assistance, and military interventions are important components of great power competition but far from an exhaustive list.

Even if one can agree on the important categories of great power competition to include in a multifaceted categorization, however, the challenge of quantifying and/or qualifying these activities is immense. While great power competitors are decent at reporting the volume of their activities in the states of Mali, Burkina Faso, and Ghana, there are intentional gaps in the information for competitive reasons. A bigger problem than hidden data is that this state-level information rarely gets reliably reported at the subnational level and almost never at the level of the community. This reality makes it impossible to tie great power competition causally to local perceptions and governance in an optimal way.

These caveats are important. The communities and governance environments reported on here are complex and varied. Great power competition is a contested concept whose impact at the community level is extremely difficult to measure. Characteristics like these make it impossible to be extremely confident about specific recommendations. These muddied waters do, however, point to three general takeaways: (1) much of the impact of great power competition is experienced and interpreted at the individual level; (2) communities are intricate evolutionary governance environments that are substantially independent of national actors; and (3) in these complex governance environments predicting the popularity and success of great power competitions is profoundly difficult.

First takeaway, great power competition is about who brings the most utility to people and how they understand this utility. People are not synonymous with formal governments in the capital city. Certainly, bilateral relationships occurring on formal government-to-government channels can trickle down to impact individuals, but the character of this impact varies from place to place and issue to issue. When adding to these formal channels the full roster of international actors (including, but not limited to, multilateral organizations, nongovernmental organizations, corporations, and strategic influencers), the complexity increases exponentially. Respondents near Chinese mines tilt negative in their impressions of Chinese influence, whereas Western mines induce slightly more positive impressions of US interests. Meeting a Chinese or an American has consistently positive impacts on perceptions in the sample. Meeting French citizens, likely due to the residuals of the colonial and neocolonial experience, engenders negative perceptions of France. Across the board, foreign troop encampments seem to be viewed neutrally or slightly positively in terms of perceptions of great power competitors. Though the sample includes more than 1,200 individuals spread across three West African countries, the likelihood of even a single respondent playing an integral part in negotiating the form or scope of activities of these international actors at a formal level is extremely low. Most, however, feel the impact of these activities and have positive perceptions and/or negative grievances about them. People encountered on the street and in the bush in the region are individuals likely similar to those in our sample, not the elite few who negotiate diplomatic ties or with general connections to formal channels of the state.

Second takeaway, individuals live in communities, and it is in these communities that many of the most important decisions impacting their lives and livelihoods are made. This chapter uses the lens of governance to capture these decisionmaking processes and based on observations embraces a fluid and adaptable understanding of governance. NiklasLuhmann describes this governance as "a mode of communication, self-referential and specialized, specialized in the preparing of collectively binding decision, in the production and use of instruments serving that purpose. Actors are constituted in this specialized communication and coordination takes places in it. Communities are intricate evolutionary governance environments that are substantially independent of national actors" (Beunen et al. 2015, 9; Luhmann 1995). This evolutionary environment is quite crowded in the regions under study here. Depending on the problem, residents might go to a nongovernmental organization or a parliamentarian, a traditional chief or an imam, a friend or a police officer. Grievances will emerge and solutions will be constructed, often completely independent of large foreign-funded infrastructure projects or military interventions. The literature has largely been deficient in recognizing how these complicated and diverse local governances react to external shocks. This book is a tentative entry into this exploration.

Third takeaway, careful consideration and humility are necessary when predicting the impact of great power competition on localized grievances and governance. The societies under consideration here are higher-order social systems with no easily identifiable or fixed center of gravity. Both in terms of international grievances and impact on governance, evidence suggests consequences of cross-border activities are scattershot. Respondents have affinities and aversions to great power competitors that do not follow a pattern suggested by the assumption that foreign policy is designed to win friends and allies. Nor do perceptions follow a pattern suggested by either the assumption that global interconnectedness follows the liberal model and floats all boats or the assumption that it follows the Marxist model and leads to exploitation. Where tentative patterns do arise (e.g., Canadian gold mines improve sense of community and do not seem to reduce support for local governance providers, whereas a heavy Chinese presence shows signs of diminishing formal and traditional governance providers in the eyes of the citizenry), they are best extrapolated with caution. The N in this study is small enough and the variables measured suboptimally enough not to put too much weight in finding identical circumstances elsewhere. Nevertheless, actors in international relations place themselves in a diverse array of communities for a multitude of diverse activities. There are undoubtedly instances where these activities engender positive feelings and support adaptable and capable local governance institutions to promote regional peace and other strategic goals. The pendulum does, however, not always swing this way and it can be difficult to predict.

Note

1. This question was asked in a battery of questions on international celebrities. Ten percent of the sample thinks Beyoncé is generally a good global influence, 16 percent are neutral on the topic, and 3 percent find her a bad influence. Seventy percent of the sample do not know who Beyoncé is.

8

The Convergence of Violent Extremism and Great Power Competition

WEST AFRICA STANDS AT A CRITICAL JUNCTURE, WHERE THE CONVERGENCE OF great power competition and the continuing spread of jihadist terrorism has brought a complex series of challenges that reverberate deeply through the region's governance structures. This is a multidimensional struggle that impacts local communities in different ways. Across Mali, Burkina Faso, and Ghana, it is evident that some communities display remarkable resilience in the face of exogenous shocks, proving adept at finding solutions to mitigate the impact of violence and instability, while others seemingly fall apart. The questions we have sought to answer in this book are twofold. First, why are some communities more resilient to exogenous shocks than others—in other words, why is it that some communities remain stable in the face of jihadist violence and/or GPC activities while others, sometimes close neighbors, do not? Second, can violent extremist organizations and GPC be viewed through the same lens of "external shocks," or are the activities of great powers and jihadist terrorists of such a distinct nature that they require their own academic literatures?

The answers to these questions lie in the intricate web of governance across the region. Governance, in its diverse forms, plays a pivotal role in determining a community's ability to withstand shocks and can work to bind a community, giving members the resilience to band together in the face of adversity—whether jihadist violence or the activities of external powers. Governance, through formal institutions, informal arrangements, and the capacity to manage common affairs, effectively stands out as a key variable in the success of some local communities over others. Importantly, it is governance at the local level rather than at the national level that counts for most. Perceptions of legitimacy for actors and institutions at the national level in Mali, Burkina Faso, and Ghana are all relatively low when compared to those at the local level. This is because for the most part communities govern themselves, and the community is understood as the most relevant environment for a governance configuration. Even at the local level, there is a degree of variety, with some governance actors proving more popular than others. The most resilient communities often possess robust local governance structures that foster cooperation, manage conflicts, and deliver essential services even in the most challenging of circumstances.

Throughout the book we have argued that governance modes at the local level are often fluid or somewhat evolutionary—that is, communities can be self-referential and represent complex and evolving governance systems that operate with a substantial degree of independence from national governments (Beunen et al. 2015, 9; Luhmann 1995). Chapters 2 and 3 illustrate how crowded this environment is in the regions under study here. Independence-era nodes of power were layered over colonial-era nodes of power, which were layered over precolonial nodes of power. Depending on the problem, residents might go to a nongovernmental organization or a parliamentarian, a traditional chief or an imam, a friend or a police officer. Grievances will emerge and solutions will be constructed, often with the activities of external actors droning in the background. At the time of surveying, respondents in Ghana were a bit more likely to approach their formal and traditional local government providers than their neighbors in Burkina Faso and Mali, but evaluations of these providers are not markedly different. Across the board, police and security services were not seen as dependable. Given the level of importance placed on the most local forms of governance by respondents, both the academic literature and Western governments have been deficient in engaging at this level, instead focusing on the national level, often because this is the way international relations typically operate.

Through taking a grassroots approach and focusing on governance at the local level, this book addresses some of the issues that arise with the more traditional state-centric ways of engaging the issues that tend to dominate both academic and policy discussions. The state-centric perspective prioritizes competing over governments against state and nonstate actors while working with allied and partner forces with often fraught historical relationships with local populations. Through our approach, we demonstrate that linkages between strategic competition and violent extremism are more organic when viewed from the perspective of local populations. This is especially so when looking at how actors attempt to exploit grievance narratives and at the conditions necessary for their resonance with target audiences.

Over the past decade, jihadist groups affiliated with Islamic State and al-Qaeda have cemented their presence across the Sahel and have made Mali and Burkina Faso the epicenter of global jihadist violence. The rapid metastasizing of jihadist actors in the region has led to the establishment of a grim record of violence, destabilizing entire communities and challenging the authority of governments across the region. The repercussions of jihadist terrorism extend beyond the immediate loss of life; they fundamentally disrupt the governance mechanisms that are vital for maintaining peace, order, and development. In the face of jihadist violence, both national governments and local communities in the region are testing the resilience of governance mechanisms. Governments, already struggling with issues of corruption, nepotism, and political instability, have found themselves ill-equipped to counter the rising tide of jihadism, while jihadist groups have thrived on exploiting weaknesses in governance, capitalizing on disenfranchisement, and exploiting perceptions of state failure to present themselves as an alternative authority.

JNIM focuses its narratives and actions on the dismantlement of nation-states and on the destruction of the current sociopolitical and moral order. They call for new forms of governance as an alternative model to what currently exists, which they argue has failed the people of the region. Though seemingly iconoclastic, jihadists are careful to directly tie this narrative to the historical trajectory of governance in the region, arguing that the establishment of Islamic states is not something new, but rather a return to a more authentic form of governance, one that colonialism destroyed in the nineteenth century. Jihadist groups recognize that invoking the "myth of a golden age" (A. Smith 1997) in which societies flourished under the sociopolitical and legal governance of Islamic law is a powerful tool, especially when juxtaposed with the currently fraught nature of many of these same communities. It is in this context that former Islamic kingdoms and empires of West Africa gain salience. Indeed, groups such as Boko Haram in Nigeria, Macina Liberation Front in Mali, and Ansarul Islam in Burkina Faso have drawn direct inspiration from former

Islamic states in the region such as Usman dan Fodio's Sokoto Caliphate and Seku Ahmadu's Macina Empire. The histories of these empires continue to reverberate in West Africa today and, when instrumentalized by jihadists, can act as social structures in the making for populations aggrieved by current state borders and with a historical memory of an alternative governance option.

The extent to which jihadist groups and their narratives around historic empires draw in populations, however, should not be exaggerated. Our chapters that focus on the perceptions and impacts of governance show that many of our survey respondents from across Mali, Burkina Faso, and Ghana believe their countries would be better places if more people followed the laws of the land. This was even a more popular response than those who believe that following the laws of God would improve the country (though the number of those who thought this to be the case was also significant). This is noteworthy because it shows, for the most part, populations do not have an issue with existing laws, legislation, and governance modes, but rather believe that, for whatever reason, these are not being implemented or enforced effectively. Because of this, it is important to find ways to bolster legal frameworks and ensure that the frameworks in place are followed. Despite leveraging grievances around corruption, jihadist groups did not seem to benefit from this when respondents were asked what they believed the primary goals of such movements were; almost no one said that it was to combat corruption.

Corruption, though, is perhaps the biggest issue facing good governance across Mali, Burkina Faso, and Ghana, with significant numbers of our respondents stating that corruption in their country has personally held them back from success. Combating endemic corruption is a difficult task and requires a whole of government approach. Corruption exacerbates a myriad of factors that leads to deepening perceptions of the illegitimacy of the three states. All three states must essentially professionalize—by making their civil service a fair and just bureaucracy accountable to the needs of the populace; creating an independent military and police agencies that work to protect citizens irrespective of their social position, ethnic affiliation, or ability to pay; and providing a general accountability to the needs of national citizens, rather than a commitment to self-enrichment (Delia Deckard and Pieri 2017, 382). Such changes are unlikely to happen quickly and as such external powers seeking to effect peace, security, or development in the region should focus on leveraging relationships across different levels of governance and, in particular, with local governance actors that have the most legitimacy among communities.

As governance started to fray in the region and jihadist violence deepened, a further dynamic was added to the mix—that of GPC. Major global powers, including the United States, China, and Russia, found renewed interest in West Africa and vied for influence and resources. The post–Cold War world looked less and less unipolar as the twenty-first century entered its second decade. These external actors engage in diplomacy, secure lucrative contracts, and bolster their military presence, often without fully considering the impact of their activities on local governance. One of the most visible manifestations of GPC in the region has been both the presence and changing dynamics of foreign military forces. In Mali, the intervention of French and UN troops over the past decade that aimed at stemming the tide of jihadist violence in that country brought to the fore questions about the limits of Mali's national sovereignty and the extent to which foreign military intervention was (or was not) succeeding. While the true effects of foreign military intervention may not be realized until both French and UN troops have fully vacated from the region (a process being undertaken at the time of this writing), it is clear that such military intervention fueled anti-Western and specifically anti-French sentiments, often centered around narratives (sometimes spread by jihadists or in some cases Russian disinformation campaigns) of the West acting again in a neocolonialist way.

Thrown in the mix of foreign military intervention, which has traditionally come in the form of nation-state actors, is the Russian-affiliated mercenary company Wagner Group. As Wagner Group came to hold more prominence in Mali and Burkina Faso, coups followed in those states, and French and UN forces were ejected. This also happened in Niger in 2023. Following a coup in that country French troops vacated, with President Macron of France arguing that the new regime was not serious about tackling violent extremism (France 24 2023c). Though best available evidence suggests Wagner Group had not officially begun operating in any of the three countries under study in spring of 2021 when surveys were conducted, there were strong indications that Wagner was in Mali's future at that time (Baché 2021).

As French troops were withdrawing from Mali, several hundred Wagner mercenary troops were stationed there. For Vladimir Putin,

Russia's president, Wagner Group acts as a "low-cost bridgehead for spreading Russia's influence across West Africa," with the logic being that in a "zero-sum great power game, if it is Russian mercenary forces providing protection and counterterrorism services to governments rather than the French or American militaries, then Moscow's clout and economic opportunities in the region will grow" (Nasr 2022, 22). Wagner Group forces were quickly deployed to the most volatile region in Mali, around Mopti, where the first recorded interactions between Wagner mercenaries and JNIM militants occurred on January 3, 2022 (Nasr 2022, 23). Wagner forces have not yet managed to stem the tide of jihadist violence and have found themselves becoming the target of jihadist groups, who after seeing the exit of France from Mali, do not want that power replaced by Russia. In April 2022, JNIM issued a statement saying that its own fighters had captured mercenary fighters from Russia's Wagner Group, described as "criminals," making it the first incident of this kind in Mali.

This has only intensified the intersection of GPC and jihadist terrorism in Sahelian West Africa and is shaping the region in new ways. The renewed interest and presence of external powers, driven by their geopolitical interests, introduces a new layer of complexity into an already volatile region. The competition for control over territory, resources, and strategic alliances can inadvertently exacerbate local grievances and destabilize fragile governance structures. This has already been seen in the discourse and actions of some jihadist groups. Whereas in the past the ire of jihadist groups was almost exclusively focused on France, the United States, and other Western allies, now Russia is coming under closer scrutiny as it begins to dominate in some areas.

While the presence of foreign troops elicits a certain type of response in local communities, the role of great powers in the extraction of resources can elicit others. Gold mining has become a lucrative business in all three countries under close study here and is often seen as one of the foci for external powers seeking to secure strategic minerals and resources. External powers such as China, France, Canada, and Australia have all made significant investments in the region to secure mineral assets. While it is sometimes posited that such extraction of resources colors perceptions of external powers in negative ways, our survey found something a little more nuanced. This was most evident with those who lived close to mines operated by foreign companies. The data shows that those who reported living within 5 kilometers of a Chinese mine generally reported more negative impressions of Chinese influence of their country, while those who lived closer to Western-owned mines reporting slightly more positive impressions of US influence of their country.

One of the biggest factors contributing to the ways in which foreign actors are perceived is personal interaction between locals and foreign nationals. Having that interpersonal interaction often engenders more positive feelings for the country that the foreign national comes from. This was seen with those who met either a Chinese or an American. In both cases this type of interaction consistently had positive impacts on perceptions in the sample. The exception to this rule was with those who met French citizens, with this often resulting in more negative perceptions of France as a power. As discussed throughout this book, the fact that France is often an outlier is likely due to the residual negative effects of its historic role as a colonial power in the region, mixed with its continued involvement in regional affairs. The actions of France are often held to a different standard than those of other powers—for example, the United States quietly kept its drone base in Niger for nearly a year, while France was forced to vacate the country immediately.

If we view VEO and GPC through a common lens as external shocks that may alter a community's governance equilibria, instead of as separate categories of events with their own libraries explaining causes and effects, we can more easily view interactions in the West African international affairs environment. Table 8.1 demonstrates the relationship between VEO and GPC activity on respondents' sense of community. The dependent variable is sense of community, which is measured by respondent's feeling that their community is a good place to live, they can recognize most of the people who live in their community, they care about what the community thinks of their actions, and they believe it is very important that they live in their community.[1] Answers to these four questions range from 1 (strongly disagree) to 5 (strongly agree) and are averaged across the four elements of sense of community to produce our sense of community index (SCI). We want to see how VEO and GPC variables correlate with SCI individually, as part of VEO and GPC models, and as part of models incorporating both VEO and GPC variables. This will help us better understand how VEO and GPC potentially interact to shape local governance environments.

Table 8.1 Predicting Respondents' Sense of Community

	Bivariate Pearson Correlation	VEO OLS Standardized Coefficient	GPC OLS Standardized Coefficient	VEO + GPC OLS Standardized Coefficient
ACLED	−.130**	−.080*		−.074*
Western gold mine	−.120**		−.132**	−.141**
Chinese gold mine	−.006		−.047	−.047
Foreign troops	−.075**		−.126**	−.113**
Met American	−.021		−.014	−.016
Met Chinese	−.030		−.028	−.026
Met French	−.070*		−.018	−.011
Mali	−.145**	−.109**	−.110**	−.079*
Ghana	−.065*	−.013	−.096**	−.073
Burkina Faso	−.073**			
Adjusted R^2		−.023	−.043	−.045

Note: **p < 0.01, *p < 0.05. VEO = violent extremist organization; GPC = great power competition; OLS = ordinary least squares; ACLED = Armed Conflict Location and Event Data.

The first data column in the table shows bivariate correlations. Armed Conflict Location and Event Data (ACLED) data represent the number of political violence-related deaths recorded from April 2020 to March 2021, the year before the survey, at the level of district/province/commune (ACLED, n.d.). Though this dataset does not cover VEO-related deaths exclusively, given the region and the time period, terrorism and counterterrorism account for the vast majority of deaths included. Deaths recorded for most of the home areas of respondents in northern Ghana and southern Burkina Faso are 0. The largest number of deaths was 799 in Koro, Mali. Variables that explore GPC ask whether or not respondents are in a community with a Western or Chinese mine and whether or not there is a sustained foreign troop presence in the area. Respondents were also asked if they had personally met an American, Chinese, or French citizen. To control for country-level factors, dummy variables for Ghana, Burkina Faso, and Mali are also included.[2]

By themselves, about half of our variables are reasonably good predictors of SCI. All the country controls are statistically significant. This means we can be reasonably confident citizens of Mali have SCI scores lower than the average in the sample and citizens of Burkina Faso and Ghana have scores higher than average. Given the conditions in Mali at the time of the survey in relation to those in Burkina Faso, these results are not surprising. VEO data in the form of ACLED-reported deaths from political violence is negatively related to SCI, meaning as the number of violent deaths increases, community members feel less connected to each other. Anxiety produced by violent disruptions has been known to tear apart social fabric (Collier et al. 2003). Being located near a Western gold mine and having foreign troops stationed in the vicinity are positively correlated with SCI. The theoretical reasons for this connection are less clear. They might be residuals of a particular time and place or patterns, if observed often and elsewhere, that deserve further exploration. Having met someone who is French is negatively correlated with SCI, but the significance of this relationship is relatively weak and disappears in ensuing models where a control variable for country is added, indicating a potential spurious effect. Malians' dislike of the French is likely driving this relationship (Bancel et al. 2017).

In VEO and GPC multivariate regression models (data columns two and three, respectively), higher levels of terrorism remain negatively correlated and significant, and the presence of foreign troops and a Western mine remain positively correlated and significant. Given the addition of fixed effects for country of survey, these results suggest a certain level of robustness in the relationships. The GPC model has more variables in it and also explains a bit more variance than the more parsimonious VEO model. The fourth data column throws all the VEO variables and GPC variables into a prediction of sense of community. What is remarkable here is the additive effect of the VEO and GPC models. All three of the aforementioned significant predictors remain significant and are signed in the identical direction. VEO and GPC activities impact respondents' perceptions of their communities and their places in it, but they do so in ways that are independent of each other. It is not the VEO and GPC variables that diminish in predictive power as more variables are added to the final model, but the fixed-effect country variables. This finding suggests that GPC may mitigate the damage VEOs inflict on local communities' governance or perhaps amplify their negative effects. The two types of intervention, one conducted by internationalized jihadist groups and the other by great powers from the West, even with the handful of control variables added, impact local communities simultaneously.

We have stressed that the communities we discuss in this book constitute complex social systems lacking easily discernible or fixed focal points (Ellis 2022). Ethnic, sociolinguistic, and cultural and religious groups often span across borders, with some people feeling more connected to those living just across an international border than with those living in distant regions of their own country. There is also no set or uniform response to external actors. Our respondents exhibit preferences for and aversions to external great power competitors that defy a pattern consistent with foreign policies crafted to win friends and allies, or at the least create a positive image of the external power. Perceptions fail to conform to the assumptions of the liberal model, which pushes exploitation of the periphery by the core. Where tentative patterns do emerge—for example, as seen with Canadian gold mines improving a sense of community and not seeming to reduce support for local governance providers, or where a heavy Chinese presence shows signs of diminishing formal and traditional governance providers in the eyes of the citizenry—they are best extrapolated with caution.

Historically, violent extremism and GPC have been treated as separate or distinct trends. This book, however, has sought to navigate these complexities in a more holistic manner, recognizing the sometimes interdependent relationships among jihadist terrorism, GPC, and governance. Resilience in the face of exogenous shocks is not just a matter of individual determination but also a reflection of a community's ability to access resources, engage in conflict resolution, and trust local leadership. Consequently, strengthening local governance structures and empowering community leaders stand as critical imperatives for the region's future prosperity.

Notes

1. Our sense of community index is a paired-down version of the Chavis et al. (2008) index. It is four questions as opposed to twenty-four.
2. Because development assistance cannot be measured below the country level, it is excluded from analysis.

Bibliography

Abitol, Michael. 1992. "The End of the Songhay Empire." In *Africa from the Sixteenth to the Eighteenth Century*, vol. 5 of *General History of Africa*, edited by B. A. Ogot, 300–326. University of California Press.

Abramitzky, Ran, Leah Boustan, Elisa Jacome, and Santiago Perez. 2021. "Intergenerational Mobility of Immigrants in the United States over Two Centuries." *American Economic Review* 111 (2): 580–608.

Acemoglu, Daron, Simon Johnson, and James A. Robinson. 2001. "The Colonial Origins of Comparative Development: An Empirical Investigation." *American Economic Review* 91 (5): 1369–1401.

Ackah-Baidoo, Abigail. 2012. "Enclave Development and 'Offshore Corporate Social Responsibility': Implications for Oil-Rich Sub-Saharan Africa." *Resources Policy* 37 (2): 152–159. https://doi.org/10.1016/j.resourpol.2011.12.010.

Acker, Kevin, and Deborah Brautigam. 2021. *Twenty Years of Data on China's Africa Lending*. China-Africa Research Initiative Briefing Paper 4. China Africa Research Initiative at Johns Hopkins University Paul H. Nitze School of Advanced International Studies.

ACLED (Armed Conflict Location and Event Data). n.d. "ACLED Data." https://www.acleddata.com/.

Adama, Hamadou. 2009. "The Hajj: Between a Moral and a Material Economy." *Afrique Contemporaine* 231 (3): 119–138.

Adeleye, R. A. 1971. *Power and Diplomacy in Northern Nigeria 1904–1906: The Sokoto Caliphate and Its Enemies*. Longman.

Adi, Hakim. 2018. *Pan-Africanism: A History*. Bloomsbury.

Adibe, Jideofor. 2019. "What Does Russia Really Want from Africa?" *Africa in Focus*. https://www.brookings.edu/blog/africa-in-focus/2019/11/14/what-does-russia-really-want-from-africa/.

Africa Center for Strategic Studies. 2021. "Spike in Militant Islamist Violence in Africa Underscores Shifting Security Landscape." Infographic, January 29.

African Development Bank. 2000. *Bank Group Policy on Good Governance*. African Development Bank.

Bibliography

AfricaNews and Agence France-Presse. 2022. "G5 Sahel Seeks 'New Strategy' After Mali Withdrawal." *Africanews*, September 23.

Agence France Presse. 2012. "Sharia Law Enforced in Mali." *N World* (blog). July 31. https://www.thenationalnews.com/world/africa/sharia-lawenforced-in-mali-1.441694.

Ahmed, Baba. 2015. "Suspected Islamic Militants Destroy Mausoleum in Mali That Was Proposed World Heritage Site." *U.S. News and World Report*, May 4.

Akyeampong, Emmanuel, Robert H. Bates, Nathan Nunn, and James A. Robinson, eds. 2014. *Africa's Development in Historical Perspective*. Cambridge University Press.

Al Jazeera. 2020. "Mali Camp Attacked as West Africa Struggles with Jihadist Revolt." April 17. https://www.aljazeera.com/news/2020/4/17/mali-army-camp-attacked-as-west-africa-struggles-with-jihadist-revolt.

Allen, Kenneth W., John Chen, and Phillip Charles Saunders. 2017. *Chinese Military Diplomacy, 2003–2016: Trends and Implications*. National Defense University Press.

Allen, Nathaniel D. F. 2018. "Assessing a Decade of U.S. Military Strategy in Africa." *Orbis* 62 (4): 655–669.

al-Qaeda in the Islamic Maghreb and Jama'at Nasr al-Islam wal Muslimin. 2019. "Statement of Condolences and Incitement." *Al-Andalus Foundation for Media Productions and Az-Zallaqa Foundation for Media Productions*, March 18.

Anderson, Mary R. 2009. "Beyond Membership: Sense of Community and Political Behavior." *Political Behavior* 31 (4): 603–627.

Anderson, Mary R. 2010. *Community Identity and Political Behavior*. Vol. 31. Palgrave Macmillan.

Anderson, Mary R., and Kevin S. Fridy. 2022. *Community, Civic Engagement and Democratic Governance in Africa*. Palgrave Macmillan.

Andersson, Magnus, Ola Hall, and Niklas Olén. 2015. *Does Large-Scale Gold Mining Reduce Agricultural Growth? Case Studies from Burkina Faso, Ghana, Mali and Tanzania*. World Bank.

Anter, Tarig. 2013. "Special Report: Who Are the Fulani People and Their Origins?" *Point Blank News* (blog). June 13. http://pointblanknews.com/pbn/exclusive/special-report-who-are-the-fulani-people-and-their-origins/.

Antwi-Boateng, Osman, and Mamudu Abunga Akudugu. 2020. "Golden Migrants: The Rise and Impact of Illegal Chinese Small-Scale Mining in Ghana." *Politics & Policy* 48 (1): 135–167.

Appiah, Josephine, Nyamekye Sanny, and Carolyn Logan. 2020. *Citizens' Negative Perceptions of Police Extend Well Beyond Nigeria's #EndSARS*. Afrobarometer Dispatches, no. 403.

Arieff, Alexis, Marian L. Lawson, and Susan G. Chesser. 2021. *Coup-Related Restrictions in US Foreign Aid Appropriations*. Congressional Research Service, Library of Congress. https://apps.dtic.mil/sti/pdfs/AD1171956.pdf.

Ariotti, Margaret H., and Kevin S. Fridy. 2020. *Informal Governance as a Force Multiplier in Counterterrorism: Evidence for Burkina Faso*. MacDill AFB: Joint Special Operations University.

Asala, Kizzi. 2021. "Ghana: Opposition Youth Activists Rally Against Federal Police Force." *Africa News*, July 6, 2021.

Asante, Richard. 2017. "China's Security and Economic Engagement in West Africa." *China Quarterly of International Strategic Studies* 3 (4): 575–596.

Asiwaju, Anthony Ijaola. 1976. *Western Yorubaland Under European Rule, 1889–1945: A Comparative Analysis of French and British Colonialism*. London: Longman Publishing Group.

Associated Press. 2019. "13 Miners Die in Ghana After Blast, Regional Official Says." January 23. https://apnews.com/article/dcfd7e5b27b5411596bd86342 e801403.

Austin, Dennis. 1961. "The Working Committee of the United Gold Coast Convention." *Journal of African History* 2 (2): 273–297.

Austin, Dennis. 1964. *Politics in Ghana, 1946–1960*. Oxford University Press.

Ba, Boubacar. 2010. *Pouvoir, Ressources et Développement Dans Le Delta Central Du Niger*. L'Harmattan.

Baché, David. 2021. "Mali: le déploiement de soldats russes, voire de Wagner, a-t-il commencé?" Radio France Internationale, December 31. https://www.rfi.fr /fr/afrique/20211231-mali-le-d%C3%A9ploiement-de-soldats-russes-voire -de-wagner-a-t-il-commenc%C3%A9.

Baldor, Lolita C. 2021. "China's Africa Outreach Poses Threat from Atlantic." Associated Press, May 6.

Bancel, Nicolas, Pascal Blanchard, and Dominic Thomas. 2017. *The Colonial Legacy in France: Fracture, Rupture, and Apartheid*. Indiana University Press.

Bates, Robert H. 1981. *Markets and States in Tropical Africa: The Political Basis of Agricultural Policies*. University of California Press.

Bazemo, Maurice. 1990. "Une approche de la captivité par le vocabulaire chez les Peuls du Djelgoji (Djibo) et du Liptaako (Dori) à l'époque précoloniale et coloniale." *Dialogues d'histoire ancienne* 16 (1): 403–423. https://doi.org /10.3406/dha.1990.1473.

BBC. 2013. "Mali and France Push Back Islamists." *BBC News*, January 12.

Becker, Laurence C. 1994. "An Early Experiment in the Reorganisation of Agricultural Production in the French Soudan (Mali), 1920–40." *Africa* 64 (3): 373–390.

Bening, Raymond Bagulo. 1995. "Land Policy and Administration in Northern Ghana 1898–1976." *Transactions of the Historical Society of Ghana* 16 (2): 227–266.

Bening, Raymond Bagulo. 2015. *The History of Education in Northern Ghana*. 2nd ed. Accra, Ghana: Gavoss.

Benson, Susan. 2007. "'They Came From the North': Historical Truth and the Duties of Memory Along Ghana's Slave Route." *Cambridge Anthropology* 27 (2): 90–101.

Beunen, Raoul, Kristof Van Assche, and Martijn Duineveld, eds. 2015. *Evolutionary Governance Theory*. Springer.

Blain, Keisha N. 2020. "Black Lives Matter and the Global Fight Against Racism." *Foreign Affairs*, September/October.

Blair, Robert A., Robert Marty, and Philip Roessler. 2022. "Foreign Aid and Soft Power: Great Power Competition in Africa in the Early Twenty-First Century." *British Journal of Political Science* 52 (3): 1355–1376. https://doi.org /10.1017/S0007123421000193.

Blanchard, Ben. 2018. "China Wins Back Burkina Faso, Urges Taiwan's Last African Ally to Follow." Reuters, May 26.

Blankenship, Brian D., and Benjamin Denison. 2019. "Is America Prepared for Great-Power Competition?" *Survival* 61 (5): 43–64.

Boafo, James, Sebastian Angzoorokuu Paalo, and Senyo Dotsey. 2019. "Illicit Chinese Small-Scale Mining in Ghana: Beyond Institutional Weakness?" *Sustainability* 11 (21): 5943.

Boahen, A. Adu. 1987. *African Perspectives on Colonialism*. Johns Hopkins University Press.

Bonnecase, Vincent. 2015. "Sur La Chute de Blaise Compaoré. Autorité et Colère Dans Les Derniers Jours d'un Régime." *Politique Africaine*, no. 1, 151–168.

Boone, Catherine. 2005. *Political Topographies of the African State: Territorial Authority and Institutional Choice*. Cambridge University Press.

Boston University Global Development Policy Center. 2022. "Chinese Loans to Africa Database." http://bu.edu/gdp/chinese-loans-to-africa-database.

Botchway, Francis N. N. 1995. "Pre-colonial Methods of Gold Mining and Environmental Protection in Ghana." *Journal of Energy & Natural Resources Law* 13 (4): 299–311.

Bratton, Michael. 2007. "Formal Versus Informal Institutions in Africa." In "Democratization in Africa," edited by Larry Diamond and Marc F Plattner, special issue, *Journal of Democracy* 18 (3): 96–110.

Bratton, Michael, and Nicolas van de Walle. 1997. *Democratic Experiments in Africa: Regime Transitions in Comparative Perspective*. Cambridge University Press.

Brautigam, Deborah. 2009. *The Dragon's Gift: The Real Story of China in Africa*. Oxford University Press.

Brottem, Leif. 2022. "Jihad Takes Root in Northern Benin." ACLED. https://acleddata.com/2022/09/23/jihad-takes-root-in-northern-benin/.

Brown, William. 1969. "The Caliphate of Hamdullahi, 1818–1864: Study in African History and Tradition." PhD thesis, University of Wisconsin.

Brukum, Nana James Kwaku. 1999. "Chiefs, Colonial Policy and Politics in Northern Ghana, 1897–1956." *Transactions of the Historical Society of Ghana*, no. 3, 101–122.

Buchanan, Elsa. 2017. "Radical Muslim Preacher Malam Ibrahim Dicko Wants to Rebuild the Peulh Kingdom in Burkina Faso." *IBTimes*, January 4.

Bukart, Audu. 2020. "The West in Africa's Violent Extremists' Discourse." *Hudson Institute*, October 28.

Burgess, Stephen. 2018. "Military Intervention in Africa: French and Us Approaches Compared." *Air and Space Power Journal* 9:5–25.

Bybee, Ashley N. 2017. "In Burkina Faso, An Extremist Fulani Struggle Sprouts." *IDA Africa Watch* 15 (May): 2–3.

Cabestan, Jean-Pierre. 2018. "China's Involvement in Africa's Security: The Case of China's Participation in the UN Mission to Stabilize Mali." *China Quarterly* 235 (September): 713–734. https://doi.org/10.1017/S0305741018000929.

Calderón, César, and Albert Zeufack. 2020. *Borrow with Sorrow? The Changing Risk Profile of Sub-Saharan Africa's Debt*. January 30. World Bank Policy Research Working Paper, no. 9137.

Callimachi, Rukmini. 2014. "Underwriting Jihad: Paying Ransoms, Europe Bankrolls Qaeda Terror." *New York Times*, July 29.

Campbell, John. 2019. "Problems in the Sahel Only Growing, Says ACLED." Council on Foreign Relations, February 12. https://www.cfr.org/blog/problems-sahel-only-growing-says-acled.

Castillo, Roberto. 2020. "'Race' and 'Racism' in Contemporary Africa-China Relations Research: Approaches, Controversies and Reflections." *Inter-Asia Cultural Studies* 21 (3): 310–336.
Charbonneau, Bruno. 2017. "Intervention in Mali: Building Peace Between Peacekeeping and Counterterrorism." *Journal of Contemporary African Studies* 35 (4): 415–431. https://doi.org/10.1080/02589001.2017.1363383.
Chauzal, Gregory, and Thibault van Damme. 2015. *The Roots of Mali's Conflict: Moving Beyond the 2012 Crisis*. Netherlands Institute of International Relations. https://www.clingendael.org/sites/default/files/pdfs/The_roots_of_Malis_conflict.pdf.
Chavis, David M., K. S. Lee, and J. D. Acosta. 2008. "The Sense of Community (SCI) Revised: The Reliability and Validity of the SCI-2." 2nd International Community Psychology Conference, Lisbon, Portugal.
Cheru, Fantu, and Cyril Obi, eds. 2010. *The Rise of China and Africa in India: Challenges, Opportunities and Critical Interventions*. London, UK: Zed.
Chilson, Peter. 2019. "The Holy War of Amadu Koufa." *Consequences Magazine*, no. 11, 191–208.
China Africa Research Initiative. 2021. "Chinese Loans to Africa Database." https://chinaafricaloandata.bu.edu/.
Chivvis, Christopher S. 2016. *The French War on Al Qa'ida in Africa*. Cambridge University Press.
Cissé, Modibo Ghaly. 2020. "Understanding Fulani Perspectives on the Sahel Crisis." *African Center for Strategic Studies*, April 22.
Clark, Andrew. 1999. "Imperialism, Independence, and Islam in Senegal and Mali." *Africa Today* 46 (3): 149–167.
Clarke, Peter. 1982. *West Africa and Islam: A Study of Religious Development from the 8th to the 20th Century*. Edward Arnold.
Cline, Lawrence E. 2021. "Jihadist Movements in the Sahel: Rise of the Fulani?" *Terrorism and Political Violence* 35 (1): 175–191.
Cocks, Tim. 2019. "How a Preacher Sent Gunmen into Burkina Faso's Schools." Reuters, November 13.
Cohen, Roger. 2022. "Putin Wants Fealty, and He's Found It in Africa." World, *New York Times*, December 24.
Colebatch, Hal K. 2014. "Making Sense of Governance." *Policy and Society* 33 (4): 307–316.
Collier, Paul, V. L. Elliott, Håvard Hegre, Anke Hoeffler, Marta Reynal-Querol, and Nicholas Sambanis. 2003. *Breaking the Conflict Trap: Civil War and Development Policy*. World Bank Policy Research Report, no. 41181.
Collins, Neil, and David O'Brien. 2022. "Neo-Mercantilism in Action: China and Small States." *International Politics* 60:1–24.
Commission on Global Governance. 1995. *Our Global Neighborhood*. Oxford University Press.
Comolli, Virginia. 2015. *Nigeria's Islamist Insurgency*. Hurst.
Conrad, David C. 2010. *Empires of Medieval West Africa: Ghana, Mali, and Songhay*. Chelsea House.
Cook, Nicolas, Alexis Arieff, Lauren Ploch Blanchard, Brock R. Williams, and Tomas F. Husted. 2017. *Sub-Saharan Africa: Key Issues, Challenges, and US Responses*. Congressional Research Service.
Coulibaly, Nadoun. 2021. "Endeavour Mining Is Ready to Face the Terrorist Threat in the Sahel." *The Africa Report*, January 7. https://www.theafricareport

.com/57586/endeavour-mining-is-ready-to-face-the-terrorist-threat-in-the-sahel/.

Crawford, Gordon, Coleman Agyeyomah, and Atinga Mba. 2017. "Ghana—Big Man, Big Envelope, Finish: Chinese Corporate Exploitation in Small-Scale Mining." In *Contested Extractivism, Society and the State*, edited by Bettina Engels and Kristina Dietz, 69–99. Palgrave Macmillan.

Crawford, Gordon, and Gabriel Botchwey. 2017. "Conflict, Collusion and Corruption in Small-Scale Gold Mining: Chinese Miners and the State in Ghana." *Commonwealth & Comparative Politics* 55 (4): 444–470.

Crowder, Michael. 1964. "Indirect Rule: French and British Style." *Africa* 34 (3): 197–205.

Custer, Samantha, Axel Dreher, Thai-Binh Elston, Andreas Fuchs, Siddharta Ghose, Joyce Jiahui Lin, et al. 2021. *Tracking Chinese Development Finance: An Application of AidData's TUFF 2.0 Methodology*. Williamsburg, VA: AidData at William & Mary.

Dahir, Abdi Latif. 2018. "The Reason American Presidents Keep Visiting the Same Few African Countries." *Quartz Africa*, October 9.

Dahir, Abdi Latif. 2019. "The African Countries Not Signed to China's Belt and Road Plan—Quartz Africa." *Quartz*, September 30. https://qz.com/africa/1718826/the-african-countries-not-signed-to-chinas-belt-and-road-plan/.

Dahiru, Aliyu. 2022. "JNIM Calls for More Offensive Against ISGS As Battle for Supremacy Continues in the Sahel." *HumAngle* (blog), November 7. https://humanglemedia.com/jnim-calls-for-more-offensive-against-isgs-as-battle-for-supremacy-continues-in-the-sahel/.

Dallal, Ahmad. 1993. "The Origins and Objectives of Islamic Revivalist Thought, 1750–1850." *Journal of the American Oriental Society* 113 (3): 341–359.

D'Aquino, Patrick. 1996. "Du Sable à l'argile: L'occupation de l'espace Dans Le Djelgodji (Nord-Burkina Faso)." *Cahiers Des Sciences Humaines* 32 (2): 311–333.

D'Avignon, Robyn. 2018. "Primitive Techniques: From 'Customary' to 'Artisanal' Mining in French West Africa." *Journal of African History* 59 (2): 179–197. https://doi.org/10.1017/S0021853718000361.

Davis, Charles. 2012. "Islam and Identity: The Role of the Mosque in Identity Negotiation Among African Fulani Immigrants." PhD diss., ETD Collection for Fordham University, no. AAI3542748.

De Guttry, Andrea, Francesca Capone, and Christophe Paulussen, eds. 2016. *Foreign Fighters Under International Law and Beyond*. The Hague: T.M.C. Asser Press. https://doi.org/10.1007/978-94-6265-099-2.

De Riviere, Nicolas. 2022. "The G5 Sahel Is in Crisis." Speech to the United Nations Security Council, New York, NY, November 16. https://onu.delegfrance.org/the-g5-sahel-is-in-crisis.

Debrah, Emmanuel, and Richard Asante. 2019. "Sino-Ghana Bilateral Relations and Chinese Migrants' Illegal Gold Mining in Ghana." *Journal of Asian and African Studies* 27 (3): 286–307.

Delafosse, Maurice. 1904. "The Mystery of the Fulani: New and Startling Theory of Origin." *West African Mail*, no. 29.

Delia Deckard, Natalie, and Zacharias Pieri. 2017. "The Implications of Endemic Corruption for State Legitimacy in Developing Nations: An Empirical Exploration of the Nigerian Case." *International Journal of Politics, Culture, and Society* 30 (4): 369–384.

Denisov, Igor, Andrei Kazantsev, Fyodor Lukyanov, and Ivan Safranchuk. 2019. "Shifting Strategic Focus of BRICS and Great Power Competition." *Strategic Analysis* 43 (6): 487–498. https://doi.org/10.1080/09700161.2019.1669888.

Der, Benedict G. 1998. *The Slave Trade in Northern Ghana*. Accra, Ghana: Woeli.

Diouf, Sylviane A., ed. 2003. *Fighting the Slave Trade: West African Strategies*. Ohio University Press.

Dreher, Axel, Andreas Fuchs, Bradley Parks, Austin M. Strange, and Michael J. Tierney. 2021. "Aid, China, and Growth: Evidence from a New Global Development Finance Dataset." AidData Working Paper. *American Economic Journal: Economic Policy* 13 (2): 135–174.

Dreher, Axel, Andreas Fuchs, Bradley Parks, Austin M. Strange, and Michael J. Tierney. 2022. *Banking on Beijing: The Aims and Impacts of China's Overseas Development Program*. Cambridge University Press.

Early, Bryan R., and Amira Jadoon. 2019. "Using the Carrot as the Stick: US Foreign Aid and the Effectiveness of Sanctions Threats." *Foreign Policy Analysis* 15 (3): 350–369.

Economist. 2022a. "How Al-Qaeda and Islamic State Are Digging into Africa." August 12.

Economist. 2022b. "West Africa's Coastal States Are Bracing for a Jihadist Storm." February 24.

Economist. 2023a. "After Niger's Coup, the Drums of War Are Growing Louder." August 7.

Economist. 2023b. "Niger Spoils Macron's Plan for an African Reset." August 2.

Economist. 2023c. "Rampant Jihadists Are Spreading Chaos and Misery in the Sahel." April 27.

Economist. 2023d. "What Next for Wagner's African Empire?" June 27.

Economist. 2023e. "The World's Deadliest War Last Year Wasn't Ukraine." April 17.

Ekeh, Peter P. 1992. "The Constitution of Civil Society in African History and Politics." In *Proceedings of the Symposium on Democratic Transition in Africa*, edited by Bernard Caron, Alex Gboyega, and Eghosa E. Osaghae. Ibadan, Nigeria: Centre for Research, Documentation and University Exchange.

Elischer, Sebastian. 2022. "Populist Civil Society, the Wagner Group, and Post-Coup Politics in Mali." OECD West African Papers. https://www.oecd-ilibrary.org/content/paper/b6249de6-en.

Ellis, David C. 2022. *The Network Illusion*. MacDill AFB: Joint Special Operations University.

Eltantawi, Sarah. 2017. *Shari'a on Trial: Northern Nigeria's Islamic Revolution*. University of California Press.

Eltis, David. 2009. "Trans-Atlantic Slave Trade—Estimates." Slave Voyages: The Trans-Atlantic Slave Trade Database. https://www.slavevoyages.org/assessment/estimates.

Engels, Bettina. 2020. "Not Normal, Not Just: Protest Against Large-Scale Mining from a Moral Economy Perspective." *Canadian Journal of African Studies/Revue Canadienne Des Études Africaines* 54 (3): 479–496.

Englebert, Pierre. 1999. *Burkina Faso: Unsteady Statehood in West Africa*. Westview Press.

Englebert, Pierre. 2000. "Pre-colonial Institutions, Post-colonial States, and Economic Development in Tropical Africa." *Political Research Quarterly* 53 (1): 7–36. doi

Engler, Yves. 2015. "Canada as Mining Superpower." In *The Harper Record: 2008–2015*, edited by Teresa Healy and Stuart Trew, 423–427. Canadian Centre for Policy Alternatives.

Ergano, Degele, and Seshagiri Rao. 2019. "Sino-African Bilateral Economic Relation: Nature and Perspectives." *Insight on Africa* 11 (1): 1–17.

Ericsson, Magnus, Olof Löf, and Anton Löf. 2020. "Chinese Control over African and Global Mining—Past, Present and Future." *Mineral Economics* 33:153–181.

Extractive Industries Transparency Initiative. 2023. "Open Data." https://eiti.org/open-data.

Fage, John D. 1969. *A History of West Africa: An Introductory Survey*. 4th ed. Cambridge University Press.

Fauvelle, François-Xavier, and Troy Tice. 2018. *The Golden Rhinoceros: Histories of the African Middle Ages*. Princeton University Press. https://doi.org/10.2307/j.ctvc77kzq.

Fearon, James D., and David D. Laitin. 1996. "Explaining Interethnic Cooperation." *American Political Science Review* 90 (4): 715–735.

Förster, Stig, Wolfgang J. Mommsen, and Ronald Robinson, eds. 1988. *Bismarck, Europe, and Africa: The Berlin Africa Conference 1884–1885 and the Onset of Partition*. Oxford University Press.

France 24. 2023a. "Attempted Bombing in North Ghana Fuels Jihadist Fears." February 9.

France 24. 2023b. "French Army Officially Ends Operations in Burkina Faso." February 20.

France 24. 2023c. "French Army Says It Will Begin Withdrawing Troops from Niger 'This Week.'" October 5.

France 24. 2024. "France to Reduce Military Presence in West and Central Africa." June 18.

French, Howard W. 2022. "A Little Great-Power Competition Is Healthy for Africa." *Foreign Policy*, August 10.

Fridy, Kevin S., and William M. Myers. 2019. "Challenges to Decentralisation in Ghana: Where Do Citizens Seek Assistance?" *Commonwealth & Comparative Politics* 57 (1): 71–92.

Friesen, Paul, Jaimie Bleck, and Kevin Fridy. 2022. "Personality, Community, and Politics: Relating the Five Factor Model to Political Behaviour in an African Setting." *Commonwealth & Comparative Politics* 60 (2): 190–211.

Gauthier Vela, Vanessa. 2021. "MINUSMA and the Militarization of UN Peacekeeping." *International Peacekeeping* 28 (5): 838–863. https://doi.org/10.1080/13533312.2021.1951610.

Gegout, Catherine. 2018. *Why Europe Intervenes in Africa: Security, Prestige and the Legacy of Colonialism*. Oxford University Press.

Gellar, Sheldon. 1967. "West African Capital Cities as Motors for Development." *Civilisations* 17 (3): 254–262.

Gerring, John, and Strom C. Thacker. 2004. "Political Institutions and Corruption: The Role of Unitarism and Parliamentarism." *British Journal of Political Science* 34 (2): 295–330.

Gervais, Raymond R., and Issiaka Mandé. 2000. "From Crisis to National Identity: Migration in Mutation, Burkina Faso, 1930–1960." *International Journal of African Historical Studies* 33 (1): 59–79.

Global Data Lab. 2023. "Subnational HDI (v7.0)." Global Data Lab. https://globaldatalab.org/shdi/table/shdi/BFA+GHA-MLI/.

Gomez, Michael A. 2018. *African Dominion*. Princeton University Press.
Gordon, Andrew J. 2000. "Cultural Identity and Illness: Fulani Views." *Culture, Medicine and Psychiatry* 24 (3): 297–330.
Government of Canada. 2009. "A Corporate Social Responsibility (CSR) Strategy for the Canadian International Extractive Sector." Global Affairs Canada. https://www.international.gc.ca/trade-agreements-accords-commerciaux/topics-domaines/other-autre/csr-strat-rse-2009.aspx?lang=eng.
Government of Ghana. 2006. *Minerals and Mining Act. Act 703*. https://resourcegovernance.org/sites/default/files/Minerals and Mining Act 703 Ghana.pdf.
Gowan, Richard. 2020. "China's Pragmatic Approach to UN Peacekeeping." Brookings, September 14. https://www.brookings.edu/articles/chinas-pragmatic-approach-to-un-peacekeeping/.
Grätz, Tilo. 2004. "Les Frontières de l'orpaillage En Afrique Occidentale." *Autrepart* 2 (30): 135–150.
Grimm, Sven. 2014. "No China–Africa Cooperation: Promises, Practice and Prospects." *Journal of Contemporary China* 23 (90): 993–1011.
Guichaoua, Yvan. 2020. "The Bitter Harvest of French Interventionism in the Sahel." *International Affairs* 96 (4): 895–911.
Gurr, Ted. 1970. *Why Men Rebel*. Princeton University Press.
Gwatiwa, Tshepo, and Justin Van der Merwe, eds. 2020. *Expanding US Military Command in Africa: Elites, Networks and Grand Strategy*. Routledge.
Gyimah-Brempong, Kwabena. 2002. "Corruption, Economic Growth, and Income Inequality in Africa." *Economics of Governance* 3 (3): 183–209.
Haffa, Robert P. 2018. "The Future of Conventional Deterrence: Strategies for Great Power Competition." *Strategic Studies Quarterly* 12 (4): 94–115. https://doi.org/10.2307/26533617.
Han, Xiao, and Michael Webber. 2020. "From Chinese Dam Building in Africa to the Belt and Road Initiative: Assembling Infrastructure Projects and Their Linkages." *Political Geography* 77:102102.
Headrick, Daniel R. 1979. "The Tools of Imperialism: Technology and the Expansion of European Colonial Empires in the Nineteenth Century." *Journal of Modern History* 51 (2): 231–263.
Heidenheimer, Arnold J., ed. 1970. *Political Corruption: Readings in Comparative Analysis*. Routledge.
Heinrigs, Philipp. 2020. "Africapolis: Understanding the Dynamics of Urbanization in Africa." In "Water, Waste and Energy: Prospects for Essential Services in Africa," special issue, *Field Actions Science Reports: The Journal of Field Actions*, no. 22, 18–23.
Herbst, Jeffrey. 1990. "Migration, the Politics of Protest, and State Consolidation in Africa." *African Affairs* 89 (355): 183–203.
Herbst, Jeffrey. 2000. *States and Power in Africa: Comparative Lessons in Authority and Control*. Princeton University Press.
Hicks, Marcus, Kyle Atwell, and Dan Collini. 2022. "Great-Power Competition Is Coming to Africa." *Foreign Affairs*, July 4. https://www.foreignaffairs.com/articles/africa/2021-03-04/great-power-competition-coming-africa.
Hill, Magari. 2009. "The Spread of Islam in West Africa: Containment, Mixing, and Reform from the Eighth to the Twentieth Century." *SPICE Digest* (Spring): 1–5.
Hilson, Abigail, Gavin Hilson, and Suleman Dauda. 2019. "Corporate Social Responsibility at African Mines: Linking the Past to the Present." *Journal of*

Environmental Management 241 (July): 340–352. https://doi.org/10.1016/j.jenvman.2019.03.121.

Hilson, Gavin, Abigail Hilson, and Eunice Adu-Darko. 2014. "Chinese Participation in Ghana's Informal Gold Mining Economy: Drivers, Implications and Clarifications." *Journal of Rural Studies* 34 (April): 292–303. https://doi.org/10.1016/j.jrurstud.2014.03.001.

Hirschman, Albert O. 1970. *Exit, Voice, and Loyalty: Responses to Decline in Firms, Organizations, and States.* Harvard University Press.

Hiskett, Mervyn. 1984. *The Development of Islam in West Africa.* Longman.

Hopkins, J. F. P., and Nehemia Levtzion, eds. 2000. *Corpus of Early Arabic Sources for West African History.* Markus Wiener Publishers.

Hou, Zhenbo, and Jane Kennan. 2013. "Graduation out of Aid Research." Overseas Development Institute, working paper. https://odi.org/en/publications/graduation-out-of-aid/.

Huifeng, He. 2013. "Low Costs and Huge Profits Irresistible Lure for Chinese to Mine Ghana's Gold." *South China Morning Post,* June 7. https://www.scmp.com/news/china/article/1255126/low-costs-and-huge-profits-irresistible-lure-chinese-mine-ghanas-gold.

Huillery, Elise. 2009. "History Matters: The Long-Term Impact of Colonial Public Investments in French West Africa." *American Economic Journal: Applied Economics* 1 (2): 176–215.

Huillery, Elise, ed. 2010. "Data_huillery_historymatters.Zip." *History Matters: The Long Term Impact of Colonial Public Investments in French West Africa [Dataset].* Harvard Dataverse. https://dci.org/10.7910/DVN/2ZQD63/MLW3K3.

Human Rights Watch. 2020. "China: Covid-19 Discrimination Against Africans." May 5. https://www.hrw.org/news/2020/05/05/china-covid-19-discrimination-against-africans.

Hunwick, John Owen, ed. 1999. *Timbuktu and the Songhay Empire: Al-Sa'dī's Ta'rīkh Al-Sūdān Down to 1613 and Other Contemporary Documents.* Vol. 27. Brill.

Ibrahim, Ibrahim Yahaya. 2017. "The Wave of Jihadist Insurgency in West Africa: Global Ideology, Local Context, Individual Motivations." OECD West African Papers, no. 7. https://doi.org/10.1787/eb95c0a9-en.

Ibrahimov, Mahir J., ed. 2020. *Great Power Competition: The Changing Landscape of Global Geopolitics.* US Army Command and General Staff College Press.

Iliasu, A. A. 1971. "The Origins of the Mossi-Dagomba States." *Research Review of the Institute of African Studies* 7 (2): 95–113.

Institute for Economics & Peace. 2024. *Global Terrorism Index 2024: Measuring the Impact of Terrorism.* https://www.economicsandpeace.org/wp-content/uploads/2024/02/GTI-2024-web-290224.pdf.

International Crisis Group. 2019. *Speaking with the "Bad Guys": Toward Dialogue with Central Mali's Jihadists.*Report no. 276.

Isichei, Elizabeth Allo. 1997. *A History of African Societies to 1870.* Cambridge University Press.

Jama'at Nasr al-Islam wal Muslimin. 2019a. "Audio Speech."

Jama'at Nasr al-Islam wal Muslimin. 2019b. "Message on the Raid." *Az-Zallaga Media Foundation,* September 5.

Jama'at Nasr al-Islam wal Muslimin. 2019c. "A Sweeping Attack on the G5 Forces Base in Dioura." *Az-Zallaqa Media Foundation,* March 22.

Jama'at Nasr al-Islam wal Muslimin. 2020a. "Statement 149: Colonial France Returns to the Policy of Genocide." *Az-Zallaqa Media Foundation*, February 18.

Jama'at Nasr al-Islam wal Muslimin. 2020b. "Statement 152." 2020.

Jama'at Nasr al-Islam wal Muslimin. 2020c. "Statement 153: Statement on the Tarkint Raid in Mali." *Az-Zallaga Media Foundation*, March 21.

Jama'at Nusrat al-Islam wal Muslimeen. 2021. "Targetting MINUSMA and Bamako Government Forces with Several Mines in Various Regions of Mali." *Az-Zallaqa Media Foundation* (blog). February 7.

Jama'at Nusrat al-Islam wal Muslimeen. 2022. "Our Jihad Is Ongoing and Our Operations Continue." *Az-Zallaqa Media Foundation* (blog). April 24.

Jenkins, Michael. 2018. *Does the U.S. No-Concessions Policy Deter Kidnappings of Americans?* Rand Corporation.

Johnston, Hugh Anthony Stephen. 1967. *The Fulani Empire of Sokoto*. Oxford University Press.

Johnston, Hugh Anthony Stephen, and D. J. M. Muffett. 1973. *Denham in Bornu: An Account of the Exploration of Bornu Between 1823 and 1825 by Major Dixon Denham, Dr. Oudney, and Commander Hugh Clapperton, and of Their Dealings with Sheik Muhammad El Amin El Kanemi*. Duquesne University Press.

Jones, Bruce, Fiona Hill, Tanvi Madan, Amanda Sloat, Mireya Solis, and Contanze Stelzenmüller. 2020. *Balancing Act: Major Powers and the Global Response to US-China Great Power Competition*. Interview by Bruce Jones. Edited by Jesse I. Kornbluth, with Emilie Kimball and Ted Reinert. Brookings Institution.

Joseph, Richard, and Jeffrey Herbst. 1997. "Responding to State Failure in Africa." *International Security* 22 (2): 175–184.

Kaba, Lansiné. 1984. "The Pen, the Sword, and the Crown: Islam and Revolution in Songhay Reconsidered, 1464–1493." *Journal of African History* 25 (3): 241–256. https://doi.org/10.1017/S0021853700028152.

Kagumire, Rosebell. 2020. "Black Lives Matter Resonates with Africans Pushing for Decolonisation." *IDEAS: Global Reporting Centre*, June 29.

Kajjo, Sirwan, and Boubacar Toure. 2021. "Malians Divided Over France's Decision to Close Bases, Reduce Forces." Voice of America, July 14.

Kassim, Lanre. 2015. "The Impact of Trade Liberalization on Export Growth and Import Growth in Sub-Saharan Africa." In *Regional Integration and Trade in Africa*, edited by Mthuli Ncube, Issa Faye, and Audrey Verdier-Chouchane, 47–68. Palgrave Macmillan.

Kelly, Fergus. 2020. "France Boosts Barkhane Force to 5,100 Troops to Further Focus on Mali-Burkina Faso-Niger Tri-Border Area." *The Defense Post*, February 2.

King, Isabelle. 2023. "How France Failed: The End of Operation Barkhane." *Harvard International Review* (blog), January 30. https://hir.harvard.edu/how-france-failed-mali-the-end-of-operation-barkhane/.

Kironska, Kristina, and Thiombiano Dramane. 2022. "How Taiwan Lost Africa, and What the Future Holds for Its Last Remaining Alliance with Eswatini." In *Africa-China-Taiwan Relations, 1949–2020*, edited by Sabella Ogbobode Abidde, 171–192. Lexington Books.

Klein, Martin A. 1998. *Slavery and Colonial Rule in French West Africa*. ACLS Humanities E-Book. Cambridge University Press.

Klein, Martin A. 2001. "The Slave Trade and Decentralized Societies." *Journal of African History* 42 (1): 49–65.
Kondratenko, Tatiana. 2020. "Russian Arms Exports to Africa: Moscow's Long-Term Strategy." Deutsche Welle, May 29. https://www.dw.com/en/russian-arms-exports-to-africa-moscows-long-term-strategy/a-53596471.
Koning, Edward Anthony. 2016. "The Three Institutionalisms and Institutional Dynamics: Understanding Endogenous and Exogenous Change." *Journal of Public Policy* 36 (4): 639–664.
Korkmaz, Tuğba. 2019. "'La Françafrique': The Special Relationship Between France and Its Former Colonies in Africa." *İnsani ve Sosyal Araştırmalar Merkezi*, August 2.
Kumi, Emmanuel, Thomas Yeboah, and Yaa Ankomaa Kumi. 2020. "Private Sector Participation in Advancing the Sustainable Development Goals (SDGs) in Ghana: Experiences from the Mining and Telecommunications Sectors." *Extractive Industries and Society* 7 (1): 181–190. https://doi.org/10.1016/j.exis.2019.12.008.
Lake, David A. 2018. "Economic Openness and Great Power Competition: Lessons for China and the United States." *Chinese Journal of International Politics* 11 (3): 237–270.
Langan, Mark. 2018. *Neo-Colonialism and the Poverty of "Development" in Africa*. Palgrave Macmillan.
Lavallee, Guillaume. 2019. "WhatsApp Becomes Battleground in Mali's Jihad Conflict." *Rappler*, November 5.
Lecocq, Baz, and Georg Klute. 2013. "Tuareg Separatism in Mali." *International Journal: Canada's Journal of Global Policy Analysis* 68 (33): 424–434.
Lecocq, Jean Sebastian. 2002. *That Desert Is Our Country: Tuareg Rebellions and Competing Nationalisms in Contemporary Mali (1946–1996)*. Universiteit van Amsterdam.
Le Roux, Pauline. 2019. "Ansaroul Islam: The Rise and Decline of a Militant Islamist Group in the Sahel." Africa Center for Strategic Studies.
Levtzion, Nehemia. 1973. *Ancient Ghana and Mali*. Methuen.
Levtzion, Nehemia, and Randall L. Pouwels, eds. 2000. *The History of Islam in Africa*. Ohio University Press.
Lijphart, Arend. 1971. "Comparative Politics and the Comparative Method." *American Political Science Review* 65 (3): 682–693.
Locherer, Theo. 2020. "Russia's Strategy in Africa." Global Risk Insights, October 4. https://globalriskinsights.com/2020/10/russias-strategy-in-africa/.
Lovejoy, Paul E. 1982. "The Volume of the Atlantic Slave Trade: A Synthesis." *Journal of African History* 23 (4): 473–501.
Lovejoy, Paul E. 2011. *Transformations in Slavery: A History of Slavery in Africa*. Cambridge University Press.
Lu, Hairong Yan, Barry Sautman, and Yao Lu. 2020. "Chinese and 'Self-Segregation' in Africa." In "Chinese in Africa: 'Chineseness' and the Complexities of Identities," special issue, *Asian Ethnicity* 20 (1): 40–66.
Luhmann, Niklas. 1995. *Social Systems*. Stanford University Press.
Lutz, Georg, and Wolf Linder. 2004. *Traditional Structures in Local Governance for Local Development*. University of Berne, Switzerland.
Macaulay, Cecilia, and Joseph Winter. 2023. "Burkina Faso Unrest: France Agrees to Pull Its Troops Out." Africa, *BBC News*, January 25.

MacEachern, Scott. 2018. *Searching for Boko Haram: A History of Violence in Central Africa*. Oxford University Press.

Mackinnon, Amy. 2020. "Why Russia and Turkey's Proxy War in Libya Is Heating Up." *Foreign Policy*, June 19.

Maclean, Ruth, Elian Peltier, and Eric Schmitt. 2023. "France to Pull Troops Out of Burkina Faso, as Its Unpopularity in Africa Grows." World, *New York Times*, January 25.

Mahoney, James, and Kathleen Thelen, eds. 2009. *Explaining Institutional Change: Ambiguity, Agency, and Power*. Cambridge University Press.

Mallet, Victor, Neil Munshi, and David Pilling. 2020. "Why Macron's Attempt to Reset French Ties to Africa Has Hit Trouble." *Financial Times*, October 27.

Mamdani, Mahmood. 1996. *Citizen and Subject: Contemporary Africa and the Legacy of Late Colonialism*. Princeton University Press.

Manning, Patrick. 2006. "Slavery and Slave Trade in West Africa, 1450–1930." In *Themes in West Africa's History*, edited by Emmanuel Kwaku Akyeampong, 99–117. Ohio University Press.

Marten, Kimberly. 2019. "Russia's Back in Africa: Is the Cold War Returning?" *Washington Quarterly* 42 (4): 155–170. https://doi.org/10.1080/0163660X.2019.1693105.

Mbaku, John. 2020. "Good and Inclusive Governance Is Imperative for Africa's Future." Brookings Institution, January 8.

McAlexander, Richard J., and Joan Ricart-Huguet. 2022. "State Disengagement: Evidence from French West Africa." *International Studies Quarterly* 66 (1): sqab040.

McGowan, Patrick J. 2003. "African Military Coups d'état, 1956–2001: Frequency, Trends and Distribution." *Journal of Modern African Studies* 41 (3): 339–370.

McKay, Andy, and Priya Deshingkar. 2014. "Internal Remittances and Poverty: Further Evidence from Africa and Asia." Migrating out of Poverty Working Paper 12, March. https://opendocs.ids.ac.uk/opendocs/handle/20.500.12413/14882.

McMillan, David W., and David M. Chavis. 1986. "Sense of Community: A Definition and Theory." *Journal of Community Psychology* 14 (1): 6–23.

Medeiros, Evan S. 2019. "The Changing Fundamentals of US-China Relations." *Washington Quarterly* 42 (3): 93–119. https://doi.org/10.1080/0163660X.2019.1666355.

Mednick, Sam. 2019. "In Burkina Faso, US Troops Train Local Soldiers." Pulitzer Center, August 11. https://pulitzercenter.org/stories/burkina-faso-us-troops-train-local-soldiers.

Mednick, Sam. 2023. "More Than 2 Million People Displaced, Burkina Faso's Government Says, As Aid Falls Short." Associated Press, June 5.

Meierding, Emily, and Rachel Sigman. 2021. "Understanding the Mechanisms of International Influence in an Era of Great Power Competition." *Journal of Global Security Studies* 6 (4): ogab011. https://doi.org/10.1093/jogss/ogab011.

Messier, Ronald A., and James A. Miller. 2015. *The Last Civilized Place: Sijilmasa and Its Saharan Destiny*. University of Texas Press.

Ministère de l'Europe et des Affaires étrangères. 2020. "G5 Sahel Joint Force and the Sahel Alliance—Ministry for Europe and Foreign Affairs." Ministère de l'Europe et Des Affaires Étrangères. https://web.archive.org/web/20211026103800/https://www.diplomatie.gouv.fr/en/french-foreign-policy

/security-disarmament-and-non-proliferation/crises-and-conflicts/g5-sahel-joint-force-and-the-sahel-alliance/.

Ministry of Finance. 2022. "2021 Debt Data." Government of Ghana. https://web.archive.org/web/20220713190743/https://mofep.gov.gh/sites/default/files/debt-data/2021-Debt-Data.xlsx.

MINUSMA. 2020. *Division Des Droits De L'Homme De La Protection.*

Mo, Pak Hung. 2001. "Corruption and Economic Growth." *Journal of Comparative Economics* 29 (1): 66–79.

Mohamed, Hamza. 2023. "Analysis: What's Next for Mali After MINUSMA Withdrawal?" Al Jazeera, July 3.

Morgan, Andy. 2012. "The Causes of the Uprising in Northern Mali." *Think Africa Press*, February 6.

Morgan, Pippa, and Yu Zheng. 2019. "Tracing the Legacy: China's Historical Aid and Contemporary Investment in Africa." *International Studies Quarterly* 63 (3): 558–573.

Morgan, Wesley. 2018. "Behind the Secret U.S. War in Africa." *Politico.* https://www.politico.com/story/2018/07/02/secret-war-africa-pentagon-664005.

Morgenthau, Ruth Schachter. 1964. *Political Parties in French-Speaking West Africa.* Clarendon Press.

Müller-Crepon, Carl. 2020. "Continuity or Change? (In)direct Rule in British and French Colonial Africa." *International Organization* 74 (4): 707–741.

Muvunyi, Fred. 2020. "Was Russia Behind the Coup in Mali?" Deutsche Welle, August 26. https://www.dw.com/en/was-russia-behind-the-coup-in-mali/a-54705282.

Myers, William M., and Kevin S. Fridy. 2017. "Formal Versus Traditional Institutions: Evidence from Ghana." *Democratization* 24 (2): 367–382.

Nantulya, Paul. 2019. "Implications for Africa from China's One Belt One Road Strategy." Africa Center for Strategic Studies, March 22, 2019. https://africacenter.org/spotlight/implications-for-africa-china-one-belt-one-road-strategy/.

Nasr, Wassim. 2022. "How the Wagner Group Is Aggravating the Jihadi Threat in the Sahel." *CTC Sentinel*, no. 11 (November–December): 21–30.

Naval Intelligence Division. 1944. *The Colonies.* Vol. 2 of *Geographical Handbook Series: French West Africa.* Oxford University Press.

Neethling, Theo. 2020. "Why Foreign Countries Are Scrambling to Set up Bases in Africa." *The Conversation,* September 15.

Neggaz, Nassima. 2012. "Dan Fodio, Usman (1754–1817)." In *The Princeton Encyclopedia of Islamic Political Thought*, edited by Gerhard Bowering, 125. Princeton University.

Newmont. 2022. *Sustainable Business. Enduring Value. 2022 Annual Report and Form 10-K.* Denver, CO. https://s24.q4cdn.com/382246808/files/doc_financials/2022/ar/Newmont-2022-Annual-Report.pdf.

Nexon, Daniel H. 2021. "Against Great Power Competition: The US Should Not Confuse Means for Ends." *Foreign Affairs,* February 15. https://www.foreignaffairs.com/articles/united-states/2021-02-15/against-great-power-competition.

Niane, Djibril Tamsir. 2016. "The Golden Age of Islam in the Sahel: The Example of Songhay Humanism." In *Islam in the World Today,* vol. 6 of *The Different Aspects of Islamic Culture*, edited by Abdulrahim Ali, Iba Der Thiam, and Yusof A. Talib, 52–62. UNESCO.

Nixon, Sam, Thilo Rehren, and Maria Filomena Guerra. 2011. "New Light on the Early Islamic West African Gold Trade: Coin Moulds from Tadmekka, Mali." *Antiquity* 85:1353–1368.

Nobili, Mauro, and Amir Syed. 2021. "Introduction. The Caliphate of Ḥamdallāhi: A History from Within." *Afriques*, no. 12 (December): 1–14. https://doi.org/10.4000/afriques.3203.

North, Douglass C. 1990. *Institutions, Institutional Change, and Economic Performance*. Cambridge University Press.

Nsaibia, Héni. 2023. "The Islamic State Sahel Province." ACLED, January 13. https://acleddata.com/2023/01/13/actor-profile-the-islamic-state-sahel-province/.

Nsaibia, Héni. 2024. "The Sahel: A Deadly New Era in the Decades-Long Conflict." ACLED Conflict Watchlist 2024, January 17. https://acleddata.com/conflict-watchlist-2024/sahel/.

Nunn, Nathan, and Leonard Wantchekon. 2011. "The Slave Trade and the Origins of Mistrust in Africa." *American Economic Review* 101 (7): 3221–3252.

Nur-Awaleh, Mohamed. 2006. "The Fulani Jihad and the Rise to Power in Hausaland in the 19th Century." In *The Histories, Languages, and Cultures of West Africa: Interdisciplinary Essays*, edited by Akua Sarr, 95–114. Edwin Mellon.

Nye, Joseph S. 1967. "Corruption and Political Development: A Cost-Benefit Analysis." *American Political Science Review* 61 (2): 417–427.

Nye, Joseph S. 1991. *Bound to Lead*. Basic Books.

Obaji, Philip. 2020a. "A Coup Won't End Mali's Corruption and Insecurity." *Foreign Policy*, August 19.

Obaji, Philip. 2020b. "Russia Trained the Mali Coup Leaders." *Daily Beast*, August 21.

Obaji, Philip. 2021. "How These Mali Coup Plotters Staged a False Flag Pro-Russia March." *Daily Beast*, June 2.

OECD (Organisation for Economic Co-operation and Development). 2019. *Converged Statistical Reporting Directives for the Creditor Reporting System (CRS) and the Annual DAC Questionnaire*. OECD. https://one.oecd.org/document/DCD/DAC/STAT(2018)9/ADD3/FINAL/en/pdf.

OECD. 2023a. "OECD.Stat." https://stats.oecd.org/.

OECD. 2023b. "Official Development Assistance—Definition and Coverage." OECD. http://www.oecd.org/development/financing-sustainable-development/development-finance-standards/officialdevelopmentassistancedefinitionandcoverage.htm.

Ofosu-Mensah, Emmanuel Ababio. 2011. "Historical Overview of Traditional and Modern Gold Mining in Ghana." *International Research Journal of Library, Information and Archival Studies* 1 (1): 6–22.

Oliver, Roland, ed. 1977. *From c. 1050 to c. 1600*. Vol. 3 of *The Cambridge History of Africa*. Cambridge University Press.

Onapajo, Hakeem, Ufo Okeke Uzodike, and Ayo Whetho. 2012. "Boko Haram Terrorism in Nigeria: The International Dimension." *South African Journal of International Affairs* 19 (3): 337–357.

Ortmann, Georges. 2017. "Deconstructing the Business of Terrorism: A Case Study of JNIM in Mali." Master's thesis, CERIS, Brussels.

Osoba, Segun O. 1996. "Corruption in Nigeria: Historical Perspectives." *Review of African Political Economy* 23 (69): 371–386.

Pan, Xiping, Jinghua Sha, Hongliang Zhang, and Wenlan Ke. 2014. "Relationship Between Corporate Social Responsibility and Financial Performance in the Mineral Industry: Evidence from Chinese Mineral Firms." *Sustainability* 6 (7): 4077–4101. https://doi.org/10.3390/su6074077.
Paquette, Danielle. 2020. "Mali Coup Leader Col. Assimi Goita Was Trained by U.S. Military." *Washington Post,* August 21.
Patterson, Soren. 2018. "Mapping China's Global Development Footprint." AidData. https://www.aiddata.org/china-project-locations.
PBS. 1999. "The Slave Kingdoms." *Wonders of the African World.* http://www.pbs.org/wonders/Episodes/Epi3/slave.htm.
Pieri, Zacharias. 2015. *Tablighi Jamaat and the Quest for the London Mega Mosque: Continuity and Change.* Routledge.
Pieri, Zacharias. 2019. *Boko Haram and the Drivers of Islamist Violence.* Routledge.
Pieri, Zacharias. 2021a. "The Islamic State in the Maghreb." In *Oxford Research Encyclopedia of African History.* Oxford University Press. https://doi.org/10.1093/acrefore/9780190277734.013.992.
Pieri, Zacharias. 2021b. "Tablighi Jamaat." In *Handbook of Islamic Sects and Movements,* edited by M. Afzal Upal and Carole Cusack, 49–72. Brill.
Pieri, Zacharias P., and Jessica M. Grosholz. 2023. "'Soldiers of the Faith': A Comparative Analysis of White Power Songs and Islamic State Nasheeds." *Deviant Behavior* 44 (1): 1–19. https://doi.org/10.1080/01639625.2021.1994359.
Pieri, Zacharias, and Jacob Zenn. 2016. "The Boko Haram Paradox: Ethnicity, Religion, and Historical Memory in Pursuit of a Caliphate." *African Security* 9 (1): 66–88. https://doi.org/10.1080/19392206.2016.1132906.
Pieri, Zacharias, and Jacob Zenn. 2018. "Under the Black Flag in Borno: Experiences of Foot Soldiers and Civilians in Boko Haram's 'Caliphate.'" *Journal of Modern African Studies* 56 (4): 645–672. https://doi.org/10.1017/S0022278X18000447.
Pokalova, Elena. 2023. "The Wagner Group in Africa: Russia's Quasi-State Agent of Influence." *Studies in Conflict & Terrorism,* 1–23.
Prezza, Miretta, and Stefano Costantini. 1998. "Sense of Community and Life Satisfaction: Investigation in Three Different Territorial Contexts." *Journal of Community & Applied Social Psychology* 8 (3): 181–194.
Ramani, Samuel. 2020a. "France and the United States Are Making West Africa's Security Situation Worse." *Foreign Policy,* September 12.
Ramani, Samuel. 2020b. "Why Russia Is a Geopolitical Winner in Mali's Coup." Foreign Policy Research Institute, September 16.
Ratha, Dilip, Supriyo De, Eung Ju Kim, Sonia Plaza, Ganesh Seshan, and Nadege Desiree Yameogo. 2019. "Data Release: Remittances to Low- and Middle-Income Countries on Track to Reach $551 Billion in 2019 and $597 Billion by 2021." *World Bank Blogs,* October 16.
Reid, Helen, and Kane Wu. 2021. "Hostility to Beijing Drives Chinese Gold Diggers into New Territory." Reuters, March 4.
Rempfer, Kyle. 2020. "How US Troops Survived a Little-Known al-Qaeda Raid in Mali Two Years Ago." *Military Times,* April 16.
Reuters. 2018. "Islamic State Claims Deadly Attack on Niger Army Base." March 4.
Reuters. 2019. "Burkina Faso's Latest Jihadist Threat: A Preacher Who Finds New Audience." November 11.

Reuters. 2020. "Jihadists Kill 28 in Attack on Military Convoy in Northeast Mali." December 16.
Reuters. 2021. "Suspected Islamist Militants Kill Eight in Attack in Niger Aid Convoy." November 15.
Reuters. 2022. "Russian Gold Miner Nordgold Shuts Burkina Faso Mine Citing Insecurity." April 11.
Reuters. 2023. "Burkina Faso Denies Favouring Russia's Nordgold over Gold Mine Permit." February 6.
RFI (Radio France Internationale). 2018. "Mali: Trois Chefs Jihadistes Ensemble Dans Une Video de Proagande." September 11.
RFI. 2025. "Cote d'Ivoire Announces French Military Exit After Decades-Long Stay." January 1.
Ricart-Huguet, Joan. 2022. "The Origins of Colonial Investments in Former British and French Africa." *British Journal of Political Science* 52 (2): 736–757.
Roberts, Richard L. 1996. *Two Worlds of Cotton: Colonialism and the Regional Economy in the French Soudan, 1800–1946*. Stanford University Press.
Robinson, David. 1985. *The Holy War of Umar Tal: The Western Sudan in the Mid-nineteenth Century*. Oxford University Press.
Robinson, David. 2000. *La Guerre Sainte d'Al-Hajj Umar—Le Soudan Occidental Au Milieu Du XIXe Siècle*. Paris, France: Karthala.
Rodney, Walter. 1967. *West Africa and the Atlantic Slave-Trade*. East African Publishing House.
Rodney, Walter. 1981. *How Europe Underdeveloped Africa*. Howard University.
Rodríguez, Francisco Medina. 2007. "Precisions on the History of Quinine." *Reumatología Clínica* 3 (4): 194–196. https://doi.org/10.1016/S2173-5743(07)70246-0.
Rolbiecki, Tomasz, Pieter Van Ostaeyen, and Charlie Winter. 2020. "The Islamic State's Strategic Trajectory in Africa: Key Takeaways from Its Attack Claims." *CTC Sentinel* 13 (8): 31–40.
Rothstein, Bo, and Eric M. Uslaner. 2005. "All for All: Equality, Corruption, and Social Trust." *World Politics* 58 (1): 41–72.
Roy, Porter. 1998. *The Greatest Benefit to Mankind: A Medical History of Humanity*. W. W. Norton.
Sachs, Jeffrey. 2005. *The End of Poverty: Growing The World's Wealth in an Age of Extremes*. Penguin Press.
Sangare, Boukary. 2019. "Fulani People and Jihadism in the Sahel and West African Countries." Fondation Pour La Recherche Strategique, February 8.
Savell, Stephanie. 2021. *United States Counterterrorism Operations: 2018–2020*. Costs of War, Watson Institute for International and Public Affairs, Brown University. https://watson.brown.edu/costsofwar/files/cow/imce/papers/2021/US Counterterrorism Operations 2018-2020%2C Costs of War.pdf.
Schatzberg, Michael G. 2001. *Political Legitimacy in Middle Africa: Father, Family, Food*. Indiana University Press.
Schmidt, Elizabeth. 2013. *Foreign Intervention in Africa: From the Cold War to the War on Terror*. Cambridge University Press.
Sears, Caitlyn. 2019. "What Counts as Foreign Aid: Dilemmas and Ways Forward in Measuring China's Overseas Development Flows." *Professional Geographer* 71 (1): 135–144.
Security Council Report. 2023. "Mali: Vote on Resolution Ending the UN Multidimensional Integrated Stabilization Mission in Mali." *What's in Blue*, June

29. https://www.securitycouncilreport.org/whatsinblue/2023/06/mali-vote-on-resolution-ending-the-un-multidimensional-integrated-stabilization-mission-in-mali.php.

Selmier, W. Travis. 2015. "Writing the Social Contract: Integrating the UN Global Compact and Mining CSR." In *The UN Global Compact: Fair Competition and Environmental and Labour Justice in International Markets*, 83–101. Emerald Group Publishing.

Selmier, W. Travis, and Aloysius Newenham-Kahindi. 2021. "Communities of Place, Mining Multinationals and Sustainable Development in Africa." *Journal of Cleaner Production* 292 (April): 125709. https://doi.org/10.1016/j.jclepro.2020.125709.

Sèni, Lazoumou. 1985. *La Lutte Du Burkina Contre La Colonisation: Le Cas de La Région Ouest, 1915–1916*. Ouagadougou: Imprimerie des Forces Armées Nationales.

Serwat, Ladd. 2024. "Burkina Faso: Escalating JNIM and Military Operations Lead to Deadliest Month of 2024." ACLED, June 10. https://acleddata.com/2024/06/10/africa-overview-may-2024/#keytrends1.

Sibiri, Hagan. 2021. "The Emerging Phenomenon of Anti-Chinese Populism in Africa: Evidence from Zambia, Zimbabwe and Ghana." *Insight on Africa* 13 (1): 7–27.

Sieff, Kevin. 2017. "The World's Deadliest U.N. Mission." *Washington Post*, February 17.

Singh, Ajit. 2020. "The Myth of 'Debt-Trap Diplomacy'and Realities of Chinese Development Finance." *Third World Quarterly* 42 (2): 239–253.

Singh, Naunihal. 2014. *Seizing Power: The Strategic Logic of Military Coups*. Johns Hopkins University.

Singh, Naunihal. 2021. "Stagnation in US-Africa Military Policy After US Servicemembers' Deaths in Niger." *Orbis* 65 (3): 448–466.

SIPRI (Stockholm International Peace Research Institute). 2023a. "Arms Transfers Database." SIPRI. https://www.sipri.org/databases/armstransfers.

SIPRI. 2023b. "SIPRI Arms Transfers Database - Sources and Methods." SIPRI. https://www.sipri.org/databases/armstransfers/sources-and-methods.

Smith, Anthony. 1997. "The 'Golden Age' and National Renewal." In *Myths and Nationhood*, edited by Geoffrey Hosking and George Schöpflin, 36–59. Routledge.

Smith, H. 1962. "Nineteenth-Century Arabic Archives of West Africa." *Journal of African History* 3 (2): 333–336.

Stepansky, Joseph. 2020. "Challenges Ahead as UN Set to Extend 'Most Dangerous' Mission." Al Jazeera, June 26.

Stiglitz, Joseph E. 1999. "Formal and Informal Institutions." In *Social Capital: A Multifaceted Perspective*, edited by Partha Dasgupta and Ismail Serageldin, 59–70. World Bank.

Stone, Gilbert. 1920. "The Mining Laws of the West African Colonies and Protectorates." *Journal of Comparative Legislation and International Law* 2 (3): 259–266.

Stride, George T., and Caroline Ifeka. 1971. *Peoples and Empires of West Africa: West Africa in History, 1000–1800*. Africana Publishing Corporation.

Stronski, Paul. 2019. *Late to the Party: Russia's Return to Africa*. Carnegie Endowment for International Peace. https://carnegieendowment.org/2019/10/16/late-to-party-russia-s-return-to-africa-pub-80056.

Swindell, Kenneth. 1995. "People on the Move in West Africa: From Pre-colonial Polities to Post-independence States." In *The Cambridge Survey of World Migration*, edited by Robin Cohen, 196–202. Cambridge University Press.

Syed, Amir. 2021. "Political Theology in Nineteenth-Century West Africa: Al-Ḥājj ʿUmar, the *Bayān Mā Waqaʿa*, and the Conquest of the Caliphate of Ḥamdallāhi." *Journal of African History* 62 (3): 358–376. https://doi.org/10.1017/S0021853721000505.

Tastekin, Fehim. 2020. "Does France's Failure in Mali Spell a Victory for Turkey?" *Al-Monitor*.

Telepneva, Natalia. 2018. "Saving Ghana's Revolution: The Demise of Kwame Nkrumah and the Evolution of Soviet Policy in Africa, 1966–1972." *Journal of Cold War Studies* 20 (4): 4–25.

Thomas, Dominic. 2006. *Black France: Colonialism, Immigration, and Transnationalism*. Indiana University.

Thomas, Roger G. 1973. "Forced Labour in British West Africa: The Case of the Northern Territories of the Gold Coast 1906-1927." *Journal of African History* 14 (1): 79–103.

Thomas, Roger G. 1974. "Education in Northern Ghana, 1906–1940: A Study in Colonial Paradox." *International Journal of African Historical Studies* 7 (3): 427–467.

Thompson, Brad. 2020. "China Snares Aussie Gold Player, $660m Russia Offer Too Slow." *Australian Financial Review*, December 24.

Thompson, Jared. 2021. "Examining Extremism: Jama'at Nasr al-Islam Wal Muslimin." Center for Strategic & International Studies (blog post), July 15.

Thompson, Jared, Catrina Doxsee, and Joseph S. Burmudez. 2022. "Tracking the Arrival of Russia's Wagner Group in Mali." Center for Strategic Studies, February. https://www.csis.org/analysis/tracking-arrival-russias-wagner-group-mali.

Thornton, John. 1998. *Africa and Africans in the Making of the Atlantic World, 1400–1800*. Cambridge University Press.

Thurston, Alex. 2015. "On Seku Amadu and the Movement for the Liberation of Masina." *Sahel Blog*, May 8. https://sahelblog.wordpress.com/2015/05/08/on-seku-amadu-and-the-movement-for-the-liberation-of-masina/.

Tilly, Charles. 1985. "War Making and State Making as Organized Crime." In *Bringing the State Back In*, edited by Peter B. Evans, Dietrich Rueschemeyer, and Theda Skocpol, 169–191. Cambridge University Press.

Transparency International. 2021. "Global Corruption Barometer." https://www.transparency.org/en/gcb.

Transparency International. 2022. "Corruption Perception Index." https://www.transparency.org/en/cpi/2022.

Trimingham, J. Spencer. 1959. *Islam in West Africa*. Clarendon Press.

Trimingham, J. Spencer. 1962. *A History of Islam in West Africa*. Oxford University.

Tsai, Kellee S. 2006. "Adaptive Informal Institutions and Endogenous Institutional Change in China." *World Politics* 59 (1): 116–141.

Tsikudo, Kwame Adovor. 2021. "Soft Powering the China Water Machine: The Bui Dam and China–Ghana Relations." *Canadian Journal of African Studies* 56 (2), 319–339. https://doi.org/10.1080/00083968.2021.1929360.

Turse, Nick. 2020. "Pentagon's Own Map of U.S. Bases in Africa Contradicts Its Claim of 'Light' Footprint." *The Intercept*, February 27.

Turse, Nick. 2023. "American Trained Soldiers Keep Overthrowing Governments in Africa." *Rolling Stone*, February 25.

Unger, Richard W. 1995. "Portuguese Shipbuilding and the Early Voyages to the Guinea Coast." In *The European Opportunity*, edited by Felipe Fernández-Armesto, 43–63. Routledge.

United Nations. 2018. "Report of the Secretary General on the Threat Posed by ISIL (Da'esh) to International Peace and Security and the Range of United Nations Efforts in Support of Member States in Countering the Threat." https://undocs.org/S/2018/705.

United Nations Department of Economic and Social Affairs. 2023. "UN Comtrade Database." https://comtradeplus.un.org/TradeFlow.

United Nations Peacekeeping. 2023. "MINUSMA Fact Sheet." https://peacekeeping.un.org/en/mission/minusma.

United States Africa Command. 2019. *FY20 Theater Posture Plan*. https://www.africom.mil/document/33250/fy20-theater-posture-plan-october-2019.pdf.

United States House of Representatives. 2016. "10 USC 127e: Support of Special Operations to Combat Terrorism." Office of the Law Revision Counsel United States Code. https://uscode.house.gov/view.xhtml?req=granuleid:USC-prelim-title10-section127e&num=0&edition=prelim.

USAID. 2014a. *Country Development Cooperation Strategy: Mali Forward, 2015–2020*. USAID Mali Mission.

USAID. 2014b. *West Africa: Regional Development Cooperation Strategy, 2015–2020*. USAID West Africa Regional Mission.

USAID. 2019. *Ghana: Country Development Cooperation Strategy, 2020–2025*. USAID Ghana Mission.

US Department of State and USAID. 2023. "Data." ForeignAssistance.gov. https://foreignassistance.gov/data.

Usman, Zainab. 2021. "What Do We Know About Chinese Lending in Africa?" Carnegie Endowment for International Peace, June 2. https://carnegieendowment.org/2021/06/02/what-do-we-know-about-chinese-lending-in-africa-pub-84648.

Uzoigwe, G. N. 1985. "European Partition and Conquest of Africa: An Overview." In *Africa Under Colonial Domination, 1880–1935*, vol. 7 of *General History of Africa*, edited by Albert Adu Boahen, 19–44. ,. UNESCO.

Vaillant, Janet G. 2006. *Vie de Léopold Sédar Senghor: Noir, Français et Africain*. Karthala.

Valkenier, Elizabeth Kridl. 1980. "Great Power Economic Competition in Africa: Soviet Progress and Problems." *Journal of International Affairs* 34 (2): 259–268.

van de Camp, Esther. 2016. "Artisanal Gold Mining in Kejetia (Tongo, Northern Ghana): A Three-Dimensional Perspective." *Third World Thematics* 1 (2): 267–283.

van Staden, Cobus. 2022. "Fears of a Chinese Naval Base in West Africa Are Overblown." *Foreign Policy*, March 3.

Vermeersch, Elise, Julie Coleman, Meryl Demuynck, and Elena Dal Santo. 2020. "The Role of Social Media in Mali and Its Relation to Violent Extremism: A Youth Perspective." The International Center for Counter-Terrorism.

Vertin, Zach. 2020. *Great Power Rivalry in the Red Sea: China's Experiment in Djibouti and Implications for the United States*. Brookings Institution.

Waddington, Conway. 2013. "AFRICOM-Led Multinational Training Exercises in West Africa." *Africa Conflict Monthly Monitor*, no. 05 (May): 45–49.
Walker, Andrew. 2016. "Join Us or Die: The Birth of Boko Haram." *The Guardian* (blog), February 4. https://www.theguardian.com/world/2016/feb/04/join-us-or-die-birth-of-boko-haram.
Wallerstein, Immanuel. 1974. *The Modern World System: Capitalist Agriculture and the Origins of the European World Economy in the Sixteenth Century*. Academic Press.
Wang, Rong, François Bar, and Yu Hong. 2020. "ICT Aid Flows from China to African Countries: A Communication Network Perspective." *International Journal of Communication* 14:26.
Wang, Yaqiu. 2021. "From Covid to Blackface on TV, China's Racism Problem Runs Deep." Human Rights Watch, February 18.
Wang, Yi. 2022. "China and Africa: Strengthening Friendship, Solidarity and Cooperation for a New Era of Common Development." Ministry of Foreign Affairs of the People's Republic of China. https://www.fmprc.gov.cn/eng/zxxx_662805/202208/t20220819_10745617.html.
Warner, Jason. 2017. "Sub-Saharan Africa's Three New Islamic State Affiliates." *CTC Sentinel* 10 (1): 28–32.
Warner, Jason. 2020. "A View from the CT Foxhole: Brigadier General Dagvin R. M. Anderson, Commander, U.S. Special Operations Command Africa." *CTC Sentinel* 13 (2): 9–14.
Warner, Tobias. 2016. "Para-Literary Ethnography and Colonial Self-Writing: The Student Notebooks of the William Ponty School." *Research in African Literatures* 47 (1): 1–20. https://doi.org/10.2979/reseafrilite.47.1.1.
Webster, James Bertin, A. Adu Boahen, and H. O. Idowu. 1967. *The Revolutionary Years: Africa Since 1800*. Longmans.
Wegenast, Tim, Mario Krauser, Georg Strüver, and Juliane Giesen. 2019. "At Africa's Expense? Disaggregating the Employment Effects of Chinese Mining Operations in Sub-Saharan Africa." *World Development* 118 (June): 39–51.
Whatley, Warren C. 2018. "The Gun-Slave Hypothesis and the 18th Century British Slave Trade." *Explorations in Economic History* 67:80–104.
Whitehouse, Bruce. 2012. "The Force of Action: Legitimizing the Coup in Bamako, Mali." *Africa Spectrum* 47 (2–3): 93–110.
Whittlesey, Derwent. 1937. "British and French Colonial Technique in West Africa." *Foreign Affairs* 15 (2): 362–373.
Wilkins, Henry. 2022. "Deaths, Instability Increase Across the Western Sahel in 2022." Voice of America, December 29.
Wilks, Ivor. 1975. *Asante in the Nineteenth Century: The Structure and Evolution of a Political Order*. Cambridge University Press.
Wilks, Ivor. 1982a. "Wangara, Akan and Portuguese in the Fifteenth and Sixteenth Centuries. I. The Matter of Bitu." *Journal of African History* 23 (3): 333–349.
Wilks, Ivor. 1982b. "Wangara, Akan and Portuguese in the Fifteenth and Sixteenth Centuries. II. The Struggle for Trade." *Journal of African History* 23 (4): 463–472. https://doi.org/10.1017/S0021853700021307.
Wilks, Ivor. 1999. "The History of the Sunjata Epic: A Review of the Evidence." In *In Search of Sunjata: The Mande Oral Epic as History, Literature, and Performance*, edited by Ralph A. Austen, 25–58. Indiana University Press.
Wing, Susanna D. 2013. "Mali: Politics of a Crisis." *African Affairs* 112 (448): 476–485. https://doi.org/10.1093/afraf/adt037.

Winter, Charlie. 2015. *Documenting the Virtual Caliphate*. Quilliam.
World Bank. 2023a. "General Government Final Consumption Expenditure (Current US$)." World Bank Open Data. https://data.worldbank.org.
World Bank. 2023b. "World Integrated Trade Solution (WITS)." https://wits.worldbank.org/.
World Gold Council. 2023. "Gold Mine Production." https://www.gold.org/goldhub/data/historical-mine-production.
Zajontz, Tim. 2022. "The Chinese Infrastructural Fix in Africa: Lessons from the Sino-Zambian 'Road Bonanza.'" *Oxford Development Studies* 50 (1): 14–29.
Zenn, Jacob. 2017. "AQIM's Alliance in Mai: Prospects for Jihadist Preeminence in West Africa." *Terrorism Monitor*, no. 15.
Zenn, Jacob, and Colin P. Clarke. 2020. "Al Qaeda and ISIS Had a Truce in Africa—Until They Didn't." *Foreign Policy*, May 26.
Zenn, Jacob, and Zacharias Pieri. 2017. "How Much Takfir Is Too Much Takfir? The Evolution of Boko Haram's Factionalization." *Journal of Deradicalization* 11 (2): 281–308.
Ziegler, Charles E., and Rajan Menon. 2014. "Neomercantilism and Great-Power Energy Competition in Central Asia and the Caspian." *Strategic Studies Quarterly* 8 (2): 17–41.
Zimmerer, Megan. 2019. "Terror in West Africa: A Threat Assessment of the New Al Qaeda Affiliate in Mali." *Critical Studies on Terrorism* 12 (3): 491–511.
Zounmenou, David. 2013. "The National Movement for the Liberation of Azawad Factor in the Mali Crisis." *Africa Security Review* 22 (3): 167–174.

Index

Abidjan, 52, 54, 55
Accra, 54, 55, 119
ACLED. *See* Armed Conflict Location and Event Data
Afghanistan, 81–82
Africa Command (AFRICOM), 119
Africa Corps, 14*n*1
African Command, 9
African Development Bank, 89, 131
African Lion, 119
Ahmad II, 29, 30, 31
Ahmad III, 29, 31, 32
Ahmadu, Seku, 7, 15, 18, 38, 174; dan Fodio and, 25, 26; Macina Empire and, 20, 24–28, 31, 37, 68, 174; in Mali, 22
Al-Ansari, al-Hasan, 66
Ali, Sonni, 44–47
Amir al-mu'minin (commander of the faithful), 17, 27
Anderson, Dagvin, 39–40, 80
AngloGold Ashanti, 136
Ansar Dine, 3, 65, 66, 67, 68
Ansarul Islam (Defenders of Islam), 13, 19, 21, 38; in Burkina Faso, 30–31, 62, 70–71; Fulani in, 77–80; in Mopti Region, 85; precolonial caliphates and empires and, 173–174; in Sahel Region, 91
AQIM. *See* Al-Qaeda in the Islamic Maghreb
Ariotti, Margaret H., 30

Armed Conflict Location and Event Data (ACLED), 9, 63, 178, 178*tab*
Asante kingdom, 44–45, 52–53
Australia, gold and, 135–136, 176
Az-Zallaqa media center, 64

B2Gold, 136
Babatu, 53
Al-Baghdadi, Abubakar, 71
Bakka'iyya, 30
Bamako, 8, 54, 79, 119
Bambara kingdom, 17, 21, 26, 27
Bandiagara cliff, 27
Barkahe force, 3, 78
Bassam, 52
Battle of Kirina, 43
Bello, Muhammad, 28, 32, 33
Belmokhtar, Mokhtar, 66, 71
Belt and Road Initiative, 39, 120, 151
Ben Muhammad, Ahmad. *See* Ahmadu, Seku
Ben Said, al-Hajj Umar. *See* Umar, al-Hajj
Benin, 61, 73
Berlin Conference, 49–50
Beyoncé, 167, 169*n*1
Biden, Joe, 151
Bight of Benin, 47
Boko Haram, 6, 7, 38; corruption and, 89–93; Islamic State and, 16; ISWAP and, 61, 71–72; Kanuri kingdom and, 24; in Lake Chad

Basin, 88; local perception of, 109–111; perspectives on the West by, 73–77; precolonial caliphates and empires and, 173–174
Bolduc, Donald, 9
Borno Empire, 32, 33, 35
Brazil, 48
Britain (United Kingdom), 44, 50; in Burkina Faso, 51–52; in Ghana, 50, 52–53, 57–58; gold and, 136; GPC perceived behaviors of, 152–157, 153*fig*; mega-cities and, 54; ODA from, 130–131
Brown, William, 25, 26, 37
Brown University, 119
Burkina Faso (Upper Volta), 1–14, 10*fig*, 25; Ansarul Islam in, 30–31, 62, 70–71; China in, 13; colonialism in, 6, 51–52; corruption in, 91–93, 100–103, 101*tab*, 115, 174–175; coups in, 1, 3, 8, 56, 57, 83, 87; data on, 9–11; debt burden in, 131; France in, 31, 50, 51–52, 57, 73, 76, 83; Fulani in, 34, 46, 70, 77–80; GPC Global South impact and, 165–169; GPC governance impact on, 157–165, 159*fig*, 161*fig*–163*fig*, 164*tab*, 166*fig*; GPC in, 2, 117–140; GPC military relations in, 118–125, 122*tab*, 140*tab*; GPC mineral extraction in, 132–137, 132*fig*, 139, 140*tab*; GPC perceived behaviors by, 152–157, 153*fig*, 155*tab*; GPC perceived impact of, 147–152, 149*fig*, 150*fig*; GPC perceived nature in, 143–152, 144*fig*–146*fig*, 148*fig*–150*fig*; grievances in, 88, 91, 93–104, 94*tab*, 101*tab*; independence of, 56–57; ISGS in, 62–63, 109; jihadists in, 3, 12–13, 30–31, 38, 87–116, 173; jihadists perception in, 108–112; JNIM in, 62–63, 76, 108–109; local resistance in, 87–116; Macina Empire and, 30–31; Mossi in, 46, 51, 85; ODA for, 125–131, 126*fig*, 129*fig*, 138–139, 140*tab*; Ouagadougou in, 3, 52, 54, 55, 91, 119; perspectives on the West in, 112–114, 113*tab*; Sahelian empires in, 47; SCI in, 177–179, 178*tab*; security perception in, 104–108, 106*tab*; Slave Kingdom of, 49; in Songhai Empire, 45–46; US in, 13; VEOs in, 2, 65–73; violence perception in, 105–108, 107*tab*; Wagner Group in, 175. *See also* Centre-Sud Region; Sahel Region
Bush, George W., 151
By France, 48
Bybee, Ashley N., 31

Cameroon, 18, 33
Canada, gold and, 136, 176
Canary Islands, 48
Censor of Public Morals, 29
Center (*markaz*), 69
Central African Republic, 33, 40
Centre-Sud Region, 11; GPC in, 117–140, 140*tab*; GPC military relations in, 140*tab*; independence for, 55; mineral extraction in, 134; ODA for, 128, 138
Chad, 1, 8, 18, 121
Cheru, Fantu, 157
Chifeng Jilong Gold Mining, 135
Chilson, Peter, 68–69, 78
China, 13; Belt and Road Initiative of, 39, 120, 151; Global South and, 40; gold and, 135–136, 137, 156, 176–177; GPC perceived behaviors of, 152–157, 153*fig*, 155*tab*; jihadists and, 83; military relations with, 120–121; mineral extraction and, 132–137, 132*fig*, 133*fig*, 139; naval base for, 140*n*1; ODA from, 128–130, 129*tab*, 138–139; perceived impact of, 147–152, 149*fig*, 150*fig*; perceived nature of, 143–147, 144*fig*–146*fig*, 148*fig*; in Upper East Region, 57; US and, 39–40; in West Africa, 7
Christchurch, New Zealand mosque shooting, 74–75
Cline, Lawrence E., 36
Clinton, Bill, 151
Cold War, 40; mineral extraction in, 132; in West Africa, 1. *See also* Post-Cold War
Colonialism: Cold War and, 54–57; direct and indirect rule in, 47–54;

GPC and, 39–59; grievances and, 40–41; independence from, 54–57; Islamic states and, 173; of Macina Empire, 19; of Sokoto Caliphate, 19. *See also* Neocolonialism; *specific colonized and colonizing countries*
Commander of the faithful (*amir al-mu'minin*), 17, 27
Compaoré, Blaise, 56–57
Corporate social responsibility (CSR), 136–137
Corruption, 89–93, 100–103, 101*tab*, 115, 174–175
Costs of War project, 119
Côte d'Ivoire, 3, 8, 52, 61, 63, 121
Counterterrosism, 83, 119, 121–123
Coups, 1; in Burkina Faso, 3, 8, 56, 57, 83, 87; in Chad, 8; in Ghana, 56; in Mali, 8, 56, 83, 87, 123–124, 144
Covid-19 pandemic, 147
CSR. *See* Corporate social responsibility

DAC. *See* Development Assistance Committee
Dagomba, 46, 52, 54
Dahomey kingdom, 44–45
Dakar, 52, 55
Damiba, Paul-Henri, 119
Dan Fodio, Usman, 7, 17, 22–25, 38, 174; Ahmadu and, 25, 26; books by, 28; Hausa kingdoms and, 22, 26
Davis, Charles, 35
Debt burden, 131
Déby, Mahamat Idriss, 8
Defenders of Islam. *See* Ansarul Islam
Delafosse, Maurice, 34
Development Assistance Committee (DAC), 125
Dicko, Ibrahim, 30–31, 69–70, 79, 91
Dicko, Jafar, 71
Diendéré, Gilbert, 119
Digital media, 64–65
Dina, 29
Djelgoji, 24–25, 30, 31
Djenne, 45
Djibo, 30
Dogon ethnic group, 11
Droukdel, Abdelmalek, 66

École William Ponty, 54
Emigration (hijra), 23–24
Endeavor, 136
Essakane, 139
European Union, 121, 140*tab*, 143–147, 144*fig*–146*fig*, 148*fig*
Excommunication (*takfir*), 23–24
Exit, Voice, Loyalty game, 58
Extrajudicial killings, 92–93

Facebook, 3, 78
Firearms, 49
Flintlock, 119
Food insecurity, 63
Forum on China-Africa Cooperation, 40
France, 2, 44, 60*n*3; Barkahe force of, 3, 78; in Burkina Faso, 31, 50, 51–52, 57, 73, 76; Burkina Faso and, 83; Chad and, 8; in Ghana, 53; gold and, 176; GPC perceived behaviors of, 152–157, 153*fig*, 155*tab*; jihadist attitudes toward, 73–74; JNIM and, 67; in Mali, 4, 8–9, 50, 57, 67–68, 73, 81, 82–83, 175–176; mega-cities and, 54; military relations with, 121–122; in Mopti Region, 50, 51; neocolonialism of, 8, 74; Niger and, 83; ODA from, 130–131; as outlier, 177; perceived impact of, 147–152, 149*fig*, 150*fig*; in post-Cold War, 39; in Sahel Region, 8–9, 50, 76–77; in Sudan, 51, 52; Tukolor Empire and, 33
Fridy, Kevin S., 30
Fulani, 3, 4, 11; Ahmadu and, 26, 27; Ansar Dine and, 68; in Ansarul Islam, 69; in Burkina Faso, 30–31, 46, 70; conceptualization of, 33–36; dan Fodio and, 24; Djelgogi and, 24–25; GPC governance impact on, 157–165, 159*fig*, 161*fig*–163*fig*, 164*tab*, 166*fig*; grievances of, 33, 62, 68, 77–80; jihadists and, 17, 33, 77–80, 85–86; in Macina Empire, 17–18, 25, 36, 37, 51; in Macina Liberation Front, 66, 85; in Mali, 23, 124; origins of, 34–35; slave trade and, 45–46; in Sokoto Caliphate, 37; in Timbuktu, 30

Futa Jallon, 18
Futa Toro, 18
Futi Tall, al-Hajj Umar. *See* Umar, al-Hajj

G5, 76, 78, 121–123
Gabon, 1
Galamsey, 135
Gao, 16, 21, 45
Germany, 50; in Burkina Faso, 51–52; in Ghana, 53; GPC perceived behaviors of, 152–157, 153*fig*; ODA from, 130–131; perceived impact of, 147–152, 149*fig*, 150*fig*
Al-Ghali, Muhammad, 33
Ghaly, Iyad Ag, 66, 69, 80, 81
Ghana, 10*fig*; Britain in, 50, 52–53, 57–58; China in, 13, 121; colonialism in, 6; corruption in, 91–93, 100–103, 101*tab*, 115, 174–175; coups in, 56; Dagomba in, 46, 52, 54; data on, 9–11; debt burden in, 131; Fulani in, 34; GPC Global South impact and, 165–169; GPC governance impact on, 157–165, 159*fig*, 161*fig*–163*fig*, 164*tab*, 166*fig*; GPC in, 2, 117–140; GPC military relations in, 118–125, 122*tab*, 140*tab*; GPC mineral extraction in, 132–137, 133*fig*, 139, 140*tab*; GPC perceived behaviors by, 152–157, 153*fig*, 155*tab*; GPC perceived impact of, 147–152, 149*fig*, 150*fig*; GPC perceived nature in, 143–152, 144*fig*–146*fig*, 148*fig*–150*fig*; grievances in, 88, 93–104, 94*tab*, 101*tab*; independence for, 54–57; ISGS in, 109; jihadists in, 63, 87–116; jihadists perception in, 108–112; local resistance in, 87–116; ODA for, 125–131, 126*fig*, 129*fig*, 138–139, 140*tab*; perspectives on the West in, 112–114, 113*tab*; Portugal in, 47–48; Sahelian empires in, 47; SCI in, 177–179, 178*tab*; security perception in, 104–108, 106*tab*; Slave Kingdom of, 49; slave trade in, 53; US in, 13; VEOs in, 2; violence perception in, 105–108, 107*tab*; Wagadou empire in, 42–43, 59n1. *See also* Upper East Region
Global Corruption Barometer, 91–92
Global South: China and, 40; GPC in, 165–169
Global war on terror, 2, 119–120
Gobir, 22–23, 25
Goïta, Assimi, 82, 119
Gold, 42–44, 47–48, 53, 134–135, 137, 139; China and, 135–136, 156, 176–177
Gold Coast, 53, 55
Gold Fields, 136
Gold Star, 136
Gonja, 52
Governance: defined, 5; endogenous factors in, 6; GPC and, 157–165, 159*fig*, 161*fig*–163*fig*, 164*tab*, 166*fig*. *See also specific topics*
Great power competition (GPC), 117–140; colonialism and, 39–59; in Global South, 165–169; governance and, 157–165, 159*fig*, 161*fig*–163*fig*, 164*tab*, 166*fig*; grievances and, 13–14; military relations in, 118–125, 122*tab*, 140*tab*; in mineral extraction, 132–137, 132*fig*, 133*fig*, 139, 140*tab*; ODA in, 125–131, 126*fig*, 129*fig*, 140*tab*, 157; perceived behaviors of, 152–157, 153*fig*, 155*tab*; perceived impact of, 147–152, 149*fig*, 150*fig*; perceived nature of, 143–148, 144*fig*–146*fig*, 148*fig*–150*fig*; VEOs and, 171–180, 178*tab*; in West Africa, 2–14. *See also specific countries*
Grievances: of Boko Haram, 88; in Burkina Faso, 88, 91, 93–104, 94*tab*, 101*tab*; colonialism and, 40–41; of Fulani, 33, 62, 68, 77–80; in Ghana, 88, 93–104, 94*tab*, 101*tab*; GPC and, 13–14; of jihadists, 7, 13, 33, 77–80; in Mali, 88, 90–91, 93–104, 94*tab*, 101*tab*; VEOs and, 13–14; in West Africa, 4–5, 7, 13
Guerrillas, 64
Guinea, 1, 57
Gulf of Guinea, 11
Gur, 46

Gurune, GPC governance impact on, 157–165, 159*fig*, 161*fig*–163*fig*, 164*tab*, 166*fig*

Hamdullahi, 26–30
Harris, Kamala, 151
Hausa kingdoms, 17, 21, 22, 24–25, 26, 35, 36
Al-Hayat media center, 64
Hijra (emigration), 23–24
Hiskett, Mervyn, 21
Huillery, Elise, 60*n*3
Hummingbird, 136

Iam Gold, 136
ICT. *See* Information and communication technology
Indirect military intervention, 119–120
Information and communication technology (ICT), 129–130
IS Sahel. *See* Islamic State in the Greater Sahara
ISGS. *See* Islamic State in the Greater Sahara
Islamic State (jihadist group), 1, 61; Boko Haram and, 16; digital media of, 65; ISGS and, 71; in Mali, 123; in Sahel Region, 173
Islamic State in Iraq and Syria, 124
Islamic State in the Greater Sahara (ISGS, IS Sahel), 84–85; Ansarul Islam and, 71; in Benin, 73; in Burkina Faso, 3, 13, 62–63, 109; corruption and, 89–93; Fulani in, 77–80; in Ghana, 109; JNIM and, 65, 72; local perception of, 108–111; in Mali, 62–63, 74, 80–84; negotiations with, 80–84; in Niger, 62–63, 77; perspectives on the West by, 73–77
Islamic State West Africa Province (ISWAP), 61, 71–72
Islamic State-affiliated organizations, 24, 62, 72–73. *See also specific organizations*
Islamic states, 6; Ansarul Islam and, 70; colonialism and, 173; JNIM and, 79–80; Tablighi Jamaat and, 69
ISWAP. *See* Islamic State West Africa Province

Jama'at Nusrat al Islam (JNIM), 3, 6, 13, 84–85; attitude toward US by, 75; Az-Zallaqa media center of, 64; in Burkina Faso, 62–63, 76, 108–109; corruption and, 89–93; exogenous shocks from, 6; Fulani in, 77–80; ISGS and, 65, 72; kidnapping for ransom by, 67–68; local perception of, 108–111; in Mali, 62–63, 66–68, 72, 80–84, 108–109; MINUSMA and, 82; nation-states and, 173; negotiations with, 80–84; in Niger, 62–63, 68; perspectives on the West by, 73–77; Wagner Group and, 176. *See also* Al-Mourabitoun; Al-Qaeda in the Islamic Maghreb; Ansar Dine; Macina Liberation Front
Japan, 130–131, 145*fig*
Jenne, 25–27
Jihadists, 11; attitude toward France by, 73–74; attitude toward US by, 74–75; in Burkina Faso, 3, 12–13, 30–31, 38, 87–116, 173; in Côte d'Ivoire, 61, 63; digital media for, 64–65; Fulani and, 33, 35, 36, 77–80, 85–86; in Ghana, 63, 87–116; grievances of, 7, 13, 33, 77–80; local resistance to, 87–116; Macina Empire and, 25–33, 36, 37–38; in Mali, 4, 12–13, 37, 38, 87–116, 173; in Niger, 61; in Nigeria, 37, 61; perception of, 108–112; perspectives on the West by, 73–77; in post-Cold war, 175; precolonial caliphates and empires and, 15–38, 20*fig*, 173–174; in Sahel Region, 3, 16, 61; in Sokoto Caliphate, 36, 37–38; strategies of, 61–86; territorial conquest by, 17; in West Africa, 1–2, 6–7. *See also specific organizations and individuals*
JNIM. *See* Jama'at Nusrat al Islam
Johnston, Hugh Anthony Stephen, 34–35

Kanem-Borno Empire, 12, 18, 77
Kaniaga, 43
Kanuri kingdom, 21, 24
Katiba Khalid Ibn Walid, 31

208　Index

Katiba Macina, 31
Keïta, Ibrahim Boubacar, 82, 123–124
Keïta, Modibo, 54, 56
Keita, Sundiata, 43, 47
Kitab al-Farq (dan Fodio), 22
Kitaba Macina (Macina Liberation Front). *See* Macina Liberation Front
Koufa, Ahmadu, 66, 68–69, 77–79
Koumbi Saleh, 42, 43
Kunta tribe, 30
Kurumba, 30

Lagos, 54
Lake Chad Basin, 61, 88
Large-N survey, 9, 11
Lavrov, Sergey, 124
Liberia, 50
Liptako, 30
Lugard, Lord, 50

MacDill Air Force Base, 119
MacEachern, Scott, 37–38
Macina Empire, 6, 10, 20*fig*; Ahmadu and, 20, 24–28, 31, 37, 68, 174; Ansarul Islam and, 70; Burkina Faso and, 30–31; colonialism of, 19; Fulani in, 17–18, 25, 36, 37, 51; Hamdullahi in, 26–30; jihadists and, 25–33, 36, 37–38; Sokota Caliphate and, 25, 26; Umar and, 30–33
Macina Liberation Front, 19, 21, 38, 62, 66; Ansarul Islam and, 71; Fulani and, 23, 77–79, 85; ISGS and, 80; in Mali, 15–16, 77–79; in Mopti Region, 68–69, 85; precolonial caliphates and empires and, 173–174
Macina Liberation Front (Kitaba Macina), 3, 6, 13
Macron, Emmanuel, 68, 73, 81, 83, 121, 175
Mahama, John D., 92
Mahdi, 21
Malaria, 49
Mali, 1–14, 10*fig*; Ahmadu in, 22; Ansar Dine in, 67; Bamako in, 8, 54, 79, 119; Burkina Faso and, 52; China in, 13, 121; colonialism in, 6; corruption in, 91–93, 100–103, 101*tab*, 115, 174–175; coups in, 1, 8, 56, 83, 87, 123–124, 144; data on, 9–11; debt burden in, 131; France in, 4, 8–9, 50, 57, 67–68, 73, 81, 82–83, 175–176; Fulani in, 23, 34, 77–80, 124; GPC Global South impact and, 165–169; GPC governance impact on, 157–165, 159*fig*, 161*fig*–163*fig*, 164*tab*, 166*fig*; GPC in, 2, 117–140; GPC military relations in, 118–125, 122*tab*, 140*tab*; GPC mineral extraction in, 132–137, 133*fig*, 139, 140*tab*; GPC perceived behaviors by, 152–157, 153*fig*, 155*tab*; GPC perceived impact of, 147–152, 149*fig*, 150*fig*; GPC perceived nature in, 143–152, 144*fig*–146*fig*, 148*fig*–150*fig*; grievances in, 88, 90–91, 93–104, 94*tab*, 101*tab*; independence for, 56–57; ISGS in, 3, 62–63, 74, 80–84; jihadists in, 4, 12–13, 37, 38, 87–116, 173; jihadists perception in, 108–112; JNIM in, 62–63, 66–68, 72, 80–84, 108–109; Kaniaga in, 43; local resistance in, 87–116; Macina Liberation Front in, 15–16, 77–79; MNLA in, 16; Mopti Region of, 24; ODA for, 125–131, 126*fig*, 129*fig*, 138–139, 140*tab*; perspectives on the West in, 112–114, 113*tab*; Russia and, 124, 138, 144, 175; SCI in, 177–179, 178*tab*; security perception in, 104–108, 106*tab*; Slave Kingdom of, 49; Tablighi Jamaat in, 69; US in, 13; VEOs in, 2, 65–73; violence perception in, 105–108, 107*tab*; Wagner Group in, 40, 83–84, 175–176. *See also* Macina Empire; Mopti Region; Multidimensional Integrated Stabilization Mission in Mali
Mali Empire, 43–44, 45
Mamprusi, 52
Manding, 43
Markaz (center), 69
Masked Men Brigade, 71
Mauritania, 42
Mecca, 36
Medina, 36

Mediterranean Sea, 47
Military relations, in GPC, 118–125, 122*tab*, 137, 140*tab*
Mineral extraction: in GPC, 132–137, 132*fig*, 133*fig*, 139, 140*tab*. *See also* Gold
Minerals and Mining Act of 2006, in Ghana, 135
MINUSMA. *See* Multidimensional Integrated Stabilization Mission in Mali
MNLA. *See* National Movement for the Liberation of Azawad
Mole-Dagbon ethnic group, 11
Moors, 46
Mopti Region, 37; Ansarul Islam in, 85; France in, 50, 51; GPC in, 117–140, 140*tab*; independence for, 55; Macina Liberation Front in, 68–69, 85; of Mali, 11, 24; mineral extraction in, 134; MINUSMA in, 57; ODA for, 128, 139; Songhai Empire and, 57; Wagner Group in, 176
Mordashov, Alexei, 137
Mossi, 46, 51, 85; GPC governance impact on, 157–165, 159*fig*, 161*fig*–163*fig*, 164*tab*, 166*fig*
Mossi ethnic group, 11
Al-Mourabitoun, 3, 66, 71
Mouvement pour l'Unicité et le Jihad en Afrique de l'Ouest (Movement for Oneness and Jihad in West Africa) (MUJAO), 16, 71
Muhammad (Prophet), 15, 17, 22, 32, 35–36
Muhammad, Askia, 44
Mujadid (re-newer), 21
Mujahideen, 74, 81–82
MUJAO. *See* Mouvement pour l'Unicité et le Jihad en Afrique de l'Ouest
Multidimensional Integrated Stabilization Mission in Mali (MINUSMA), 4, 67, 83, 123, 151; China in, 120; JNIM and, 82; in Mopti Region, 57

Namdini, 137, 139
National Movement for the Liberation of Azawad (MNLA), 16

Nation-states, 12; JNIM and, 173; in Sahel Region, 78. *See also specific countries*
Native Tribunals, 53
Neocolonialism, 73, 76; of France, 8, 74; ODA and, 157
The Netherlands, 44, 48
New World, slave trade to, 46, 48
The New York Times, 68
Newmont, 134, 136
Niger: Burkina Faso and, 52; coup in, 1; France and, 8, 83, 121; ISGS in, 3, 77; jihadists in, 61; JNIM in, 62–63, 68; Kanem-Borno Empire in, 18; Macina Empire of, 17–18; Tukolor Empire of, 3; US in, 177
Nigeria: corruption in, 92; GPC perceived behaviors of, 152–157, 153*fig*; GPC perceived impact of, 147–152, 149*fig*, 150*fig*, 151; Hausa kingdom of, 22; jihadists in, 37, 61; Kanem-Borno Empire in, 18; Sokoto Caliphate in, 17. *See also* Boko Haram; Sokoto Caliphate
Nkrumah, Kwame, 56
Nordgold, 137
Northern Territories, 55
Northern Territories Administration Ordinance, 53
Nouadhibou, 52

Obi, Cyril, 157
ODA. *See* Overseas development assistance
OECD. *See* Organisation of Economic Co-operation and Development
Operation Barkhane, 8, 121
Operation Serval, 4
Organisation of Economic Co-operation and Development (OECD), 125, 139, 141*n*3, 157
Ouagadougou, 3, 52, 54, 55, 91, 119
Overseas development assistance (ODA), 125–131, 126*fig*, 129*fig*, 138–139, 140*tab*, 157
Oyo kingdom, 44–45

Peace Corps, 59
Perspectives on the West by, 73–77
Petronin, Sophie, 68

Portugal, 44, 50, 57; in Ghana, 47–48; Mali Empire and, 43; slave trade by, 48
Post-Cold War, 12, 39; GPC in, 117; jihadists in, 175; Russia in, 123–124
Postcolonialism, 6
Precolonial, 21
Precolonial caliphates and empires, 15–38, 20*fig*, 42–47, 173–174. *See also* Macina Empire; Segu Empire; Sokoto Caliphate
Prigozhin, Yevgeny, 125
Putin, Vladimir, 175–176

Qadiriyya Sufism, 33
Al-Qaeda, 1, 65, 71, 75, 123, 173
Al-Qaeda in the Islamic Maghreb (AQIM), 3, 66
Al-Qaeda-affiliated organizations, 3, 16, 61; Islamic State-affiliated organizations and, 72–73; US and, 120. *See also specific organizations*
Al-Qasimi, Abu Dujana, 67
Quaraysh, 36
Quinine, 49
Qur'an, 29, 37, 67

Racism, 75, 145–147, 146*fig*
Re-newer (*mujadid*), 21
Resolute, 136
Resource-for-infrastructure, 157
Rothstein, Bo, 88
Roxgold, 136
RTIV. *See* Trend-indicator value
Russia, 2; gold and, 137; jihadists and, 83; Mali and, 124, 138, 144, 175; military relations with, 123–124; perception of, 143–152, 144*fig*–146*fig*, 148*fig*–150*fig*; in post-Cold War, 123–124; US and, 39–40; in West Africa, 7. *See also* Wagner Group

Sahara desert, 10–11; trade over, 42–47. *See also* Islamic State in the Greater Sahara
Sahel Region, 1–14, 10*fig*; Ansarul Islam in, 91; France in, 8–9, 50, 76–77; Fulani in, 33; GPC in, 117–140, 140*tab*; GPC mineral extraction in, 139; independence for, 55; Islamic history in, 19–22; Islamic State in, 173; jihadists in, 3, 16, 61; mineral extraction in, 134; nation-states in, 78; ODA for, 128, 138; al-Qaeda in, 65, 173; Russia in, 7; Wagner Group in, 124–125. *See also* Burkina Faso; Mali; Niger
Sahelian empires. *See* Precolonial caliphates and empires
Sahraoui, Adnan Abu Walid, 71
Saint-Louis, 52
Salafist Islam, 66
Samori, 53
Samori Ture, 18
Saudi Arabia, 118, 151, 152–157, 153*fig*
SCI. *See* Sense of community index
Segu Empire, 20*fig*, 26, 27
SEMAFO, 136
Senegal, 8, 33, 121
Senghor, Léopold, 54
Sense of community index (SCI), 177–179, 178*tab*, 180*n*1
Shaanxi Mining Company, 135
Shandong Gold Mining, 135
Shari'a, 22, 23, 81; Fulani and, 35
Shekau, Abubkar, 16
SIPRI. *See* Stockholm International Peace Research Institute
Slave Kingdoms, 49
Slave raiders, 48, 49, 57
Slave trade, 40, 48; Fulani and, 45–46; in Ghana, 53; in Songhai Empire, 45–46
Slaving kingdoms, 44–45
Smith, H., 18
SOCAFRICA. *See* Special Operations Command Africa
Soft power, 41
Sokoto Caliphate, 6, 20*fig*; Ansarul Islam and, 70; Borno Empire and, 32; colonialism of, 19; dan Fodio and, 7, 17, 22–25, 174; Fulani in, 37; jihadists in, 36, 37–38; Macina Empire and, 25, 26; Umar at, 33
Songhai Empire, 30, 44, 45–46
Sosso, 43
South Africa: gold and, 136; GPC perceived impact of, 151

Soviet Union. *See* Cold War
Spain, 44; slave trade by, 48
Special Operations Command Africa (SOCAFRICA), 9, 39–40, 80
Special operations forces, 9, 120
Stiglitz, Joseph E., 6
Stockholm International Peace Research Institute (SIPRI), 140*n*2
Sub-Saharan Africa, 123; ODA for, 127–128, 129, 131
Sudan, 33, 51, 52
Sufism, 33
Super Camp, 120
Syed, Amir, 32

Tablighi Jamaat, in Mali, 69
Takfir (excommunication), 23–24
Taliban, 81–82
Tanjaniyya Sufism, 33
Telegram, 3, 65, 78
Tijani Sufism, 33
Tilly, Charles, 43
Timbuktu, 16; JNIM attack at, 65; Macina Empire and, 17–18, 27–28, 29–30; Mali Empire and, 43; Songhai Empire and, 45, 46; UN Super Camp at, 120
Togo, 61
Toucouleur forces, 51
Tracking Underreported Financial Flows (TUFF), 128
Transparency International, 91
Trend-indicator value (RTIV), 121, 122*tab*, 140*n*2
Trimingham, Spencer, 36
Trump, Donald, 75
Trump, Melania, 151
Tuareg, 16, 30, 46, 56, 66, 123
TUFF. *See* Tracking Underreported Financial Flows
Tukolor Empire, 3, 33
Turkey, 7, 124, 151, 152–157, 153*fig*

Ulema, 29
Umar, al-Hajj, 18, 29, 38, 51; Macina Empire and, 30–33; Sokoto Caliphate and, 33
United Kingdom. *See* Britain
United Nations (UN): exogenous shocks from, 6; global war on terror and, 119–120; Security Council of, 123; Super Camp of, 120. *See also* Multidimensional Integrated Stabilization Mission in Mali
United Nations Human Development Index, 91
United States (US), 13; in Afghanistan, 81–82; Africa Command of, 9; global war on terror and, 119–120; GPC perceived behaviors of, 152–157, 153*fig*, 155*tab*; jihadist attitudes toward, 74–75; JNIM and, 67; military relations with, 119–120; mineral extraction and, 132–137, 132*fig*, 133*fig*, 139; in Niger, 177; ODA from, 125–128, 138–139; perceived impact of, 147–152, 149*fig*, 150*fig*; perceived nature of, 143–147, 144*fig*–146*fig*, 148*fig*; in post–Cold War, 39–40; slave trade by, 48; SOCAFRICA of, 9, 39–40, 80. *See also* Cold War
United States Agency for International Development (USAID), 9, 128, 139
Upper East Region: China in, 57; GPC for, 117–140, 140*tab*; independence for, 55; mineral extraction in, 134; ODA for, 128, 138
Upper Volta. *See* Burkina Faso
US. *See* United States
USAID. *See* United States Agency for International Development
Uslaner, Eric M., 88

Violent extremist organizations (VEOs): in Burkina Faso, 65–73; exogenous shocks by, 61; GPC and, 171–180, 178*tab*; grievances and, 13–14; in Mali, 65–73; in West Africa, 1, 2–14. *See also* Jihadists; *specific organizations*

Wagadou Empire, 42–44, 47, 59*n*1
Wagner Group, 4, 14*n*1, 39; in Burkina Faso, 175; in Central African Republic, 40; Islamic State in Iraq and Syria and, 124; in Mali, 40, 83–84, 175–176; in Sahel Region, 124–125
Wang Yi, 40

War on terror, 2, 119–120
West Africa, 1–14, 10*fig*; corruption in, 89–93, 100–103, 101*tab*, 115, 174–175; data on, 9–11; grievances in, 4–5, 7, 13; history of, 18–19; jihadists in, 6–7; precolonial caliphates and empires in, 15–38, 20*fig*; security landscape of, 62–65. *See also specific countries and topics*
Western Express, 119

WhatsApp, 3, 6, 78
White supremacism, 75

Xi Jinping, 120

Yaméogo, Maurice, 54
Yusuf, Mohammad, 92

Al-Zawahiri, Ayman, 66
Zida, Isaac, 119

About the Book

WHAT HAPPENS WHEN EXTERNAL FORCES ARE BROUGHT TO BEAR ON DOMESTIC grievances and governance institutions? In environments profoundly affected by both violent extremist organizations and powerful international actors, what attributes characterize local governments that can maintain peace and stability? Addressing these questions, Zacharias Pieri and Kevin Fridy demonstrate the surprising linkages between global strategic competition and local counterinsurgency in West Africa and show how resilient local governance structures have effectively managed the consequent challenges.

Zacharias P. Pieri is associate professor of international relations and security at the University of South Florida. **Kevin S. Fridy** is professor of political science and international studies at the University of Tampa.